MOVIE MAN

DAVID THOMSON

MOVIE MAN

STEIN AND DAY / *Publishers* / New York

© 1967 by David Thomson

Library of Congress Catalog Card No. 67–23534

All rights reserved

Stein and Day / Publishers / 7 East 48 Street, New York, N.Y. 10017

First STEIN AND DAY PAPERBACK edition 1969

Printed in the United States of America

CONTENTS

Romantic: Demy and Rivette – Consensus:
Preminger

ILLUSTRATIONS

The author and publishers would like to thank the following distributors for permission to reproduce stills: Paramount, Metro-Goldwyn-Mayer, Twentieth Century Fox, Warner Brothers, Gala, Contemporary, Columbia Anglo-Amalgamated, Universal Pictures, United Artists, Rank and Monarch, and the National Film Archive for help in obtaining them.

THIS BOOK
IS FOR KIERAN HICKEY

MOVIE MAN

I

BACKGROUND TO A VISUAL SOCIETY

The New City – Architecture –
Literature – The Scientific Personality

The association of 'movie' and 'man' in the title of this book is
intended to evoke a variety of meanings. There are four ways
one could interpret 'movie man': a man who makes films—the
director, perhaps; a man who appears in a film—the actor; a
man who is presented in a film—a character; and a man who
may watch a film or only live in a society that employs film.
These roles are generally thought of as being distinct but I
believe the phrase is capable of sustaining the merger of all the
roles into one concept that we might compare with Stone Age
man or Renaissance man. Movie man is the unit in a society
that has so assimilated the methods and effects of moving film
that they are determining his understanding of the present and
his discovery of the future.

Movie is an invention of the twentieth century, though like
the potential of the atom its possibility had always existed. It is
not sufficient to accept its discovery as chance; why was movie
brought to fruition in the years after 1890? In this chapter I
want to show to what extent it was a necessity for industrial
man, the logical consequence of the development of society and
communication. It cannot be isolated from the processes of
urbanization and mechanization which had been set in motion
over a hundred years before Lumière and Méliès, and which
had themselves been the consequence of the previous stages of
society. This evolution is concerned not only with methods
of production and increases in population but with the sort of

terms in which man thinks of himself. It is only in comparatively recent times, for instance, that terms like 'means of production', 'demography', 'urbanization' and 'equality' have become exchangeable between men.

THE NEW CITY

There was no day, or year even, in which Birmingham, Manchester or Chicago arose, but from our hindsight we can see and feel the change from parochial assortments of buildings to vigorous centres of industry and organization. There was no watershed, although now the time-charts seem littered with them. The inventions, like Crompton's mule or Bessemer's steel process, were observed as quietly by their contemporaries as real innovations are today.

Within a hundred years there were so many more people; the graph of population turns almost a right angle between 1770 and 1870. We are more able to note the increase in production and population than to distinguish exactly which caused which. But the new urban consciousness was not entirely economic. Both John Stuart Mill and Karl Marx refused to separate economic from moral welfare. They recognized that the new city gave to its inhabitants a new conception of themselves. Once a society functioned through its economy, rather than through its basic inequality of class, the common index had attained an equality man had never experienced in the pastoral existence of previous ages.

No slogan embodies Marx's unity of morality and economics more than the American colonists': 'No taxation without representation'. The fact that the idealism of neither the American nor the Russian revolutions has been fulfilled *in toto* by the present power blocs does not invalidate the original excitement of individual validity or the bitterness of the grievance that stimulated the revolutions. In both cases the socio-economic consciousness of a people was directed against the aristocratic rulers. Just as the population level had risen slowly, without dramatic alterations, in the years before 1700, so aristocratic oligarchy, whether secular or religious, had continued to shape peoples' conceptions of themselves; the only change had been in the primitiveness of the subject awe and fear. The same pattern of subjugate population and the concentration of power, riches and refinement in an *élite* existed throughout Europe. 'The divine right of kings' demonstrated the comprehensive sway of the *élite*; the last English king to make that claim credible, Charles I, was, significantly, forced to flee his own capital. By 1640 the balance of power in London had shifted from the Tower and the royal palaces to the City and the Houses of Parliament.

In concentrating population, the city generated the phenomenon of 'society'. The technological and mechanical advance has intensified a basic psychological predicament, for the development of building has deprived man of Crusoe's experience in providing his own shelter. The juxtaposition of people highlighted contrasts of behaviour and heightened the conflict between reactions in the human subconscious towards buildings: both shelter and prison, security and threat.

As shelter has expanded beyond the home and the town to the metropolis, escape has been made more difficult. We are increasingly deprived of natural landscape and more and more subject to urban claustrophobia. Long before cottage industry converged to form urban industrialization, the city, its keep and its high thick walls were resorted to for defence against enemies. In time of war the city offers company, distraction, organization and community. It also offers to the enemy the most inviting target for his most powerful weapons.

A similar ambiguity runs through our whole experience of the city now, for at the same time as its organization assists the efficiency of our lives it threatens to dehumanize them. Fritz Lang's and Joseph Losey's films, particularly their versions of *M*, show how the same methods of authority and networks of power exist above and below normal society—the one representing law and the other the underworld; the psychopathy of Losey's murderer in *M* is thus an anguished version of the surrounded individual. Man's encounter with mechanisms cannot stop short with the benefits of the water-closet, electricity and the motor car; he has to face their more destructive effects. The ideal city of prosperity, welfare and the exercise of human talents—such as stimulates the pioneers in some of

Anthony Mann's films—may become the Poisonville in Dashiell Hammett's *Red Harvest* or even Jean-Luc Godard's Alphaville.

ARCHITECTURE

The gap between the ethos of aristocracy and the response of a slave populace is expressed in the scale and soaring points of Gothic architecture. It is significant that, with very few exceptions, the Gothic buildings that remain are castles or cathedrals. Their amplitude was believed to be filled by the authority of the nobles and the Church, and in a comparatively underpopulated country the difference in riches and power that the size manifested could be accepted. The peasant dwellings were so primitive that most of them have long since collapsed.

Ironically, at a time when such social differences were becoming intolerable, a bastard Gothic style was still being employed in architecture. The 1832 Reform Act and the destruction of the old buildings by fire demanded a new parliamentary chamber that would implement the new desire for political expression. The competition for designs stipulated the Gothic or Elizabethan styles and the accepted building, as planned by Barry and Pugin, was a part of the Gothic revival. It was more functional than Strawberry Hill or Beckford's Fonthill, which were still aristocratic self-indulgence, but it did not seem to approve of the reformed political structure and even the original efficiency of its lay-out had degenerated within a hundred years into a legislative chamber that imposed absurd privations on its elected members.

The English Gothic revival was one element in the eclecticism of Victorian architecture. For although the cities and their purposes were palpably novel there was no successful new architectural form to assist them. In England the innovation of the Crystal Palace was ridiculed and potentially exciting railway stations were covered with the unnecessary decoration that makes them today so dismally filthy and archaic. It was not until the end of the nineteenth century, in Germany and America, that an urban architecture was realized by Behrens, Gropius, Sullivan and Wright that was stripped to fit need.

Frank Lloyd Wright's position is ambiguous, for while many

of his buildings were revolutionary, and many of his statements enlightened, his whole career fits a nineteenth rather than a twentieth century pattern. Wright was a Middle West romantic who loved the horizontal form because, rather like Wordsworth, he believed it helped the building to share the strength and naturalness of the earth. Yet he was the victim of a twentieth century temptation; believing himself right when so many criticized him, he felt justified in dramatizing his own inventiveness and its effect of shock upon the 'mobocracy': thus he demanded, 'Genius must dominate'. King Vidor's film *The Fountainhead*, which is loosely based on Wright's life, takes up this issue. The very size of the most revolutionary new buildings and the need for drastic innovation in the face of so many years' waste made it necessary for the patrons of the architect to be men of great power. In *The Fountainhead* the physical detail of a man quarrying rock is an image of primitive strength that Vidor's romanticism associates with the more sophisticated power of a commercial tycoon. The houses Wright built were for rich men and, because of the increased density of society, their magnificence seems more out of proportion than that of the Elizabethan or Augustan houses built for political or mercantilist leaders.

Such houses, built by the Victorians, had resorted to precedent styles because, as social buildings, they were not new. The new sort of domestic unit was the urban worker's house. In row after row in the new cities it comprised not only the slum but a fact of political implication. It is from the slums created by speculative building that we derive the credo that 'form is the function of purpose'. The conclusion to be drawn from degrading housing was that it indicated an opinion that the lower classes had only a depressed purpose; this provoked them to political consciousness. Through form people became more aware that they might have a purpose.

Out of this consciousness a sense of modernity was born. In the 1830s Barry could not have conceived of a 'modern' architecture because his society lacked a contemporary sense of itself. Instead its yardsticks were the monuments of past styles: the image of the Parthenon recurs in innumerable Victorian public buildings. Barry's Houses of Parliament was envisaged as being permanent because of a universally felt security. Its present redundancy, on the other hand, would make it impossible for any successful new legislative assembly to be built without the recognition that it served only for a limited time. It is, of course, contrary to conventional 'artistic' conceptions of the architect that his work should be only temporary: Lloyd Wright's Taliesin West Buildings were based on a stone superstructure of such durability that its monumentality as a ruin in years to come might be its finest, if Ozymandian, effect.

Against this idea there is now posed the practicality of kinetic architecture: buildings of steel, glass and plastic that can alter their shapes to suit the various functions of the inhabitants. Such an architectural form corresponds with the conditions of a film soundstage, the hangar-like building in which a large part of a film is shot. The controlling factor on a soundstage is the need of 'now'. All lights, all technical abilities, all recording equipment, the energy and creativity of actors, director and crew are concentrated in a small corner of the building and a small area of emotion and action within the larger context of a film's script. The localization of this intensity will be transferred as soon as one shot has been completed. Then another set, previously struts, paint and cardboard, will be made to take on cinematic life, and the used one broken down and parts of it employed in making another set. National architecture may yet have to acquire a similar ability to focus its materials and skills, and landscape may even become as fluctuating as skyscape.

LITERATURE

We may see two sorts of sequence in writing: the first is that of the narrative or the author's uncovering process, and the novels of Dickens, Eliot, James and Conrad are examples of it; the second is the inevitable one of words succeeding words. Every book illustrates this category but those of Burroughs, which deliberately shuffle words out of grammatical and narrative sequence into new and possibly more liberating patterns, and of Nabokov, which parody narrative with grotesque coincidence, have shifted the emphasis and in so doing have blurred fiction and fact.

In earlier ages that were confirmed in their faith, and socially static, the sequence in writing was one of enactment or of allegory. Character lacked psychological detail in such a context and was expressed in an emblematic or poetic sense. By the nineteenth century this confidence had been undermined; at the same time the rationalism of the previous century could not confront the new consciousness of inchoate masses. If the picaresque novels of Fielding or Diderot are satires on prejudice, the sort of credible naturalistic narrative of the nineteenth century, whatever its moral resources, is possible only as faith subsides. Its detail indicates a step-by-step discovery and description of a new world. Actions were no longer divinely supervised but could be measured against a social index. As Henry James said in *The Last of the Valerii*, people were, or were not, 'susceptible of a moral life'.

James is the classic discriminator of this morality, upholding a sense of personal independence and guarding against trespass on it without invoking the full Christian doctrine as support. His agnosticism is sharper because it recognizes how much its values are threatened by superficiality and selfishness. The intelligence that observes these encounters is noble, the more so because a half-century in which its standards have been overthrown has not made the stand seem foolish or pathetic. Rather, the difference that has been set up seems as poignant as that which Nanda, in *The Awkward Age*, is made to feel between herself and her grandmother.

The viciousness James sees is discreet because his world has not allowed its outward appearance to be overcome by it. It is an interior malaise made worse by the circle being so intent on itself. For is not James's society quite as enclosed as Jane Austen's? It is true that it is close to the centres of influence and cultivation as they existed in James's time, but there is so little effort to take up this responsibility. One has only to think of the cursory appearances in doorways to announce entrances of James's servants, and compare them with Renoir's recurrent theme of servants carrying on a complete duplicated life beneath, and finally among, their masters, to see that James did not appreciate servants as human beings, let alone moral beings, for all the respect with which he regarded every human potential at the level of 'possible' people. Together, the elevated social circumstances and the moral exclusiveness constitute an aristocracy that showed no presentiment of the great shadow of people that would never read a word the novelist wrote.

An aura of academism settled on the novel, in its way as romantic as the Victorian idealization of the Shelleyan poets. In neither James's prefaces nor even in Levis's elevation of James as a moral arbiter to *The Great Tradition* is there any note of the anguish or chaos that might disturb the order within which novels could be written. Instead, in the preface to *The Awkward Age,* James says that 'though the relations of a human figure or a social occurrence are what make such objects interesting, they also make them, to the same tune, difficult to isolate, to surround with the sharp black line, to frame in the square, the circle, the charming oval that helps any arrangement of objects to become a picture'. And yet for the writer or the reader is there an essential difference if material shifts from the consciously contrived to the knowingly random, when the words have effects more chance than their selection and more schematic than their fortuitousness?

The intermingling of factual and imaginative content is nowhere clearer than in the native American novel. Herman Melville's dramatization of his own experiences culminates in the practical and mystical treatise on whale-hunting, *Moby Dick.* John Dos Passos has continued to alternate the actual events of his lifetime with fictional accounts of archetypal projections with an energy that is comparable with Melville's. But with Ernest Hemingway and Norman Mailer the duality forces itself into the writer's consciousness, and Hemingway's belief that it is first necessary to be a good man before being a good writer identifies the difficulties of the characters in leading honest lives with the difficulties of the author in making an unbiased account.

It is in Hemingway's prose solution to this problem that we can see an association with the film-camera. Hemingway was intent on seeing the things that a bourgeoisie would rather not look at. *Death in the Afternoon* is a constant adjuration to observe the process closely and report the detail exactly. It was his wish to achieve a style that described action without including intention. Undoubtedly there was too much of the romantic in Hemingway for intention not sometimes to infect the account. At the ending of *A Farewell to Arms* the factual account is free of every interpretative nuance except that it is raining, and we recall how much Catherine Barkley feared the rain.

Even so, Hemingway was at pains to reject this sort of novelistic device because he believed a man could only use words honestly if he was committed to believing them. He thought a man might see an event and describe it accurately but that if emotion and subjectivity were once explored the only honest response was to collapse in doubt. The fact that he attempted to do what the camera does automatically places him at the end of a narrative tradition, and his reliance on a mechanical effect denotes the dissolution of the efficacy of the omniscient narrative. The world has passed out of the novelist's control and the terse telegram that Colonel Cantwell leaves at the end of *Across the River and into the Trees* is a last unblinking message, its factual content ready for a computer.

It is possible that Dashiel Hammett, because he was a more cynical man, went further in the process. In *The Glass Key*, for instance, the level of reportage is so devoid of interior or justifying versions from the characters, and the pressure of society so great, that a profound uncertainty surrounds Ned Beaumont's character. Perhaps more than any modern fictional character he has been observed in reality, the nature of such a process being that it is consistent to only one level. The doubt we are made to feel about him is a just equivalent of the doubt he might feel about himself. A situation has been reached whereby any attempt to discover meaning through prose will appear as an experiment: the writer has been forced to make the reader more conscious of writing than story.

THE SCIENTIFIC PERSONALITY

'Science' is a concept that still provides an obstacle. Not only Lord Snow sees our culture as divided between the artists and scientists. Even Jean-Luc Godard falls at the obstacle in *Alphaville*. After a succession of films that treated contemporary life in an exemplarily scientific way he approaches the subject with a crude directness, turning Paris into a 'scientific city' as outmoded as the versions of H. G. Wells and George Orwell, and can only combat it with the strip-cartoon certainty of Lemmy Caution. That Caution wins is incredible, for the longer 'Alpha 60', the controlling machine, speaks the more essentially Godardian it sounds, even though the temptation to humanize the brain, by adding breathing sounds to the electronic voice, has not been avoided.

Science is not, as our schooling tries to suggest, one subject among many. It is everything; because, as J. B. S. Haldane defined it, it is simply 'a body of general statements about a set of natural events which can be verified in practice'. Man is in a scientific age not because he is surrounded by machines like computers but because he realizes that computers operate in the way that he does. A scientific personality is the fitting result of the changes in experience and self-consciousness that I have already described in this chapter.

Time chastens the scientist, just as it does the artist. Atoms and electrons, for instance, existed in Galileo's time but were not identified for several hundred years. A general scientific statement on the nature of matter would be that it does not, in the scale of reasonable human experience, alter, but that man's sense of it extends. John Dalton conceived of the atom as being like a marble. His concept is the simplest and thus still the most general of atomic theories. From his solid object we derive the difficulty of 'particle'—the only suitable word we have, which evokes the corners of a crumb between our fingertips. The linguistic barrier is reached with 'particle' but the process of re-definition goes on. It became necessary to invoke an electronic nature for the atom and to suppose a duality of nature—of wave and particle—that directly contradicts a dictionary's confidence.

In the 1920s Werner Heisenberg announced his uncertainty principle. Briefly, this says that it is not possible to fix both the velocity and the position of a particle, and that the attempt at both is made impossible by the very act of measurement. Hemingway may not have known about Heisenberg but his prose solution has taken account of his findings. The real significance of Heisenberg's work lies in the admissions it makes about the reflexivity of our recording instruments. In his philosophical predicament as the definer of our nature and our knowledge of ourselves, the scientist finds himself in the position we once allotted to the artist.

The branch of science closest to the artistic end is psychology because, like narrative, it attempts to interpret events and, like morality, it hopes to improve them in the future. Freud was its pioneering genius and his own consciousness of that status reveals how far his findings were influenced by a classical culture and essentially in support of established ideals. Freud and his immediate colleagues and rivals were all, in some form or other, doctors and their function was to treat the sick. They realized a new dimension of sickness and to define it had to posit the phenomenon of 'normality'. Freud grasped his own theory not methodically but intuitively, composing a vast palace of dogma from a comparatively few cases rather in the way contemporary novels were written.

The absence of measurements in Freud's work is concomitant with the conviction that the people he is dealing with are sick victims of an alien diversion from the whole and natural life. Looking back on Freud's work one is aware of the greater social and cultural confidence he had, even though he ended his life being chased from Vienna by Hitler. Its subsequent undermining has borne down on all Western society as the distinction by which it recognized the sane and insane seemed less credible. In Vincente Minnelli's movie *The Cobweb*, which is set in a psychiatric clinic, one character sums up the film when he says you can't tell the doctors from the patients. Acknowledgement of this is increasingly appealing to analysts; there is now less conception of a sick minority than an acceptance of common patterns of character that break down the old barriers which were social in the sense that a man was termed mad when his actions isolated him socially. The new terms of reference equate the doctor and the patient, as Professor G. A. Kelly, the originator of Personal Construct Theory, points out:

'Thus the psychology of personality is not simply a matter of disinterested psychologists assessing a disinterested organism but of psychologists, who happen to be professionally and casually interested in their chosen subject matter, assessing a non-professional psychologist, who, on his part, is intimately and urgently involved with the job of making sense out of the life upon which his existence depends.'*

As a result, the scientist does not measure symptoms of confirmation but the phenomena of behaviour. The implication of whatever social power he holds over a patient may even be painful to realize. The institution in which strict distinctions were once observed between the sick and the healthy seems to the analyst an unsatisfactory microcosm of the society he inhabits outside. It becomes harder for him to offer stable ideals to the patient from that external world and, like contemporary politicians, he becomes sceptical of presenting principle and can only suggest the most pragmatic treatment of every problem. He wonders if the patient's view of reality may not be as plausible as his own as their dialogues become divergent definitions of the same word.

The blurring of distinctions between artist, scientist and layman reflects the possibility of uniting the various interpretations of 'movie man'. We have arrived at a state in which man's most engrossing occupation is epistemological. The increasing necessity for practitioners in either the arts or the sciences to adopt a style or a form of research that is modern is the result of an acceleration in all the means by which a society develops. Events move so swiftly that it is not possible to note every stage in development as a stable unit; instead one is conscious of the fact of process. Just as an eye scanning a landscape—from a railway carriage perhaps—jumps from one point of focus to another, so from a fixed emotional vantage an intelligence scans events in the same way, constructing narrative out of incidents. But a camera in the carriage passes smoothly over the panorama offering less a version of events than a record.

The American soldier who discovered a concentration camp is supposed to have said, 'The English language does not have the words to describe what I saw'. The newsreel compensated for his difficulty, and in doing so defined a human neutrality towards such events. Hitler was passed off by a humane culture

* G. A. Kelly, *Proceedings 14th International Congress on Psychology*, quoted by D. Bannister in *New Horizons in Psychology*, Penguin, 1966.

as mad and the camps as evil, although the facts of Nazism made the integrity of any code that might condemn them precarious.

The age of moving film is one that can forget nothing. The miles of newsreel footage will be shown repeatedly until, like a feedback process, they pass into the collective consciousness. The plasticity of moving film makes all its content information until there is no real distinction between its personal and public significance. As Norbert Wiener put it, 'To live effectively is to live with adequate information. Thus, communication and control belong to the essence of man's inner life, even as they belong to his life in society.'*

---

* *The Human Use of Human Beings*, Eyre & Spottiswoode, 1955.

2

CINEMATOGRAPHY

The Factual Nature – Chance –
Photographic Effects – Present
Tense – Colour – Light – *Mise-
en-scène*

THE FACTUAL NATURE

The photochemical reaction that makes a photograph is not
complex, and yet it was not controlled until the first half of the
nineteenth century. The process of cinematography is also, by
twentieth century standards, a simple one, but even when
Auguste Lumière,* one of its first exponents, had been able to
project a film in front of an audience, he doubted its usefulness.
The history of all forms of photography has a recurrent pattern :
the lone amateurs experimenting for perhaps a hundred years,
and then being suddenly usurped by commercial application ;
in 1895–6, the first programmes by Lumière and Méliès, in
1915, *Birth of a Nation* and Chaplin at Essanay. It is an advance
as rapid as those of the preceding century in urbanization,
population, the sources of power and gross national products.
Not only this speed, but the nature and potential of photography
force one to consider it as much commercially and technologi-
cally as in the artistic context. In the obvious comparison with
the development of printing, the first presses were instruments
of the age of humanism, and the photograph of the age of
science.

Lumière and Méliès offer a classic contrast between presenting the 'real' and the 'unreal'. Lumière filmed with as much

* Of the two Lumière brothers, Auguste was the businessman, Louis
the cinematographer.

fidelity as possible, simple everyday things—baby being fed, a train entering a station and workers leaving a factory. Méliès often appeared himself in the role of a conjuror and his films were 'fantastic'—heads expanding and exploding, and the first science-fiction movies. But the contrast should not obscure similarities, even though audiences ran from Lumière's train and laughed at Méliès's trickery. The different intentions had such paradoxical results that even before 1900 the cinema's ambivalence had been outlined. Two factors were clearly prerequisite to the movies—the camera's ability to record and the audience's ability to judge that recording. The most intriguing effects occurred when the apparent reality began to influence the audiences' judgement. Méliès was in this sense as scientific a photographer as Lumière. His films are essays on visual effects —particularly those of an incredible nature—and they induce an audience not to be moved or excited by the subject matter, but to consider their own methods of observation and judgement. In this respect Méliès is an antecedent of Hitchcock and Lang, while Lumière's influence is greater on Hawks and Godard.

Lumière's work does not invoke a methodological response as readily. Although he seems more intent on the recording power of the camera he obtains responses that are not especially scientific: baby being fed is charming as well as factual, his workers leaving their factory are conceptualized into archetypes, and in *L'Arroseur arrosé*, in which a prank is played on a man hosing his garden so that he drenches himself, the response changes from conceptualization of the everyman figure watering his flowers to identification with the practical joker who stands on his hose.

L'Arroseur arrosé is very short and its transference of identification is accomplished in one shot. The joke is in the action and, to maintain its amusement, the camera must be allowed to record without interruption. One could see this fragment as broadly definitive of that aspect of film's nature that was adopted in the American cinema where the realism of the camera was put to narrative use and a mass-entertainment form resulted. The European pursuit of expressionism and surrealism opened a supposed breach between commercial and intellectual cinema, but with sound the recording abilities reached a completeness that assisted the commercial cinema towards a monopoly which itself offended the consciously artistic cinema. The harm in this breach persists when commercial producers and distributors shrink from 'art' and intellectual critics sneer at the 'entertainment' movies.

It is an unreal division, because the nature of film and its effects unify more than discrepancies in ambition divide. The most impressive revelation of the director's intention is not to be found in the script but in the unity he attains of subject and method, so that it is invalid to question the camera's recording ability on the grounds that the director chooses what to present to the camera's mechanism. The relationship between camera and subject is as unitary as that between observer and phenomenon in a scientific experiment. Film justifies the word 'medium' much more than 'art' because it is connecting rather than offering. It is more related to real existence than an ideal way of life and by recording that existence it entails the possibility of an objective definition which will reflect on our ideas of truth and meaning much more than on those of love, honour or moral criteria. Cinema and television both put their spectator in the position of the scientist. They lull the consciousness of this realization by seeming to present events in a narrative form. But the spectator's response to those events, as it differs with the response he might make to them in life, constitutes a scientific statement on human perception and judgement.

Lumière's naturalism and Méliès's dreams are equal; to call one lie and the other truth is invalidated by their shared photographic existence. In Lang's *Beyond a Reasonable Doubt* the dialectic is such as to present the images alternately as truth and lies so that the ultimate effect is destructive of the whole criterion of truth and falsity. Dana Andrews is approached by a newspaper editor to collaborate in a trick to draw attention to the dangers of capital punishment, particularly the chance of wrongful conviction. Andrews is to be made to seem guilty of a murder by manufacturing evidence against him. The act of manufacture is to be recorded by photographs and documents which the editor will keep and produce only at the last minute to demonstrate the fallibility of the legal system. The plan works. Andrews is in the death-cell when the editor drives with the file of evidence to the police. He crashes and both he and the file are destroyed. The editor's daughter, who was engaged to Andrews until the 'facts' of the murder became known, discovers at the last moment among her father's papers evidence sufficient to free Andrews. But, in fact, Andrews was the real murderer; he had taken advantage of the pact. The daughter informs on him and is left shattered, as much in her judgement as in her emotion.

Compare this with *Toni*, made in 1934. Renoir read a newspaper report of a *crime passionnel*. It intrigued him and he decided to film it. The entire film was shot on location using as many non-professionals as possible. *Beyond a Reasonable Doubt* takes place on manufactured sets and employs professional actors in every part. The people and landscapes in *Toni* are free in a sense that does not apply in Lang's films. Renoir's characters aspire to the freedom of choice of real life and the action is apparently uninfluenced by the director's purpose. But Renoir is as artificial as Lang in that he has set up the whole verisimilitudinous action for the cameras. From the outset Lang is franker in his use of contrivance. It is only as his film develops that the reality of the contrivance asserts a perspective in which physical reality—which is Renoir's goal—becomes an abstract, and epistemological reality undermines the spectator in the way Renoir's realism convinces him.

Both Lang and Renoir intend to film certain events as accurately as possible. Distortion is alien to both of them: for Lang it would pervert the functional cleanliness of the study and for Renoir it would elevate one aspect of atmosphere or personality above the others. The immense difference between the two directors is in their conceptions of visible society. Renoir's is particularized to infinity so that the complexity of motive and desire promotes a sense of phenomenology, while Lang conceives of an abstract society so simplified that every character possesses the whole range of archetype. Movement interests them both as it should film directors, but for Renoir the movement is physical and for Lang it is epic.

They are contemporaries who came to movies after the First World War and their early films reflect the two narrative trends in the cinema. Renoir inherited from his father* an enjoyment in people fulfilling themselves. His actors—so often friends—are encouraged to improvise and are epitomized by Michel Simon's extrovert tramp in *Boudu Sauvé des Eaux* and Octave, in *La Règle du Jeu*, who is the social catalyst submerging his own sadness in his delight at sociability. Octave is played by Renoir himself, and in one sequence he masquerades as a bear, the brother of Boudu. The sociable atmosphere of Renoir's films excludes everything except a recording sensibility in the camera. To this end, Renoir was one of the first directors to liberate and extend the camera's powers, particularly its mobility and depth of focus. Extension of his visual range is concurrent with moral tolerance.

Lang's narratives, on the other hand, have always been a formalization of plot and his actors have consequently been more restrained. Their performances are split into individual gestures, glances and movements which are both personal and universal. *Dr Mabuse, the Gambler*, made in 1922, is a fantastic melodrama following the structure of a serial and using every plot situation of the *genre* as a ritual. Like every serial it confronts good and evil; unlike others it heightens the conflict by setting it in a limbo world the fate of which is to be decided by the energies of the protagonists. For this Lang must photograph a world of his own, invariably built on the soundstages, and limit his view to the pressurized actions of his characters. Although enforcing it with exceptional rigour he adopts a convention of the economical melodrama, which is to keep only the essentials. An action like the ascent of a staircase can thus be implied by a shot of the climber at the foot cut to a shot of him at the top of the stairs. This device, which is commonly accepted by audiences, assumes that the character is so much a creature of the plot that it is irrelevant to see him in anything other than a plot situation; it does not permit a chance diversion on the stairs.

---

* Apart from any other virtues, *Renoir, My Father* (Collins, 1962), by Jean Renoir, supplies the background and philosophy of working for Renoir films.

CHANCE

The choice either to abbreviate or to allow the camera to record the full ascent is not contradictory. Both methods employ the camera to record and transmit information. The difference reflects a distinction of purpose. A camera divergent to spontaneity—such as Renoir's—will naturally tend to naturalistic detail and the cinematic illusion of reality. A method as convergent on precise actions as Lang's is less able to include a background that is as convincing as reality. Chance is possible in Renoir's world, but in Lang's is replaced by fate. Inasmuch as all cinema has a constant level of documentary the acceptability of random events is an indication of the director's preoccupations.

Stanley Kubrick's *The Killing* is in many ways a realist film. Its characterization, though terse, is unstylized and its people are unglamorous. Its cityscape, whether exterior or interior, is recognizable. When Sterling Hayden goes to the bus depot to deposit a gun in one of the lockers the camera tracks with him from the pavement, through the depot to the lockers and then back again to the street. The association of interior and exterior is a proof of genuineness. At the race track a real meeting is on and the action is contingent on the crowd and the races. The cinematography records the reality without ever suggesting a view different from that of any bystander. Furnishing is meticulously accurate and Lucien Ballard's photography in the scenes of preparation is based on a single artificial light source from a lampshade over a table. The camera is allowed to run until action is complete. In a long scene between Elisha Cook and Marie Windsor it tracks continually from one side of the dressing-table to the other to cover Cook's worried movements around his wife.

The realism of *The Killing* is required by its subject: a plan to rob $2 million from a race-track on the day of the big race. Like the gang's plan the film has the form of a schedule which is based upon not only the tasks of the members of the gang but utilization of the mechanisms of the city, its buildings and automobiles. Their own apartments are headquarters and planning rooms and the post-boxes are part of their signalling system. The state of roads and the time a vehicle takes from A to B must be known. There is to be no violence in the robbery because, so long as the plan is adapted sufficiently to the organization of the city and the race-track, it will not be needed. The fight staged in the bar is a decoy for the police for which a professional is hired, calmly accepting the balance of his fee against ninety days in jail.

Because of the urban awareness the huge sum of racetrack money becomes a symbol of the modern city, and to get the money it is necessary for the gang to become as regular and efficient as the machines they use. In fact, human divergence threatens their success and chance finally destroys them. The actual robbery works; the whole structure of the film's *mise-en-scène* is inevitably vindicated by the mechanical efficiency of success. But even before the robbery weaknesses appear. Cook needs the money so badly to fulfil his wife's ambitions that he has dropped a hint sufficient for her to plan a double-cross with her lover. This double-cross is significantly voyeuristic; the lover plans to watch the gang carry out their complex mission—then hit them. Ironically, Cook's wife guesses the day of the robbery because of the conflict in her husband's routines. He cannot sleep and gets up much earlier than usual; to be sure that this indicates the vital day Marie Windsor, for the first time in their married life, gets up to make his breakfast. She has guessed his plan, but he sees nothing unusual in the irregularity of her behaviour.

Windsor's lover arrives at the rendezvous to make his snatch; there is a gun battle. Hayden, arriving late after having been held up in the traffic, sees the signs of violence and drives off to the airport with the money. This is still within the plan, having been prearranged in the event of trouble, but it is now an emergency routine. He buys a second-hand suitcase and drives into the country. Behind a bush he empties the mass of money from a duffle bag into the case. With the breakdown of organization the factual content of the photography is invaded by a poetic sense of panic. This is a poetry entirely inherent in the situation, not one imposed by editing or the angles of the camera. The rural setting is incongruous with the sight of so much money and the wind agitates the bundles. At the airport his case is too heavy to travel with the passengers. He becomes the victim of airline routine so that his own actions need to be adjusted frantically to the last chance of escape. The case is taken to the plane on a truck with the rest of the luggage. The truck swerves to avoid a dog, the case falls off and bursts open. The money is blown like snow in the slipstream of the jets. It is an image of disintegration, the notes becoming as populous as the inhabitants of the city—the plan finally exploded.

In *The Killing* chance is filmed as faithfully as the plan because it is a contesting element. When Ted de Corsia, the policeman in the gang, refuses a call for help from a woman because he has to be at the track by a certain time, this is a refusal of his occupation's random nature which commits him to the success of the plan. In *Rear Window*, James Stewart, Grace Kelly and Thelma Ritter face such a dilemma when the actions of two of the people they are watching both require attention at the same time. Miss Lonelyhearts appears to be on the verge of suicide: a chance intrusion on their observation of Raymond Burr. They do nothing about Miss Lonelyhearts and the camera, returning to Burr, ignores her. The incident is typical of Hitchcock's premeditated selection of events so as to subject his characters to moral pressure and to expose their indecision between the stimuli of the film and the ordinary moral code they may be presumed to share with most of the audience. That Miss Lonelyhearts is in fact saved is indicative of Hitchcock's intolerance of complication and his taunting resolution of self-confessedly artificial difficulties.

Chance is, of course, a primary impulse in Hitchcock's films, subjecting his characters to ordeal; but it is a purposeful and, ultimately, didactic chance. Cary Grant's trans-continental chase in *North by Northwest* may have been started by the fortuitousness of his calling an hotel page at a certain moment, but for Hitchcock it is a deserved accident. Grant's essential flippancy is to be stripped by events of great danger which, to tease Grant, themselves preserve an appearance of comedy.

Contrast Hitchcock's method with the precepts of the *cinéma-vérité* technique, in which a selected subject is covered by recording devices and recordists as unobtrusively as possible.

This is a method in which the chance occurrence is most likely to shape the film. One of the Drew Associates' films concerns John Grenier,* the campaign manager for Senator Goldwater in the 1964 Presidential election. Much of the film concentrates on Grenier in his office, either in conference with assistants or on the phone to local agents. During one session he is interrupted by a call from an agent who had arranged an impossible schedule for Goldwater. The quiet reprimand that Grenier administers on his amplified telephone is in front of several other organizers. One of the other men even adds his own say to Grenier's and, when the agent makes an attempt at excuse, Grenier and the other man smile despairingly at each other. This complicity is as effective a fulfilment of paranoid suspicions as any fictionalized film might achieve and a great deal of its effect comes from the tension between a spontaneous situation and a dramatically significant action. The chance incident is a revealing of character and environment as Grenier's telephone apparatus is amenable to the cinematographic recording instruments.

For the makers of the Grenier film, the telephone call from the agent was the equivalent of a scoop, and it is the hope of *cinéma-vérité* that such an incident should be generated while the cameras are turning, reproducing its time sequence for an audience and so maintaining its continuity that the spectator watches in the same circumstances as one of the men at the conference.

PHOTOGRAPHIC EFFECTS

Whether a frank mirroring of reality or the carefully selected recording of contrivance, the cinema's capacity is for achieving an accurate visual reproduction and, in most cases, for maintaining the natural time sequence. The joke in *L'Arroseur arrosé* depends upon unity of time and place just as much as John Grenier's authority or Cary Grant's realization of the menace of the crop-spraying aeroplane in *North by Northwest*. But the cinema has a unique flexibility in its handling of time, involving

* An extract from this film was shown on John Grierson's television programme *This Wonderful World* in the spring of 1965.

1. An image from Auguste Renoir appearing in his son's *Partie de Campagne*, based on Maupassant's story. The pattern of love found and lost is inseparable from the change of season and countryside.

2. A street scene from Lang's *The Woman in the Window*. A construction of wood and plaster on the studio floor, the puddles carefully put down and the light and shadow representing not only street-lights and moonlight but the landscape of legend.

3. Chance takes a hand. *The Killing*. Sterling Hayden watches the bag holding the money being taken away. The light is that of a real airport vestibule.

4. *Une Vie*. Maria Schell says goodbye to Pascale Petit as she leaves the house with the child Schell's husband has given her. Petit is intent on the child but Schell is susceptible to loss.

5. Dana Andrews laughingly poses with the manufactured evidence of the murder he has really committed. *Beyond a Reasonable Doubt*.

a constant present tense which is able to juxtapose, without any obvious photographic differences, the past, present and future. The inexorable present in which the specific image is perceived, with its echoes of the past and intimations of the future, is what associates a movie with a dream.

It is a classic solution of movies to declare that the sequence of events just witnessed was only a dream of one of the film's characters. It is possible to think of many more films as dreams than simply those admitting it. The whole of *Citizen Kane* might be Kane's own dreamed recollections in the last moments before his death. The fact that the film takes the form of investigations carried out by a representative of a newsreel company could be interpreted as showing the degree to which Kane's own publicity has conditioned his attitude to himself. Like newsreel and the sort of popular journalism Kane's own newspaper purveys the visual context of *Citizen Kane* has a constant sense of factual escape which is typical of dream experience. What determines *Citizen Kane*, in scene after scene, is the general preconception, rather than the actual realization. In other words, the events are predominantly in the past tense, and it is a characteristic of Welles's film that it ignores much of a movie's present-tense powers. What carries *Citizen Kane* along is not the physical realization but the affectionate nostalgia beneath the investigative structure. The early scene at the boy Kane's prairie home when his parents sign him away to the bank is rare for its sense of actuality. At this stage the film's perspectives are still within the bounds of naturalism and the shot of Kane's parents and the representative of the bank in the house, with young Kane seen through the window throwing snowballs, involves a directly meaningful spatial relationship which is enhanced by the sequence having opened with a shot from outside the window of the mother looking out at her son.

As the film progresses—and it has a generally chronological sequence—the perspectives become more distorted. The wide-angle lenses exceed the eye's angle of vision and distend the depth of focus, both of which are refinements of the camera's recording function, and serve to separate the area near the camera from the distance. That is, the middle distance becomes expanded and a character will appear to move from long-shot into close-up unnaturally quickly. In Xanadu, at the end of his life, Kane's world has become one of gross close-ups and huge panoramic shots in which the human scale is so dwarfed as to be close to absurdity. *Kane* is often no more than a variety of striking still photographs, in which the control of the camera is heavy with intended meaning.

These are expressionist devices, and one of the cinema's first 'dream' films is also known as one of the origins of cinematic expressionism: *The Cabinet of Dr Caligari*. In *Caligari* the dream sequence which comprises most of the film is made up of normal photography of distorted settings. But is it not unnecessary duplication to stylize one item in the visual context when the process of watching a film itself constitutes a far subtler resemblance to the state of dreaming? The shock in *Caligari* comes when the fact of the dream is revealed and the garden, in which the story is told, is shown as being part of an asylum. But as the film stands this is a gratuitous shock, because the context of the dream has been so deliberately heightened that it could only be the product of madness. The suspicion in our mind that the asylum and its authorities are really insane and the patients sane would be more worrying if the 'dream' were naturalistic. Thus in Lang's *The Woman in the Window* there is no photographic distinction between the real and the dream sequences: both have the gleaming simplicity of Lang's blacks and whites—a photographic style which at its best is always poised between the dream and the concrete—and Edward G. Robinson's normally quiet business and domestic life is balanced with the sordidness and violence of his dream. In recording the two levels of Robinson's life without distinction Lang makes the reality and the fantasy so compatible that their relationship is fluid. The fluidity suggests the overthrow of order and sanity and yet still leaves a conclusion apparently conventional and happy.

In Welles's case there has always been a tendency towards baroque photography: the contradiction in these terms is indicative of a misuse of film. This has not always brought failure for Welles; the formal inflation of his image at the expense of actual content is as appropriate to *Confidential Report* and *Touch of Evil* as it is to *Kane*. But in *The Trial* he does fail

34

because much of Kafka's horror is in its factualness. The calmer photography of *Paris Nous Appartient* is better suited to the demonstration of the inexplicable than the various devices of *The Trial*. With a few exceptions, *Citizen Kane* consists of recollections by the various characters in which a specific explanation of Kane fails to materialize. Just as Xanadu is full of treasure-troves Kane has never examined, the rapid succession of sketches, montages and chiaroscura camera effects present journalistic accounts of the incidents in his life as unpenetrative of significant details as the newsreel which opens the film and sets the reporter, Thompson, off on his round of Kane's acquaintances to discover a meaning for its subject's life and last word 'Rosebud'.

One is tempted to think that Welles has grown to resemble Kane and to relate the attractions of grandeur of the great men in his films to a personal estimation of heroic proportions. Welles's common theme is the secret of the powerful man and his cinematic method is to create an aura of mystification around these men—whether Kane or Gregory Arkadin in *Confidential Report*—that disguises a hollow centre. His characters are opportunities for him to dress up, to photograph himself from a series of odd angles and to mesmerize the other people in his film. This power undoubtedly satisfies Welles, and to leave everyone in bewildered awe would have delighted Kane.

Confidential Report follows the efforts of a young American, hired by Arkadin, to track down Arkadin's past. Ostensibly Arkadin is intent on making sure his secret is safe but the hiring is also a vicarious trick, an indulgence by which he focuses attention upon himself. The cinematic attention is very overwrought. Welles is photographed so constantly from floor level that he loses all impressiveness and degenerates into a posturing mountain. When his secret is discovered—though never revealed to the audience—Welles is flying in his aeroplane. He hears that his beloved daughter knows the secret—and vanishes. The plane is discovered flying pilotless. There is nothing at the centre but a vacuum. One's frustration with Welles is the feeling that this conclusion to the very interesting subject of the film is one that he is not conscious of. Glory seems to enchant Welles and, to achieve a reputation he may subsequently be nostalgic about, he acquires all the pomp of a magician. But the hat is really empty.

Welles's second film, *The Magnificent Ambersons*, is also a recollection, in which the director himself speaks the nostalgic narrative, instead of appearing at its centre. It also uses the cameo and sketch, particularly in the opening sequence describing the town in which the Ambersons lived. But, thereafter, it is much more immediately realized. The deep-focus photography is credibly adjusted to the Ambersons' house which, as a set, dominates the action. *Ambersons* is both a more perfect and a less interesting film than *Kane*. The interest declines with the frankness of its acceptance of Tarkington's novel's form and its beauty derives from the importance the film places on actual encounters recorded in takes as long as are necessary. The sequence between Tim Holt and his Aunt, Agnes Moorehead, and those in which Holt and Anne Baxter first ride and then walk through the streets of the town, because their continuity of events contains so many 'meanings' of character and situation, make satisfying demonstrations of the human relationships to which the movie dedicates itself. They are rich sequences, in a Jamesian sense, the complete report establishing a hierarchy that is the structure of the social system. The nostalgia of *Ambersons* is really for a magnificence constituted by the co-existence of formal and individual behaviour.

The three sequences referred to have the same exactness of event as that moment in James's *The Portrait of a Lady* when Isabel, on entering a room, sees Osmond, her husband, and Madame Merle together in such a position that intuitively she senses the nature of their relationship. That James should make so 'photographic' a scene central to his novel is one of the naturalistic portents in both plays and novels in the late nineteenth century. Just as for Isabel the sight has a physical memory which grows with understanding during the rest of the novel, so in the movies the enacting accuracy of meaningfulness in an image attaches itself to the spectator's consciousness.

Because the cinema is able to extract such concentrated attention the most subtle and important meanings may not be in the more 'signposted' items but in the most natural and unconscious gestures of the actor or the dimension of a setting. The fireside conversation between Osmond and Madame Merle is not momentous in itself. Its essence is in the naturalness of behaviour and the angle of vision that uncovers it. So in *Ambersons*, the scene between Holt and Moorehead is less important in the development of plot than many others. But in allowing us to see as simple a thing as the way Holt eats several helpings of strawberry cake it indicates his character. And it is not simply that he eats a lot of the cake, but that he eats quickly and automatically, with the selfishness and crudity of palate of an adolescent. The very behaviour—and not a literary description of it—forms our consciousness of the character.

PRESENT TENSE

The present-tense values of this sequence from *Ambersons* are, of course, distinctive of a camera, and of the spectator's own experience of looking at people. In the cinema it is a power able to transcend time and make up a sequence which may at times be narrative, but is always primarily a self-sufficient succession of images. For many years the commercial cinema had no equivalent for the literary 'I remember' other than a heightening of background music and a slow dissolve which eventually gave way to recollection, itself decorated with blurred edges, slow-motion or the manipulation of colour. It was certainly not a *flash*-back. Resnais showed in *Hiroshima Mon Amour* just how suddenly and briefly a memory might obtrude. When Emmanuelle Riva sees her Japanese lover's arm and hand as he lies asleep there is a shot of perhaps two seconds showing another hand and arm. Only later do we learn that they belong to her dead German lover. The connection between these shots is of subject-matter and, by implication, of Riva's involvement as observer in both, but immediately it is an autonomous association that stimulates speculation. The fact that they are put one after the other does not advance a running narrative line but it indicates the whole means by which the film does advance. For the cinema has made the German's arm as present as the Japanese arm. There is no sense of the 'literary' mind endeavouring to describe an earlier similar sight; it bursts straight into the film and into Riva's and the spectators' consciousnesses. As such it is an indication of the associative nature of *Hiroshima* and its use of the cinematic ability to make all time present and all events equally plausible by demonstrating them.

In Godard's *Une Femme Mariée*, the wife, Macha Meril, in her 'statement' to the camera, aligns herself with this cinematic function: 'J'aime mieux l'présent. C'est plus excitant, le présent. J'aime bien la musique . . . les choses qui s'abîment . . . J'aime bien les fleurs . . . C'est pour ça que j'aime le présent, parce que, pendant le "présent", j'ai pas le temps de réfléchir, j'peux pas penser . . . J'suis surprisé par rien de c'qui m'arrive . . .'* It is this immediateness that makes her the centre of the film's consciousness to such an extent that her wilfulness often controls its shape, particularly in that sequence in which her husband chases her through the house. There are seven 'statements' in the film, all preceded by a title. The first five are simply characters speaking to the camera much as if they were being interviewed, and of these only Meril's sequence has retained the interviewer's questions. Even though these questions are not heard, she pauses attentively while they are asked and then tries to answer them. Everything she says has been provoked by a question. Her husband's, her son's, and their friend, Roger Leenhardt's, statements, are uninterrupted. In the husband's case—a consideration of memory—it is a halting soliloquy, and in Leenhardt's, on intelligence, as fluent as a lecture. But Meril's is spontaneous, formed by the moment. Although it comprises an attitude, the attitude has to be prompted instead of being offered.

Its philosophy controls its way of delivery as much as all her behaviour. She moves from lover to husband, and back to lover again, and is always most taken with the one she is with at the moment. One could even say that she has some of the attributes of the camera: an ability to treat time in the same way as a travelling camera treats space, by moving onwards mechanically.

For Riva, just as for Meril's husband in *Une Femme Mariée*, the

* *L'Avant-Scène* (Cinema) No. 46, March 1965. Contains the whole script of *Une Femme Mariée*.

absorption of the past is a problem. The husband's statement on memory is prompted by a visit he has just made to the Auschwitz trials. *Nuit et Brouillard* is largely concerned with the potency of the concentration camps in our memory and its form is the same as Resnais establishes with the compared arms in *Hiroshima*. The controlling influence of the past is Resnais's preoccupation and it is often specified in the role played in his films by architecture. In *Nuit et Brouillard* we see the camp as it was in operation, and as the monument it is today. Hiroshima's destruction is contrasted with the city's new, post-atomic buildings and the nineteenth century architecture of Nevers.

The cinematic sequence of images is comparable not only with a kinetic concept of architecture, but with many other systems of contemporary civilization. The pattern of the celluloid strip is the universal experience of living: a constant present, in which the forms and often the content of every instant repeat the previous instant. Every moment has the complete concentration of the person, but it has also a built-in obsolescence, and not only in the overtly ephemeral aspects of life, such as fashion in clothes and the constantly renewed succession of pop records. At the apparently more fundamental levels of technological development and mass production the same impulse is evident. In the automobile industry, for instance, it shapes the annual need for new designs and the production-line system on which the vehicles are assembled. The pressure on the automobile designer is like that on the research scientist, the aircraft inventor and the rocketry physicist, while the automobile assembler is an archetype of production workers, whether the end-product be computers, transistor radios, newspapers, or even movies. There is a political equivalent in the saying 'The king is dead, long live the king', and its example in the swearing in of Lyndon Johnson as president, ninety-nine minutes after Kennedy's death, in the aeroplane that waited to carry him and his predecessor's corpse to Washington.

Macha Meril's character in *Une Femme Mariée* is a response to this condition, and her inclination to analyse her own position and the quality of events in her life is typical of modern epistemology. But a literary sense of the past, and its possible restrictions, does intrude: not only the memories of Auschwitz for her husband, but her own doubt about whose baby she is carrying. There are many similarities between Meril and Riva in *Hiroshima*. Both films explore the cinematic aptitude for the dislocation between human memory and the emphasis on the present in contemporary society. Both films have several passages in which the women's almost random experience of the present is faithfully detailed—Riva in her hotel, Meril in her apartment—hinting at an automaton existence that might exclude meditation.

In both cases, the sequence of living, by being made a cinematic sequence, is likely to be appreciated as a narrative sequence. Such a possibility is inherent in film once one decides on a subject, even if that choice is as spontaneous and non-authoritarian as possible. The tension between past and present is especially exposed by narrative forms because their events are endowed with sequence.

The opening of Hawks's *Only Angels Have Wings* shows Jean Arthur arriving in a small South American port and meeting two pilots from the local airline. One of them, Joe, makes a date with her. At the last minute he has to make a flight in thick fog. He takes off, but is ordered back. Eager to pick up his date he tries to land instead of staying in the air until the fog lifts. He is killed. The rest of the pilots, Cary Grant particularly, seem to ignore the fact. Arthur is shocked by their callousness when, in the *cantina*, Grant eats a meal that Joe had ordered. 'What about Joe?' she cries. 'Joe?' answers Grant. 'Who's Joe?' They all deny knowledge of him. Joe's death through an un-professional gamble has disqualified him from mention and memory, even though when he was in trouble in the air Grant and others were anxiously giving advice and instructions to him over the radio.

But even for the self-sufficient Grant the past may assert itself. Later in the film, Richard Barthelmess arrives as a relief pilot with his wife, Rita Hayworth. Grant once had an affair with Hayworth and knew Barthelmess at the time he won a reputation as a coward. Although short of pilots, Grant sends Barthelmess on a most hazardous flight. It involves landing a plane on a small plateau. The resolution of this sequence, in the

way that it records the crucial action, is to redeem Barthelmess:
by the pilots' code his present-tense success absolves past failure.
To do this Hawks has a shot so audacious that the spectator is
totally involved in the difficulty of Barthelmess's task and convinced of his skill. Barthelmess's plane is held in a single take
with the camera in another plane in front of him. The plane
attempts to land at a first run-in but overshoots and is forced to
lift off again. It then turns a complete circle round the sheer
faces of the plateau and comes down again successfully, halting
only yards from the brink.

Barthelmess's success indicates not only his own skill but the
method of Hawks's film. The near-mythic South American
airfield with its closed community of fortune-hunters and
adventurers, manifests the screen's isolating function but supplies the reality of the people's lives with photography that is
self-effacingly accurate. Thus Barthelmess's landing is an event
both in the narrative sequence and as an autonomous incident.
The movement of the camera is an equivalent of the film's
criteria of professionalism and honour. It is a demonstration of
skill, character, environment and the specific, narrow society in
which most Hawks movies are set.

COLOUR

Like sound, colour is an extension of the cinema's recording
powers. There are those who claim that today all films should
be in colour because to neglect it is to aim at something less than
the full potential of accuracy. But the adoption of colour has
not been universal in the way that sound quickly changed the
whole process of film-making. Neither has CinemaScope been
as totally accepted as those who note the similarity between it
and the eyes' angle of vision would like. Just as sound was once
as much a problem to many film-makers as an advantage, so
colour and wide screens are ambivalent benefits. As they
increase the recording powers they expose intentions unaware
of the importance of these powers.

Colour is like black-and-white cinematography in the situations with which it confronts its users: how can it reproduce
faithfully and how can it be employed in narrative without

restricting the freedom of the characters? Can a person in a film wear a colour without acquiring the 'meanings' of that colour to the exclusion of all else? The more accurate colour photography becomes the more this is possible and the more likely it is for colour in movies to be appreciated as it is in life. A painter selects a colour intending its value to be felt by the spectator; although he must choose, that predicament has the reward of meaning for him. The movement of film offers freedom of colour: there is no need for choice to be limiting. A character can wear one and then another colour and the colours, ideally, are not made in the camera, but transcribed from the subject.

Antonioni's *Il Deserto Rosso* is a conscious essay on film and colour and it demonstrates two functions: as a source of intrinsic, emotional or symbolic meaning, and as a sign, a piece of information. Thus in the 'orgy' sequence the walls are painted red, as later, when Harris and Vitti have made love in an hotel room, they will turn pink: the red here is intended as a poetic source of sexuality. But yellow is a signal, whether the quarantine flag on a ship or poison gas coming from a factory chimney. Vitti's alienation from Ravenna and her life there is expressed by her inability to decide on a colour for the walls of the shop she is going to open. This difficulty is, of course, the one faced by the painter.

Vitti's dream, realized in the story she tells her son, evokes conventional emotional colours: blue sea, golden sands. The sequence stands out because of its very crudity. Its recording of colour is, compared with the rest of the film, so old-fashioned that it recalls the cinema's earliest use of colour when transmission was in itself an achievement. Long before *Becky Sharp*, the first full colour movie made in 1935, tinting had been used. Renoir's *Nana*, made in 1926, has an overall tint in several sequences which demonstrates how technical limitations imposed limiting effects. Thus the green of an outdoor sequence has an overpowering 'mood'. Early Technicolor films had such problems of control that they compromised with 'theatrical' colour. The musical was beset with this problem and in *Meet Me in St Louis*, the rather harsh primary colours are diverted and diffused to fit a mood of nostalgia and childhood fantasy.

Duel in the Sun deliberately accentuates the garishness of its colour to produce a primitive and operatic effect.

However, by the time Vidor came to make *War and Peace*, which in Hollywood terms was of operatic potential, he was able to take advantage of improved processes to present a much more naturalistic colour range. When Otto Preminger made *Bonjour Tristesse*, *Exodus* and *The Cardinal*, the advance was sufficient for most of the colour not to be noticed for itself, but to constitute an extra accuracy. At the same time, Minnelli and, to some extent, Hitchcock, have continued to use colour as an emotional instrument. *Lust for Life* is a study in the colours of Van Gogh's palette often to the exclusion of all others, so that an intuitive sympathy with the painter develops and, though the images are undistorted, the colour is so concentrated that one's experience is as heightened as the painting of the reaper in a field of blazing orange corn which Van Gogh speaks about to a nun at the end of the film. In *Marnie* colour works at two emotional levels : the traumatic red as a signal, which alerts the audience as sharply as Marnie herself; and the jaundiced yellows and absinthe greens which are constantly appearing in the décor as symptoms of illness, and which correspond with Marnie's own blonde hair and the blonde bag we see at the beginning of the film containing the money she has stolen.

Both *Marnie* and *Lust for Life* have a restricted use of colour because they are so conscious of it ; they share the predicament simplified in *Nana* where one effect excludes all others. *The Cardinal* is even able to introduce a blatantly theatrical colour scene and yet resist being overwhelmed because the film's colour context is so scrupulously objective. When Tom Tryon visits the cheap vaudeville where his sister is dancing, the exotic colours of the show appear as the make-up they are. The same principle applies to the ecclesiastical richness in the scenes of Tryon's investiture : the colours of ritual are not necessarily representative of the man.

Reputation can be made colourful by rumour and in *Rancho Notorious* Lang controls the colours that surround Marlene Dietrich to illustrate this. Dietrich's first appearances are in flash-backs recounted by people Arthur Kennedy meets in his search for the man who raped and killed his girl. An exotic woman is conveyed by these anecdotes who sings in saloons in purples and greens and rides along main street in shimmering pastels. Her big win at the chuck-a-luck is represented by the revolving kaleidoscope of the wheel itself. But when Dietrich makes an actual appearance she is more ordinarily dressed in clothes that are suited to the horse ranch she owns. Kennedy is unable to see that she is a real woman—rather than a *femme fatale*. He urges her to put on her one fine dress because the vital brooch is pinned to it. Dietrich puts on this image of notoriety to please the man she loves but its sight only provokes him to vengeful rage and a cruel rejection of her.

The richest use of colour is the richest use of cinematography: such fidelity to the event that the naturalistic and symbolic meanings do not seem separate. In *Rebel without a Cause* James Dean's blue jeans and red jacket, though clearly naturalistic, are romantic expressions of his need for outsize events. They make an assertive contrast with the subdued colours of Californian suburbia and his parents' clothes just as the prophetic apocalypse in the planetarium scene is a subjective interpretation of an ordinary afternoon.

Made in 1955 in a plausible contemporary setting, *Rebel* was one of the first movies to develop the documentary qualities inherent in wide screen and colour. Its background has the neutrality of wood and stone further devitalized by the bias to brown and green of WarnerColor, the process in which the film was shot. But even in a film like *Party Girl*, in which the process was much more sophisticated, Nicholas Ray is still using colour to evoke a gulf between conscience and corruption. The reds worn by Cyd Charisse so take the place of animation in her performance that the dance routines express her character at a level of abstraction that is much more appropriate than the conventional melodrama. Hollywood's failure to respond to the colour reality that its processes have made possible is symptomatic of its inability to transcend the feature convention. The contemporary cityscape is in fact depriving itself of colours as values and either using them as signs or allowing the proper colour of an object to remain untouched. In Don Siegel's *The Killers* the outstanding colours are the turquoise of a tinted window and the orange of carrot juice: examples of colours serving their own functions, rather than emotive purposes. The basic colours in *The Killers* are the blue of tarmac and steel and the browns of wooden furniture and tanned skin.

One can believe that the characters in *The Killers* choose the colours they wear themselves. The yellow dress in which Angie Dickinson first appears is not a symbol of cowardice or seduction but a fact which one recalls as one might a colour event in life. Its meaning can be rationalized retrospectively depending on how one judges her behaviour in the film. Then, it reads not simply as a deliberately attractive device, an image of beauty, vacillation or treachery, but embodies all these associations.

The Killers is very plainly photographed, as if by an automatic camera. In a Ray or Antonioni movie the colour is, of course, being carefully controlled. In *Pierrot le Fou* Godard is content to employ every improvement that technology offers and to record all colours on the same level. There is in *Pierrot* a striking sense of the reality of the colour and none of a directorial meaning being applied through it. This factual apprehension can accommodate the contrasts of colour in advertisements, the artificial colour of an automobile, the natural colours in a landscape or the colours of a character's clothes and skin, and thus all the internal references, both significant and insignificant. The numerous white interiors make a background for the arbitrariness of colour. When Belmondo is casually tortured in the bath by having Karina's red dress tied round his head, instead of making the simple cruel association we share his sense of colour's mutability. This dress that Karina once wore she must have had to take off, so that now she would appear a different colour. Belmondo associates the soaking dress with blood because of the likeness and because he is an intellectual who schematizes his life as it happens. Colour here has been allowed to retain its private relationship with an object as in a Jasper Johns flag or the parrot that Belmondo has in *Pierrot*.

LIGHT

Light is the means of cinematography and of knowledge derived from seeing. Significantly, a flash of light experienced personally offers the sign, and even the substance, of revelation; the manipulation of light in the cinema is equally the effect of conviction and may be considered, with Welles's drama of perspective and angle, as an intentful elaboration. American feature movies between 1925 and 1945 largely employed artificial light in studios to simulate exterior as well as interior conditions. Night in these circumstances was day-for-night, shot in the equivalent of daylight and filtered. Thus a conception of night is presented which is acceptable because the technique has rendered it visible. Since 1945 improved filmstocks have gradually enabled movies to be shot under actual conditions. Night in *Alphaville* is the blackness that surrounds a city and is broken up within it only by the varieties of lighting that burn in a city through the night. Paradoxically, though genuine, it is more disorientating because it makes a direct connection with our feelings about night, freeing night's doubt to invade our imaginations.

The lighting cameraman has had to become more flexible. His function is to record an image, whereas for many Hollywood cameramen it was to establish a mood. Josef von Sternberg's films so concentrate on the potential of abstraction contained by a scheme of lighting that is adjusted to action that their emphasis shifts from the scenario to the plasticity of light on objects and people. 'Shadow is mystery and light is clarity. Shadow conceals—light reveals. To know what to reveal and what to conceal and in what degree to do this is all there is to art'* indicates the concentration of von Sternberg's cinema and the degree to which it lacks a formalized intelligence. The conceptions of action and characterization in his films would be crudely theatrical but for the entirely photographic subtlety given to them. Thus *The Scarlet Empress* is a blatant lampoon on the dignity of history, monarchy and Russia but a brilliant set of variations on the disruption of sexual relationships by inequality. The only constant is the presence of Marlene Dietrich, and the progress she makes, from the young innocent seduced by a handsome Russian officer to the Empress picking bedfellows from among her soldiers, is not one of narrative or character but of light. The young girl is photographed clearly but as the film advances shadow encroaches on her and she

* 'More Light', Josef von Sternberg, *Sight and Sound*, Autumn 1955.

becomes increasingly surrounded by veils. These make her more enchanting and perverse until she has all the Russian qualities that shocked her when she first arrived in Moscow.

The Scarlet Empress and *The Devil Is a Woman* are the climaxes of Sternberg's photography of Dietrich and they are a succession of set-pieces, the intervals between which are often staggering ellipses of motivation. Dietrich's face is less personal in these films than a primary motif, others being configurations of light and shade, veils, feathers, saturnine moustached heroes, certain lines of dialogue, the idea of disguise and symmetrical reversals of incident. Dietrich is a provocatively shy seductress, conscious of her effect, and the men are ironists observing their own infatuation.

The wit in Sternberg's movies is that he makes his realization artificial, and this is the proper expression of his fatalism, which in literary terms is banal; but because his audio-visual world is so dense the human wilfulness and stupidity that attempt to control it are true gestures of vanity in the face of destiny. The great motif of *The Scarlet Empress* is a swinging motion, to be seen in the bells of Imperial Russia, Dietrich's adolescent innocence on a garden swing, the various amulets and necklaces that are dangled before her, and in the to-and-fro shifts of power in the court. It has its finest instance in the close-up of Dietrich seen through the heavy mesh of a veil as she swings a necklace back and forth and the light regularly flares on its diamonds; the spirit is so resigned that the face is barely visible. The very essence of Sternberg's Moscow is not in the historical reality but in the jewel, the veil and the light.

It was von Sternberg's ambition to make a film in which everything photographed was artificial and his closest approach to this was his last film, *The Saga of Anatahan*, which, though made under great limitations and without the quality of playing he had in America, has a completeness that summarizes his work and a simplicity that denotes full maturity—the restrictions imposed by finance stimulated a purer abstraction. The subject is archetypal: fifteen men and one woman marooned on a volcanic island for seven years; but the film is utterly abstract: the set is a man-made jungle that shines in the light and throws a lattice of shadow on the action. The Japanese faces seem devoid of expression. To possess the woman, the men proceed to kill each other off in dynastic struggles as absurd as those in *Scarlet Empress*. The same pendulum motif of destiny taunts them: the waves that advance on and recede from the island; the swinging hammock occupied by different men in succession; the lost movements of men wandering in the jungle, and the swaying woman as she dances for the men. The narrative of *Anatahan* describes the men searching in vain for meaning on the island. Von Sternberg's world is pessimistic because it mocks the idea of meaning. Its constants are the two sexes, the patterns of their movements and the light that exposes and confuses them.

On the other hand, the manufactured images in Lang's movies show a didactic use of light and darkness that is free of Sternberg's obsessiveness if only because there is no one like Dietrich, the pre-eminent fatalist, at the centre of the light. Rather, the differences of illumination are likely to affect every character: thus Glenn Ford passes from the light of happiness to the dark of revenge in *The Big Heat* and is himself unaware of the altered light. Renoir's light has always been convincingly real just as he explored real locations before the majority of other directors. But it is like his father's light, warmly atmospheric and a perfect expression of the film's personality. There is his father's pantheism in the slight diffusion of *Partie de Campagne* that is an idealism made tangible.

Light is only beginning to be restored to the function it serves in life of falling equally upon all people. The lighting cameraman Raoul Coutard has written of the way Godard has inspired this revolution, suddenly demanding speed of the cameraman who once had been the regulating force in production schedules. Godard, said Coutard, asked one thing: 'You must rediscover how to do things simply'.* This sort of simplicity shares *cinéma-vérité*'s desire for a record and a sense of the instant in which it may be obtained. Eight-millimetre cameras are already available on which the operator does not have to deal with exposure, because of an automatic setting device. Essentially this is enhancing an objective record that does not discriminate between

* 'Light of Day', *Sight and Sound*, Winter 1965–66.

its parts. The images obtained by this sort of method—and they exist in *Lola, Vivre Sa Vie, Bande à Part, Alphaville* and *Pierrot le Fou*—make a unique presentation to the spectator in their combination of visual clarity and non-committal interpretation. The radiant sunlight in *Lola* is not the effect of radiance but the simple stratagem of photographing the sun. The streets of Paris and the *banlieue* in *Bande à Part* are not the critically tense streets built on sound-stages in Lang's *Woman in the Window* but the equal actuality susceptible to every private projection, the reproduction of the spectator's own experience and not the insinuation of an ideal.

MISE-EN-SCÈNE

Alexandre Astruc, the director of *Une Vie*, formulated the *camera-stylo* theory, which suggested that a camera can be used in the way a writer uses a pen. It is a theory illustrated by his own work and descriptive of that of F. W. Murnau, Jean Renoir, Max Ophuls, Kenji Mizoguchi and Otto Preminger. The comparison with a pen is a sign of Astruc's literary antecedents. He is closer to the point when he says, 'Je voudrais pouvoir exprimer par le moyen de la camera les rapports de l'âme et des corps'.* The pen is invoked as a comparison because the popular appeal of narrative forms has passed from written works to audio-visual media. The concentration upon visual narrative, inasmuch as it is impossible to distinguish between the photographed existence and the life we live, presents the spectator with the question of how far life takes on narrative forms and how far a narrative suppresses life's spontaneous potential. Between Guy de Maupassant's novel *Une Vie* and Astruc's version of it there is the customary difference between film and writing: the intrinsic precision of words insists on the skill of the writer, but the divergence of the moving photograph devolves upon the judgement of the spectator. The idea of the novel, that life is neither as good nor as bad as one thinks, is retained in the film, but whereas in the book it is a bitterly ironic verdict Maupassant passes on his heroine and her society, in the film it is a much more personal

* *Telerama*, No. 513, May 1961.

admission of failure and loss. Maupassant's society was unbalanced in favour of the male but Astruc's is as level as the camera's eye.

In the film the misfortunes of the woman have been halved: only her husband deceives her. The events of this deception have been heightened to show up their inherent melodrama. Schell's failure to perceive the pattern of conventional marital betrayal is symptomatic of her lack of insight. She does not understand the events as the film's spectators are expected to. Thus, whereas in the book the husband is a mean little lecher, entirely the creature of provincial life, in the film Christian Marquand makes a much more complex and sympathetic character. The fast tracking-shot with him as he strides through the woods hunting is an exciting event, a movement as appealing as Jeanne's run down to the sea at the beginning of the film and one in which the sense is conveyed through the camera rather than the contrapuntalism of camera and monologue.

Maupassant's novel is told by the woman in the first person. The film has the relevant events interspersed with Schell's account of them. The account is entirely dispassionate so that, when applied to the present sufferings, it is clearly retrospective and to some extent chilled by the final tragedy. It is as formal, and yet as simply real, as the film's colour scheme. At one level the Brittany landscape is reproduced with all Claude Renoir's skill, evoking the atmospheric context admirably and filling the role of descriptive prose. At another level it forms a series of signals which indicates the course of action, without ever seeming arbitrary or non-naturalistic.

The colour scheme of *Une Vie* is as appropriate to its setting as that of *The Killers*. But nineteenth century Brittany is an environment in which the availability of colour in dress is restrained by inhibition and economy and in which the colours of landscape are bound to predominate. No costume in the film has a colour which does not appear in the countryside or seashore, and the impressions they make depend on how they relate character and setting. Maria Schell's misfortunes are signalled by yellow: when she and Pascale Petit run down to the sea at the opening Petit wears a yellow dress and they run through yellow flowers; when Schell is in danger of drown-

ing Petit's yellow dress blows in the wind like a distress flag;
on the night Marquand first seduces Petit Schell wears a yellow
dress; when Marquand goes hunting with his prospective
mistress, Antonella Lualdi, Schell wears a yellow dress; and
during the picnic that precedes the fatal betrayal Lualdi not
only wears a yellow dress but brandishes a yellow-centred daisy.

To state the scheme as plainly as this is to reveal how
inseparable it is from the moving film's account. Further, it is to
isolate it as a device and to attribute it to Astruc's calculation
as an item of meaning. One's experience of the scheme, however,
does not distinguish the observation of the fact and the conclusion of its intention. The fatuity of using words to describe
film is more obvious in Astruc's case than with most other
directors. His camera movements illustrate this difficulty. Many
of Murnau's, Ophuls's or Anthony Mann's movements can be
described because they have an intrinsic meaning—either
lateral or circular travelling shots—that figures in several of the
directors' films and thus comes to represent a motif. Astruc's
movements, though, defy a verbal account because they take
lines and directions that 'shadow' the action without necessarily
becoming exclusively aligned with a character.

Astruc is not well known in this country but he is essential to
a consideration of the theory of cinematography. He has made
only six features and had previously written one novel and
several of the most influential articles on cinema. The literary
connection is very strong for Astruc; frequently he compares the
effects of films with the effects of Balzac, Flaubert and
Dostoevsky. The fact that he has written one novel indicates
the possible difficulty of his choice of medium, and the theory of
camera-stylo is an attempt to dissolve that difficulty: 'Il [the
cinema] devient . . . un langage . . . c'est-à-dire une forme dans
laquelle et par laquelle un artiste peut exprimer sa pensée,
aussi abstraite soit-elle, ou traduire ses obsessions exactement
comme il en est aujourd'hui de l'essai ou du roman. C'est
pourquoi en nouvel âge celui de la camera-stylo.'*

The sort of novel that Astruc refers to most often is the realist
narrative of the nineteenth century and it is for this reason that

* 'Naissance d'une nouvelle avant-garde, le camera-stylo', *Écran Français*,
No. 144, March 1948.

Une Vie is his own masterpiece. *Une Vie*, like all Astruc's films, lacks a directorial personality such as we expect from Hitchcock, Lang or Hawks. Its quality is a narrative felicity, an extreme concentration on the events so that one is made a participant in them, sharing the camera's unity with the action and its consequent reticence of judgement.—'Je cherche un cinéma non de dénonciation, mais de réconciliation avec le monde.'* This is what Astruc terms *mise-en-scène*. In fact the concept has already been partly outmoded by Godard, Rouch and Marker but it is still significant in the way it summarizes the classical cinema— of Renoir, Murnau, Hawks—that so influenced Astruc and, indeed, Godard. The essence of *mise-en-scène* is the surpassing of words by images, but I will try to convey some of its meaning with an example from *Une Vie*.

When Maria Schell is saved from drowning she is brought to a quay where Christian Marquand stands watching her. It is their first meeting. On the sound-track her monologue gives her impression—'sur le quai, il était là. Je ne le connaissais pas.'—and there is a long, slow tracking-shot that, without seeming tied to him, picks up Marquand as he moves forward, speaks to a fisherman and comes to help Schell up the steps.

This description is as bare as the shooting script. The effectiveness of the film is in the accumulation of details that are only isolated after several viewings. The flustered anxiety of Schell's movements contrasts with Marquand's calm, independent strength. While she faces the camera he has his back to it for much of the shot. His coat is a deep russet and her white dress is darkened by its drenching. At the head of the steps Marquand reaches down his hand to her which at first she ignores and then takes only shyly when he refuses to move out of the way.

Beneath the detail there is an ambiguity of atmosphere. We sense it is a crucial meeting but the dimness of early evening makes it seem casual. Marquand's involvement is brusque, the slowness of the tracking shot is proof of how much he is stimulated by mild curiosity out of boredom, and the slight lack of harmony between his own and the camera's movements suggests the element of chance. Schell's admission of ignorance and the clear impressiveness of his dark romantic appeal to

* *Cahiers du Cinéma*, No. 116, February 1961.

her inexperience already predict the pattern of deception that the film recounts.

Une Vie is a succession of cinematographic events of this kind of subtlety. The crucial importance of the natural and discreet expression is born out by the obtrusive academism in Astruc's latest work.

La Longue Marche concerns the journey of a French Resistance group across the Cevennes. Since the terrain is the site of real events it is proper that it should be described so exactly. But Astruc's camera now tracks habitually—whether or not the action is suitable—with a glassy smoothness over even the roughest hillside. The pictorial qualities in the landscape have been pursued at the expense of its human reference. Thus, it is a film concerned with violence that is graceful. It treats chaos but it is measured.

Camera-stylo's very coherence has betrayed Astruc into revealing a difference between his knowledge and that of his characters which, at its worst, amounts to knowingness. The tracking shot that follows two of the group into a village, against which the Germans have taken reprisals, and that comes to rest on a disturbed meal table on a balcony, could not have been conceived by any but a visually imaginative director. But only a director disciplined by the relationship of action and recording camera could have chosen to do without it.

3

THE SCREEN

The Barrier – Theatre – The
Television Screen and Conceptualization – Two-Dimensional
Society: *La Notte* – Spatial Relationship: Separation and Connection

In Godard's *Les Carabiniers* the two soldiers see their first film.
It is of a young woman in her bath. One of them advances on
the screen to obtain the woman and rips it apart. The image still
plays on his struggling back. This is Godard's joke, but not
seventy years earlier Lumière's first audience reacted in a similar
way to the first film shows. In *Vivre Sa Vie* the girl Nana goes to
the movies and sees Carl Dreyer's *La Passion de Jeanne d'Arc*.
Godard cuts from close-up of Anna Karina, to close-up of
Falconetti, Dreyer's Joan, to the titles of Joan's reaction to the
idea of death. These three shots are presented on our screen and
if we can believe that Joan of Arc is pertinent to Nana, then we
have admitted the possibility of their significance for us as well
as being moved to sympathy by the nature of their faces. The
screen reveals the fact of organization to us.

When Godard juxtaposes Karina and Falconetti he is certainly, in Astruc's sense, providing an intellectuality, translating
a sentence like 'Nana saw herself in the film', but he is also
making a much more general connection of two images among
all the millions mankind has accumulated. Whatever the second
image—Falconetti, Mount Vesuvius, an amoebic cell—we
would supply a link just as man sees significance in chance.
Godard is brought by this awareness to humility as much as
artistic or intellectual ambition. If the screen extracts meaning

54

it is denying choice. The profoundest quality of the screen is the perspective of understanding it allows the spectator not only on the particular image, but on the whole process of images and films. The screen convinces us that moving film is an image by focusing it, or 'descrambling it', for us. The screen can be used to embody meaning—Hitchcock and Eisenstein achieve this—but its greater function is a communication that incorporates ambiguity as well.

THE BARRIER

The same building can do service as both a theatre and a cinema, but while a stage is a spatial continuation of the interior separated by only a gangway and footlights, in the cinema attention is on an inanimate surface flat as a mirror, so cut off by the mechanical device which illuminates it as to be un-known. The theatre's physical integration gives it a more communal nature than the cinema, so that those who go to the theatre have the company of human beings on the stage who may even step outside their play and speak to them, and in the variety theatre will address them constantly. If one throws a missile at an actor it may hit and injure him. He may throw it back. It will only bounce off the screen, leaving the images as serene as before.

Groucho Marx often steps forward from the action of his films and speaks directly to the camera, probably much in the way he did in the music-hall acts the brothers performed before going to Hollywood. The early Marx Brothers films are often very close to those theatrical origins but, without having seen their stage act, I feel that cinema and the barrier of the screen offered them an extra quality. *Animal Crackers* was made in 1930 from a Broadway musical. There is one large set for the whole film that is clearly an unadapted stage set. The camera work is inert, the various set-pieces being filmed rather ponderously and edited carelessly. The other characters are as fatuously hollow as possible and, most important of all, they are quite powerless.

Their impotence is complementary to the Brothers' anarchy and to Groucho's insults. The setting is Margaret Dumont's country house-party for rich socialites. Groucho, masquerading as an African hunter, is guest of honour. Chico and Harpo are simply there. They are dressed like clowns and their actions are uninhibited and destructive. Groucho alternately insults his hostess and admires her breasts; Harpo chases the maid. The other guests are so helpless that they have to ignore this behaviour. For in the cinema they are beyond the audience's practical sympathy and possible assistance. In the theatre the outrageousness would be realized by the audience, and its unfairness would be unbearable. But in the cinema, even though the stage act has been photographed with so little embellishment, the balance has shifted. Anarchy is now reasonable because what the Brothers are doing to the other guests is what film does to an audience. Like Margaret Dumont we must sit there and take it. Very quickly we are laughing at the abuses and encouraging wilder ones, even though if we were ourselves the targets we should be as shocked as the victims. The Marx Brothers depend on the property of the cinema that what we see seems both real and absurd, overpowering and yet remote.

There is a sequence in *Animal Crackers* in which Chico and Harpo play bridge with Margaret Dumont and one of her guests. Like servants, good clothes and fashionable paintings, bridge is a part of the house-party way of life so that Chico and Harpo are attempting to enter this society. They cheat. Not subtly, but with a child's shamelessness. Harpo cuts the pack as he likes, looks at every card before dealing it, throws embarrassing cards away and plays five aces of spades in succession. Bridge is ridiculed and Dumont's polite protestations are useless. Chico and Harpo have once again gained the Marxian control of the film. All their movies have quite arbitrary and absurd plots which are always having to halt while one or all of the Brothers, by introducing their 'turn', begin a new plot which is entirely of their making and in their control. While Chaplin and Keaton are at the mercy of their plots or the sequence of events in a particular film, the Marx Brothers are unique in that their films are shaped by their personality. It is their dynamic absurdity that affronts the conventional world; with Chaplin or Keaton it is the self-pity or stoicism of the heroes that are presented to it.

But the Brothers are not alike and to compare them is to illustrate how the screen discriminates. Chico is always at the centre but as a cipher rather than a character. He can talk to Groucho, swap cracks with him and even con him; he can also communicate with Harpo. In fact it is his role to be Harpo's interpreter, piecing together the sense in Harpo's messages of gesture, grimace and whistle. But Harpo and Groucho do not share scenes in the same way. Groucho treats Harpo with some caution and unease, and in turn is regarded warily. Whenever Groucho talks to Harpo the remark is directed at him and said with half an eye on the audience as if Groucho expected us to share his attitude to Harpo. Groucho does not understand Harpo and this adds to the impression that he has most in common with an audience, whereas Harpo is the least comprehensible of the three and the most anarchical. He has the appearance of a lunatic and combines a mystic gentleness with moments of great rage. The violence in the Marx Brothers films always derives from Harpo whether he is rendering the whole cast unconscious at the end of *Animal Crackers*, or stepping away from a building in *A Night in Casablanca* and allowing it to fall. These actions conform with our estimate of Harpo because even in moments of calm his gestures are abrupt and obscene. He is the madman who justifies our fears in his potential. Like Groucho, one senses that incautious handling might provoke him.

It is in this sense that Harpo is a creature of the screen. More than either of his brothers' behaviour, his is without motive, simply the gratuitous expression of his enormous energy. The constancy and pitch of this energy distinguish him from Groucho and Chico, and indeed from us, and give him something of the quality of a machine. There are times when his actions become increasingly mechanical so that he even needs rewinding or refuelling. The lack of reason is suited to the arbitrariness of the screen and its ability to unfold events which one can do nothing to stop or control. Anything can be put on the screen from one frame to the next and its appearance will do away with the need for explanation. The Marx Brothers' films rely more than most on this autonomy, and Harpo more than any of his brothers. Even though he refuses to speak,

Harpo is the king of his films, and the silence is a sign only of confidence.

Groucho, on the other hand, conforms much more to our own sense of character. His impersonations are always aspiring to fame and power and his two impulses, sex and money, though exceptionally single-minded are recognizably human. Harpo pursues sex like an animal, but Groucho for all his lechery is inhibited. He has to follow the ritual patterns of seduction where Harpo would merely seize his target. So long as he must conform to these patterns Groucho is susceptible to the interruptions of his brothers and the greater cunning of the women he wants. In that sense Groucho is the originator of the line of American screen comedians doomed to fail: Jack Benny, Bob Hope and Jack Lemmon all illustrate this type. It is a further characteristic of the type that the failure forces the comedian to attempt to enlist the understanding of the audience. There is a running note of the 'aside' remark in Bob Hope's work and he is an example of the man who is funniest when recounting or reacting to his own humiliations. Lemmon does the same thing in *Some Like It Hot* when his response to Joe E. Brown's concluding and sublime tolerance is to appeal despairingly to the unseen audience.

The barrier constitutes a final frustration for these comedians, for when Groucho turns to the camera he is looking into a void, and if we laugh when he says after a flat pun in *Animal Crackers*, 'Don't blame me, not all the jokes can be good', there is no reassurance for him as there might be in the theatre. Groucho's whole attempt to transcend the barrier of the screen is characteristic of his frustration. Harpo ignores camera and screen, registering as some missing link, hopelessly out of its environment and yet adapting to present circumstances with a ruthless uninhibitedness and becoming the source of the dynamic for the whole action. Only Jerry Lewis has aspired to Harpo's automatic behaviour, and the richness of the Marx Brothers' films is that they manage to blend the styles of Lewis and Lemmon. In that blend we have a comparison of comic personalities which reveals the dissociative effect that the screen has upon its audience.

THEATRE

It is a common complaint of variety artists, and comedians particularly, that an act or routine which might have lasted several years being taken round the theatres can be used up in one film or in one television appearance. It is claimed that the screen over-exposes them. But the Marx Brothers made the move from vaudeville to Hollywood, as Chaplin had before them. Their movement away from theatres to the equivalent of factories which could broadcast their images to other theatres is an historical consequence of the movement of large audiences into the theatre in the nineteenth century. The sequence of events bears out how far the cinema is a medium of its time that necessarily involves the separation of performer and spectator.

One of the key changes in the progress of the presentation of plays was when the players stopped travelling to their audience and the audience began to go to a theatre. It was not an abrupt change. Shakespeare wrote plays for the London play-houses which a company could also take to court, a noble-man's house or an inn of court. All his plays are written to be performed anywhere. This is true of Racine: *Phèdre* could be done behind a proscenium, in a garden or by the roadside. It is also true of Beckett. But during the nineteenth century this range was less because exact interior setting assumed much more importance.

It was only the Industrial Revolution's discovery of the means to heat and light large interiors, the increase in population, slowly rising standards of literacy and evenings waiting to be filled after a day's work that led to the manufacture of theatre buildings on a large scale.

The focus of much nineteenth century drama is the condition of this new audience and its novelty is to attempt a realistic presentation of their lives. The protagonists need no longer be of high birth; occupation, politics, and life within the walls of the home receive increasing attention. The more democratic nature of this theatre springs naturally enough from the growing realization of concepts of emancipation in Europe, and behind

Ibsen we may see the figures of Mill, Comte, de Tocqueville and Marx. Realism of condition is characteristic of nineteenth century artistic movements and close idealistic connections with politics, like Zola's defence of Dreyfus, are not uncommon. Since the living conditions of so many were becoming primarily urban and interior, so plays came to depend more and more on sets as faithful as possible to the audiences' own homes.

While Ibsen, Chekhov and Shaw all redeemed realism of emotion and character from the waste of the early nineteenth century, they were sometimes overwhelmed by a physical reality. Chekhov's psychological realism and the narrative sequence that supports it are both as typical of his stories as his plays. He said of *The Seagull*, 'It came out like a story', and once declared his intention 'to depict life as it is and people as they are'. His director, Stanislavsky, said, 'All those who try to "act", to "pretend" when taking part in Chekhov's plays are making a sad mistake. One should become part of his plays, one should live them, have one's being in them . . .'

Shaw may not require such involvement, but his precise stage notes describe interiors against which brilliant but still plausible patterns may be constructed. His theatrical use of debate needs only to be compared with Brecht's to show how naturalistic the demonstration has to be in Shaw's plays. Ibsen relies less on realism and makes more use of archetype in his characters, but he still uses the mechanics of realism and does not always escape their restrictions. Even when Brand climbs his symbolic mountain one is distracted by the 'mountaineering' detail of the ascent, and in *Rosmersholm* the invocation of the mill-race that runs past the house luring Rebekka is so persistent that we are left with a curtain speech that has the housekeeper looking through the window and describing to us the suicide of Rebekka and Rosmer. It is ironic to think that her successors stand ready at the French windows to provide the opening cliché in so many Shaftesbury Avenue pieces.

More important is Ibsen's obvious yearning for an expansion of the medium, such as cinema would have provided. There is an anachronism in the new urban audience only able to watch a form that in its nature had not altered since Shakespeare's day. In the plays of the period we have the first use of stage-notes to describe the appearance of characters, and the consequent assumption that appearance was an expression of character. This is remote from the masks of Greek theatre and the neglect of appearance in Racine, but it is germane to the cinema. The context of real action and the nature of appearance entranced the dramatists just as they did the French impressionists. What a powerful subconscious impression the rich surface texture of early photographs, like Brady's series on the American Civil War, must have had. The first photographed wars, the Crimean and American Civil, coincided significantly with a wider recognition of war's grimness and Sherman's admission that it was hell—a line re-echoed in so many movies that its idea is now commonplace.

Brady's photographs were messages from the front but their flat autonomy could not be reproduced in the theatre. Perhaps a large gullible audience excited the dramatists to the attempt; certainly one senses this appetite for power: Ibsen uses suspense to lever moral forces in a way that is often Hitchcockian. But the theatre is to a room as protagonists are to people. The integration of character and background that Ibsen and Chekhov strove for is an achievement of *mise-en-scène*. Chekhov's unattainable stage directions are realized in films like *La Règle du Jeu* as is the credible and moving interplay of theatricality and spontaneity. For if theatre is the imitation of an action then cinema is its realization: *realisateur*, of course, is the French word for 'director'.

An example from *The Miracle Worker* may help to demonstrate this. *The Miracle Worker* tells how Helen Keller, a blind, deaf mute, is helped by Annie Sullivan, the girl who looks after her, towards some understanding of communication. One of the film's major sequences shows how Annie makes Helen eat a meal in a way that approximates to that of her parents. Helen is normally allowed to stumble about the dining-room gathering food with her bare hands where she can find it. Annie stops this. She sends the parents out of the room and begins to school Helen.

The sequence is perhaps five minutes long and the *mise-en-scène* is engrossed by the action. That is to say, there are the minimum of cuts and the camera moves round the room as

violently as Helen and Annie. This is not the peaceful en-
lightening of a handicapped child but a battle between Helen's
animal intractability and her fierce teacher. At every attempt
by Annie to sit Helen down and arrange her cutlery and napkin
the child lashes out and there is a frenzy of thrown food and
tableware. I don't think this scene could be done on the stage
as totally as it is on film without either giving offence or
degenerating into slapstick. For the violence is as essential and
critical as in a street brawl. The players, Anne Bancroft and
Patty Duke, are so unreservedly committed to the fight that
they achieve what is a sublime effect: the simultaneous particularization and generalization of the action. This duality of
meaning is part of the film's ambiguity for Arthur Penn makes
his version of the story depend upon its mixture of violence and
reason. There is a tragic irony in the conclusion that the wild
but free spirit of Helen can only be brought to enlightenment
by a process that is partly brutal. The screen is essential to the
ambiguity for it is able at the same time to present an over-
whelmingly faithful picture of the physical struggle and, by
reducing it to a flat, intangible image, allow the audience
objectivity. One sees the battle in its enactment by two im-
mersed actresses as well as its more abstract implications; that
one sees the two at the same time is the source of excitement and
tragedy.

THE TELEVISION SCREEN AND
CONCEPTUALIZATION

The degree to which the fight scene in *The Miracle Worker*
involves us may depend on other factors than the qualities of
the film: the size of the screen and the darkness of the surroundings. We are alerted and impressionable in the dark, confronted
on the screen with images that even in a conventional full-figure
shot may be three times larger than ourselves. Until television,
one could have argued unrestrictedly about the power exercised
on the audience by the size of the screen. The way in which the
cinema industrialists emphasized this factor when the competition of television encroached on their public seemed to
indicate the cinema's own belief in it. The intelligent reaction

would have been for them to welcome television as the new means of distribution because television is the logical sequel to cinema in a society that, as it increases, makes greater demands on communication. Similarly, the smaller screen and the comparative detachment that it permits are part of the progress from Lumière's patrons running away from a train to one only jumping in one's seat at the murders in *Psycho*. The smaller the screen the more emphasis is given to the conceptualization of the image and the sense of power it offers to the spectator. Thus the violence on television is not more cruel than that in the cinema but the medium allows a greater uninvolvement, whether the violence is that of *The Avengers* or of a Vietnam newsreel.

This sort of sophistication affects the medium as much as the material. Just as man may watch the transmitted pictures taken by a camera on the moon so he may become an interior being living through his most vital window, the television screen. The possibilities of television are as yet barely realized : sets might be dialled to obtain the image of any page of any book or any scene in the world; they might be equipped so that man could collect film material, instead of books, and project it himself whenever he desired. Apart from the Orwellian prophecy of how such a benefit might be turned against man as a means of inspection, there is the possibility that emotions and ideas might be viewed from a distance like places. Experience may finally succumb to the medium so that the occupation of man will be itself the evaluation of that experience rather than its performance.

Before comparing the cinema and television screens closely, consider the statistics of their recent popularity. The weekly attendance figure for British cinemas in 1946 was over 31 million; in January 1966 it was 6·2 million and in June 4·6 million.* Cinema attendances fell as television licences increased. The technological refinement has shifted the balance of communication : the audience is again static, and the performers travel, though this time by radio waves. The means of presentation is still a screen, and most individuals spend more time in watching than they ever did in the cinema. One thirty-minute episode of *Coronation Street* may be watched by more than

* There has always been a seasonal fluctuation in figures.

twice the number of cinema admissions for a week all over Britain, and many of the old movies shown on television will equal the figure.*

In America, over 19,000 old movies are available to television, and in this country the figure is growing. For at an operative level the two media have come to terms: the same actors, directors and technicians work on both and the same sound-stages are used. It is the economics of the sale of films to TV that is significant. In 1965 one such sale was of 200 films for £500,000, which is £2,500 per film, between 0·25 and 10 per cent of their original cost. In one transmission their audience will be between 5–10 million, which at four shillings a head in a cinema would bring revenue of about £1½ million. These films are often shown at peak viewing hours, and if their viewing figures indicate less a real interest in them than the fact that so many sets are turned on regardless at certain hours, this is only repeating the pattern of the cinema's halcyon period when one went to the cinema rather than to a particular movie.

What is the impression made by these films when shown on television? Certainly the rich spatial depth of *Citizen Kane* and *The Magnificent Ambersons* is harder to perceive, so that to see either in the cinema after first acquaintance had been made on television was to be enraptured by the perspectives of Xanadu and the Ambersons' house. But the idea of the buildings and their importance for Kane and the Ambersons is not lost, nor is the investigative structure of *Citizen Kane*. It is even possible that Welles's own intoxication with visual grandeur, which is what most mars his films, is less obtrusive on the smaller screen. In the same way, Westerns, or movies that use epic natural locations to contain the struggles of archetypal figures, appear on television much more as ritual. Thus *The Far Country* is diminished a little, but *Rancho Notorious* is just as effective.

Lang's films are not hurt by the reduction in size because the television screen's miniaturization of human detail increases attention on the formal values in his films. He pins down life-

* TV licences in July 1965 numbered 13·5 million. Average programme viewing figures are between 5·5 million and 7·5 million. A peak programme may attract 16·5 million.

6. Anna Karina in *Pierrot le Fou*. There is no composition or meaning in the scene, but the effect of a view seen suddenly through a door.

7. *Only Angels Have Wings*. Cary Grant, Jean Arthur. 'Who's Joe?'

8. *Vivre Sa Vie*. A real killing of no significance. Anna Karina is caught in a pimp's double-cross but her discovery of herself makes the death irrelevant. The street is chaotically natural c o m p a r e d w i t h Lang's.

9. *The Scarlet Empress*. Marlene Dietrich looks out of her coach at a strange
Russia. The fluidity of light on face and fur makes a suitable ikon for the depraved
Russian Orthodoxy.

10. *Confidential Report*. Orson Welles *alias* Gregory Arkadin *alias* Hank Quinlan
alias Charles Foster Kane. The low camera supplies our awe.

likeness as he would an insect. Lang would not distinguish the behaviour of one specimen from another; he is confident that no specimen can surprise the species. Direct human actions are isolated in Lang's films, and as purposeful as the director's observation of detail of expression in his characters. The opening of *Rancho Notorious* shows Arthur Kennedy saying goodbye to his sweetheart and giving her a brooch. As he leaves, two men ride into town, rob the assay office where the girl works, rape and kill her. The rape is as undramatic as the couple's expression of love has been non-specific—both are stated in the terms of convention as they might appear to a society with only general interest in its members. But the generalization of event is filled in with a specific visual realization such as the beautiful tilt down from the dead girl's face to her dress, from which the brooch has been torn, down the length of her arm to her hand, like an upturned spider. The girl's face, brooch and hand are both connected and itemized by this shot. Although generalization they are poetic statements of events and they constitute the themes of the movie. The rape is a condition of the whole film and a source of consequent moral flexibility. Like numbers, the items can be used on either side of the equation.

Lang does not try to disguise the strict melodramatic formulas of his films, but strips everything else away and concentrates on the developments of the action so that they achieve formal values like the demonstration and proof of theorems. The action of his films is not realized but conceptualized. His characters are without psychological depth and his chief interest is in how they respond to the events of the plot. In this sense they are characters under observation. It is the screen's ability to conceptualize which assists Lang's purpose, and if his films are sparse of spontaneous action they are rich in abstract movements which are illustrated by what seem to be real people. For Lang, as for Brecht, the screen is a means of presentation; it is the nature of the cinema that adds a plausible reality to the idea he is offering. Whether the concept can survive the reality, and vice versa, is Lang's subject.

It is in *The 1000 Eyes of Dr Mabuse* that this is most apparent and Lang acknowledges most plainly his use of the screen. There is a scene of a man and woman sitting in the restaurant of the hotel in which most of the action takes place. It is a shot that has been used earlier, but now it is grainier and less distinct. The camera pulls back to show that it is in fact an image on a television screen. The screen is one of many in some interior room. Every room in the hotel has a hidden camera that transmits an image to the control room where Dr Mabuse watches. Mabuse has a design, which in Lang's films he has followed for nearly forty years, and which in his absence from the screen has been imitated by Hitler, at least, to make every person in the world as much a cipher as the people on the screen. The independence of these people is in peril for they do not even know they are being watched.

Like Mabuse, James Stewart in *Rear Window* has almost scientific means of observing the other inhabitants of his apartment block. He sees them when they come in front of the windows of their apartments. In shape and function these windows correspond to the screen as it is used in cinema and television and to every contemporary presentation of flat visual material. Any photograph, whether studio portrait, newsreel or glossy automobile advertisement, offers a concept of its subject. Stewart in *Rear Window* is himself a photographer and his apartment walls are filled with dramatic news photographs he has taken: car crashes, accidents, explosions. Hitchcock's film shows what happens when his professional gaze is turned on people, and is a comment on all photographs of people. For just as photography first informed civilians about war, so in the variety of its forms it has become the major means of communication. The most powerful men of the last ten years— Kennedy, Khrushchev, Mao—are the best-known faces, because to achieve and exercise power they had to make their own faces their emblems and their seals. But the image will be two-dimensional and only a variety of concepts can fill this out. Once variety is attempted the emblematic unity may be lost. To move from the political to the personal scale does not alter the idea of the image as a concept. The eyes that look and the face that is watched are not only the means of communication but the signs of meaning in that communication.

TWO-DIMENSIONAL SOCIETY: 'LA NOTTE'

Antonioni's *La Notte* is a film which successfully transfers its own two-dimensional nature to human observation and communication, and yet retains a photographic realism. *La Notte* concerns a husband, Marcello Mastroianni, and his wife, Jeanne Moreau, and the sort of communication they have. They live in Milan and the city is a real presence in their lives because so many of its forms are equivalent to their relations. The wall in Milan can be hard, sheer and impenetrable, or it can be glass, transparent but reflecting. The walls are spatial units just as affairs, marriages and meetings are emotional links.

Antonioni at one level makes *La Notte* a survey of the complex inter-relations of people and architecture that is almost abstract. To balance this he uses a chronological sequence that is close to the natural one: a day and the following night in the characters' lives. There is no sense of plot; the events which occur depend on the man and his wife searching them out, but do not accumulate into something that could fully occupy them. They have the freedom of people who are financially secure and the twenty-four-hour sequence uncovers this freedom and the boredom that comes from it.

Their wandering progress is started by a visit in the opening sequence to a friend who is dying in hospital. Moreau leaves before her husband, and this is the first instance of one of her patterns of behaviour: the enquiry and retreat. When Mastroianni leaves he is accosted in the corridor by another patient, a young nymphomaniac. The girl persuades him to enter her room. Once inside she stands against a flawless white wall and, for the moment before Mastroianni appears at the edge of the screen coldly observing her, the girl is suspended against this background. The white void is an image not only of dissociative illness but of the appetite that constitutes her illness. Mastroianni's observation of her is the consequence of the disparity between the moral precepts of a Roman Catholic and humanitarian society and his lust for the girl. Indecision allowed him to be led into the room, and even when the seduction is achieved his involvement is that of an object rather than a person. The nurse who discovers them on the bed slaps the girl but ignores Mastroianni. When he leaves the hospital he finds his wife outside leaning against a wall.

Already the two elements of the film are established: the random, almost experimental, movement of the characters and the use of the wall as a separating and displaying instrument—exactly the functions of the cinema screen. This is emphasized by photography that accentuates the two-dimensionality. The lack of fill-in lighting to indicate perspective compresses foreground and background so that doorways, walls and characters appear on the same level, and until a door or a wall is defined by the movement of a person it often has the properties of an optical illusion. Thus, when Mastroianni and Moreau are going up in the hospital lift, the doors shut on the ground floor and after a few seconds open again on one of the upper storeys. The opening doors uncover another half-open doorway through which the nymphomaniac is watching the entrance of the lift. There is so little distinction of depth that the doors pull back like the curtains on a screen, so that even in her watchfulness the girl is made remote by being conceptualized. The alienation of the city is its domination by this condition; characters in the same frame are separated by walls and partitions and presented as flatly to each other as the whole film is to us.

The frustrated attempt at communication is used throughout and it is a measure of Antonioni's integration of it with the plausible movements of Milanese society that he makes this contemporary cliché meaningful. Much of his success is due to the idea he sustains that these characters are autonomous, wandering into every situation by their own inclination rather than at his symbolic design.

The pattern of Moreau's behaviour is exemplarily consistent with this illusory reality and the abstract design. On leaving the hospital she goes with her husband to a party to launch his latest book. Her unease with her husband's work is shown by the blown-up photographs of the book's jacket in front of which she stands before leaving on her own. The walls in the streets carry on the idea of an alien background. Either they are blank concrete façades, or plate windows through which she stares and, when stared back at, moves away from disconcerted. In the slum quarter of the town her hand peels layers of flake from the old plaster walls. On a building site she comes upon two men fighting. She tries to intervene but has to run away when the winner stands up and pursues her. Finally she goes by taxi to an old haunt of hers and her husband's, dismisses the taxi and telephones her husband so that he will collect her.

The whole movement of Moreau through Milan, primarily away from her husband but finally returning, even though by a deliberate device to make him aware of her feelings, is naturalistically aimless. Chance encounters, like a child crying in a yard or the men fighting, divert her temporarily but are ultimately the impetus to her moving away. Her attitude to the fight is complementary to her husband's encounter with the nymphomaniac. Both are originally fortuitous. The husband's prime response is pusillanimous, whereas Moreau's is purposeful, but in nature they are not so different. For she looks once at the fight, turns away, but then moves towards it, a little entranced by the animality so that her cry 'Enough!' is both admonishing and provocative, just as her husband's surrender to the girl is helpless and willing. When the victor stares at her she is no longer humanitarian but the aroused female. Her retreat is in character and it must be self-conscious and frustrating.

The idea of sexual frustration is resumed when Mastroianni takes her back to their apartment. She has a bath and deliberately calls him into the bathroom. But even when she gets out of the bath and dries herself in front of him, he is unresponsive. She puts on a new dress and models it for him, but his kiss on her shoulder is perfunctory. The scene ends with Moreau standing in front of a window outlined against the night that is to dominate the rest of the film and represents the failure of her various 'enquiries' in the first part. By this stage a living condition of coexistence and alienation has been established, and it is stated in the next sequence in which the couple watch a Negress dancing in a nightclub. It is an absurd sex dance involving the contortions of the girl while drinking from a glass. It suggests the impossibility of simple eroticism and both Mastroianni and Moreau have bitterly to accept this.

There follows the long party sequence, one of Antonioni's

triumphs of *mise-en-scène*, although compared with Astruc's the director's pessimistic personality is much more tangible. It is held in the gardens and house of a rich industrialist. Again there is a complete freedom of movement and relationship and the same intrusion of façades alternately to divide and display the characters. The constant black sky is one such background, others are the ornate tapestries in some of the rooms, the blown-up photograph of machinery in the industrialist's study and the various partitioning devices of open-plan architecture. When Mastroianni first meets Monica Vitti, the industrialist's daughter, we see Vitti playing a game of her own device, sliding a powder compact across a chequered marble floor. Mastroianni's reflection appears in the plate-glass surrounding the floor. He watches for a moment and when he moves towards her the camera moves and we discover that he is actual and Vitti reflected. This is not virtuosity but the essence of the film: the confusion between people and their images.

Moreau is no more at ease here than she was at the publisher's party and she responds similarly. She wanders around, is stared at—by one blonde, in particular, as if she were an inanimate object—and herself stares at Vitti who is sitting on a staircase reading. The first confrontation of the two women is particularly flat so that the line of the staircase has no perspective, but is laid 'on' the screen. It concurs with the final lack of jealousy between the two by withholding a natural spatial context. Moreau watches her husband as he meets and talks with Vitti and sees them kiss. She is still watching Vitti when another guest calls out to her by name so telling Vitti that Mastroianni has a wife. This stops the growing affair between the two but admits the beginning of a triangular relationship.

Moreau takes the kiss as signal for an adventure of her own. When it starts to rain she goes for a drive with a young man who has been following and watching her. They drive slowly in pouring rain. We cannot hear what they say but only see their faces, appearing alternately as faces and silhouetted heads as the car passes from the light of street-lamps to the dark between them. She refuses to sleep with the man and they return to the house. There she and the man confront Mastroianni and Vitti in a pattern of what has been on both sides unfulfilled adultery.

Vitti helps Moreau dry and when Mastroianni collects her there is a clear possibility of a triangular relationship that might be powered on the idea of the different sexual pairings without their fulfilment: Mastroianni strokes Vitti's cheek and Moreau kisses it. They leave Vitti standing as a silhouette against the rising dawn—a shot that is sequel to the one of Moreau in her own apartment against the night.

Mastroianni and Moreau walk through the garden on to a golf course. They sit in a bunker and she reads a love-letter he once wrote to her. The shots of the couple during this scene are close and flat, rejecting the normal diagonals used for dialogues. Both people are facing the same way and the camera is directly in front of them. As Moreau reads there is a close-up of her profile which outlines her head as if it were a thing. There are shots of the neckline of her dress that have no physical associations but are abstract patterns in black and white. In this last sequence the camera achieves most explicitly what has been happening throughout the film: the treatment of people as objects. The impossibility of genuine emotional contact has led to their being incorporated in the architectural pattern of the city. They have become two-dimensional, living up to their nature on the screen. Thus, *La Notte*, while being about marriage in Italian society, is also about a way of considering people that is essentially cinematic. No pretence of the third dimension is offered; instead the two-dimensionality is explored more rigorously than in most other films. Like the plate-glass and the marble walls, *La Notte* moves on the screen blending and distinguishing reality and concept.

SPATIAL RELATIONSHIP: SEPARATION AND CONNECTION

There are screens within screens. At the opening of *Citizen Kane* our screen is filled with the obituary newsreel compiled by 'News on the March'. At the climax of *Fury* the accused citizens see their own savagery projected on a screen put up in the courtroom. These screens are apparent and their meaning is intended to be direct but there are those that are not supposed to be seen.

Back-projection is an industrial technique. It is proof of both the mechanical ingenuity and the interpretative power of the film industry. It enables people to be filmed in front of a background without actually taking expensive stars and equipment to a distant location. A small but well-briefed unit goes out—to Africa perhaps, or the streets of New York—and photographs a background from a concealed vantage so that the lions come closer without attacking and the other citizens without staring at the stars. This strip of film is then projected on to a translucent screen in the studio in front of which stand the stars. One of its commonest uses occurs when the actors are moving, in a car, on horseback or simply walking, and the back-projection is a travelling shot behind rocking horses, the mock-up of a car or even a treadmill.

Back-projection is always apparent to the experienced eye. Even somebody unaware of how the device works, or even of its existence, might sense from the nature of the image a dislocation between actor and place. That dislocation is of the same sort as Mastroianni and Jeanne Moreau experience in Milan. Person and place are both more noticeably conceptualized when back-projection is used than when a real union has existed between them at the time of filming.

The most interesting use of back-projection is to be found in the work of Hitchcock. It is an expression of the unsustaining but judicial society that exists in his films. If one considers that back-projection is a lazy and clumsy device it is a paradox that one of the most technically intelligent directors should employ it. *Marnie*, for instance, on the one hand uses a most original effect, obtained by simultaneously tracking in and zooming out, which Hitchcock had been striving to perfect for over twenty years; at the same time its back-projection of Tippi Hedren's horse ride and her fall at a brick wall are blatantly faked. It is difficult to believe that so astute a director could tolerate such alienating technical inefficiency unless it obtained an effect he wanted.

Hitchcock's characters are isolated by examination and, rather than establish an articulated physical existence, events are made to loom before them as confrontations which their subjectivity has filled with emotional significance. The effect of flatness is in keeping with the concentrated psychic force that people and objects manifest in Hitchcock's movies. The wall that appears before Marnie on her horse is intended as a psychological block and her fall is a descent into trauma rather than a physical tumble.

The cutting in the riding sequence, from a close-up in front of Marnie to a shot approaching the wall as if from her position in the saddle, is characteristic of Hitchcock's method at moments of crisis. It also illustrates his confrontation of flat surfaces, or antagonistic ideas. When Vera Miles advances on the house at the end of *Psycho* and when Joan Fontaine ventures towards Rebecca's bedroom in *Rebecca* similar cutting is employed. In both cases the sense of physical encounter has been eliminated by the suction of ideological fear. The process is akin to that of the child on the darkened staircase whose daytime experience is confident enough but finds at night that the stairs become occupied by the source of every fear he has. No specific fear detaches itself but all concentrate in the dark into an amorphous and enclosing pressure. Both Vera Miles and Joan Fontaine experience something of the child's reaction to what they finally discover. The decayed head of Mrs Bates that stares back at Vera Miles is certainly horrific but more potentially terrifying is the wig that is knocked off Perkins's head and, as it lies beneath a violently swinging bulb, seems to writhe with life. At the beginning of *Rebecca* the camera is in a car driving by night to the house, Manderley. The headlights pass across its façade and, as every window reflects them, a thrill of energy seems to slide over its front. Manderley's energy and Anthony Perkins's wig threaten the characters in the two films and in both cases the threat is connected with the possibility of a mind's surrender to an obsessive view of life. As a child, Perkins has been so dominated by his mother that the rest of his life is a battleground between his contradictory feelings for her. His own personality has been stopped just as Joan Fontaine's status at Manderley is menaced by the ghost of Rebecca.

Rebecca and *Psycho* are both ghost stories and in watching them one should be more alert to psychic affairs than to naturalistic encounters. Credibility is bound to be subjective and to say that *Psycho* is absurd is itself absurd if one has been frightened while watching it. Hitchcock's cinema reaches out to primitive responses and operates effectively on them because his use of the medium convinces us as being representative of so controlling a power that any observing intelligence reverts to a more emotional bias. And yet this primitiveness is achieved by a uniquely sophisticated awareness of the screen's function. One way of explaining Hitchcock's genius is by realizing how directly he has denied the idea of spatial integration that is consistent with the mainstream of the cinema.

Like the people in Antonioni's later films Hitchcock's characters do not have a mutually supporting spatial relationship. The idea of a flat screen is multiplied so that every character is shut in his own plane, relating to the other characters by contrast or reflection. Fundamental to Hitchcock's world is an impossibility of communication and understanding so that physical relationships are no more than appearance. The spiritual and psychological personality is superior to the social and it is for this reason that Hitchcock's society is so unconvincing as a replica of any we know but so engrossing as a presence that contributes to a private world. When Joan Fontaine goes into Rebecca's room we see not an inhabitable bedroom but a shrine. The housekeeper, Judith Anderson, becomes in the room less a servant than an intermediary between Rebecca's shrine and her ghost. Fontaine's movement into the room is gripping because of its sense of moral effort. The scene works through the psychological richness of its images: of Anderson admiring Rebecca's bed, stroking the sleeve of Rebecca's fur coat against her cheek and gazing at her hand through Rebecca's transparent underclothes. Such behaviour is ludicrous if Anderson is really Joan Fontaine's housekeeper and this is a real room in a real home, but the scene does suggest that the house is truly haunted, that the relationship between Rebecca and Anderson was unnatural and that the ambience of the room is thoroughly evil.

As she becomes entranced by Rebecca's things Judith Anderson grows increasingly unaware of Joan Fontaine's presence. Fontaine herself is oppressed by the room and its infringement on her as mistress of Manderley so that by being ignored she is in danger of ceasing to exist. The lighting in *Rebecca* does in fact lend recess and perspective to the images, whereas in *La Notte*

Antonioni deliberately increases their flatness. The alienation of Mastroianni and Moreau is much closer to an everyday reality than the dramatic spiritual incompatibility between Fontaine and Anderson, but both films are intent on depriving their characters of physical relationships. To do this they are asserting one property of the screen—its flatness—which the photographic illusion of a spatial relationship is attempting to disguise.

In Renoir, Hawks and Preminger the spatial relationship is the manifestation of a social contingency and its instrument is an unobtrusive camera amenable to the intervals between people. These intervals become bonds if an intention or understanding passes across them in which the comprehension and the distance are integrated. Norah Gregor seeing her husband kiss another woman during the shoot in *La Règle du Jeu* and John Wayne looking down the street at the figure he takes to be Dean Martin in *Rio Bravo* observe this principle holding over a hundred yards. In the still from *Anatomy of a Murder* (facing page 97) only a few feet separate Lee Remick and James Stewart as they glance at each other. The moment of the still is critical. Remick is about to give evidence in the trial of her husband for the murder of a man who, Remick says, raped her. Stewart who is defending is uneasy with Remick's open sensuality: he wonders if she might not have willingly acquiesced. For the trial he makes her wear a hat over her long, loose hair, and large spectacles. But George C. Scott, prosecuting, demands that the disguise be removed. As Stewart watches the removal his doubts are visible, the closeness embarrassing. The ambiguity of this bond unites and separates the characters simultaneously.

Preminger's juxtaposition of these two characters is for the very purpose of conveying ambiguity, but in Howard Hawks's *Red River* there is a spatial bond that is anecdotal and fatalistic because it senses its own meaning. John Wayne and his adopted son, Montgomery Clift, had planned to drive the first herd of cattle north from Texas. Wayne's rule of the cowboys is as harsh as his ownership of the cattle is total but, when he intends to whip a deserter, Clift assumes command, takes the herd on and leaves Wayne to follow. The pursuit by Wayne, who has promised revenge, is a remote but constant spatial association.

75

Clift reaches Abilene and waits. Wayne arrives and proceeds to walk through the herd and up the street towards his adopted son. Wayne shoots down one man who tries to help Clift. When challenged, Clift will not draw his gun and Wayne is not prepared to shoot. They are still father and son but they realize their separateness. They fight savagely and are stopped by Joanne Dru's angry scorn at their obvious friendship. The quarrel is over but the new relationship is a different one. Youth and age, severity and reason, have been compared but failed to equalize; the society continues because the various parties know it is an inevitable form for human beings.

Hawks perfects the sort of spatial relationship that the naturalistic cinema allows. Like Renoir he emphasizes the illusion of reality. Spatial identity in their movies is relative within a social *milieu*. In Lang's and Hitchcock's movies the screen's power of abstraction is more directly important.

Lang's characters take up general positions just as they stand for everyman. When Spencer Tracy plans his revenge in *Fury* the actual details of his isolation are less important than the idea of it. Previously he has been an ordinarily good man within a society, but when that society harms him he turns in upon himself. The increased concentration of the camera on his loneliness leads to the malevolent introspection of vengeance. His determination to remain in hiding is a trick that has lost contact with the decency he originally enjoyed and the isolation is self-encouraging.

Hitchcock's characters take up psychological positions. During *The Birds*, Tippi Hedren's mobility is gradually restricted from the smart, sophisticated woman's ability to move about freely to the stunned child being forced into an attic corner by the birds, all her responses dulled, her liberty immobilized by terror.

The bonds in Hawks and Renoir are more spontaneous and transient—their movies are in that sense more plastic. But even in their films the screen underlines the implication of the spatial contiguity. In bull-fighting there is a term, *querencia*, which means the part of the ring the bull chooses to go to, where it feels most at ease. As soon as one films people and projects the film on to a screen their *querencias* become apparent although in life they would be adopted without one being conscious of the decision. In films that have moral criteria—such as Lang's and Hitchcock's—the screen is the grid for measurement and spatial discreteness will be more emphatic, although the illusions of movement and depth are necessary to bring life to them.

4

PLACE AND LOCATION

Power over Place – Editing:
Montage or Flow – The Frontier
Community: Anthony Mann –
The Restriction of Organization:
Losey

The combined circumstances of cinema—of life-like photography and conceptualizing withdrawal—affect place in the way that any photographed landscape or interior is, at the same time, a record of that place and a manifestation of it to the imagination. A place will always exist, susceptible to infinite interpretation; but a location exists for only a short time during which other energies are concentrated on it, even to the extent that the general public are kept away from it, so that it may contribute as an item to an effect or to meaning.

Place may very often have been a film's original inspiration. Renoir's *The River* is more about the director's sense of India than a formal narrative. The human events are episodic and informal but the progress of the river is constant and mysterious. The river seems simple, but its surface is so varied that the human consciousness of the film is identified with the unreasoning children. Few films have captured so well a child's acceptance of place and simultaneous primitive awe of it. It is a film that interprets *mise-en-scène* literally, for the movements of plot and camera seem to emanate from the hot countryside and in the superbly brief siesta sequence, as the children sleep in uninhibited postures and the image consists of dissolved shots from marginally closer to farther away, and in again, the rhythm of sleeping breathing is like a primeval pulse in India itself.

Hitchcock, on the other hand, has little sense of actuality in his places. Even when an event occurs at a well-known urban landmark, like the United Nations building in *North by Northwest* any recollection we may have of the place is destroyed by the sense of illusion with which Hitchcock surrounds it. The U.N. building is no safer than the desolate prairie where Cary Grant is later marooned. Both locations have been 'treated' for the mystification of Grant and the audience. They are both the landscape of nightmare, and the elements of reality they retain are there to disorientate us.

The cinema's power over place is particularly relevant to man's powers of understanding. All the Earth is now known, although we are less conversant with some areas than others. Consequently a personal experience of a new place is less likely. The wonders of the world have been described beforehand so that when we reach a place we feel less a contact with nature than an appreciation of what men have done to the place and of what it has meant to previous generations. Nicholas Ray in recent years has set his films outside the commonly photographed America—in the Florida Everglades, in the Far North and in the African desert. On every occasion, though, the explorer is brought to feel how far the wilderness has been spoiled. In *Bitter Victory* Richard Burton discovers an ancient ruined city in the desert and moves on to raid a German-occupied town. In *The Savage Innocents* Anthony Quinn carries the wounded mountie to civilization and leaves him on the outskirts of the settlement of shacks as the juke-boxes echo over the snowy plain.

The more natural habitat of advanced man today is the interior setting of Fritz Lang's movies and his response to them is as untrusting as Lang persuades us to be. In *The 1000 Eyes of Dr Mabuse* Lang discovered his purest setting: the Hotel Luxor modelled on Nazi headquarters. Its public rooms possess space but no identity and its private rooms conceal cameras and two-way mirrors. A city can be constructed less as a place of living than a means of observation.

POWER OVER PLACE

Lumière and Méliès demonstrated the different attitudes that
the cinema could take towards place. Lumière took his camera
into the streets and into his garden; Méliès set up his apparatus
in a purposefully blackened room, conceived and prepared to
aid his illusions—the prototype of a film set. Throughout *Birth
of a Nation* Griffith used sets which his titles proudly announced
as 'facsimile reproductions' of actuality. His version of Ford's
Theater on the night of Lincoln's assassination might be the
real thing, certainly the actor who plays the President and the
audience of extras seem unaware of any fabrication, and for
the spectator today Griffith has an antiquity not easily discernible from that surrounding Lincoln.

Whether Lumière's or Méliès's, the context is equally real,
for if an illusion is to be effected it must be created before the
cameras. While Méliès's context may be that of a magician's
cavern, it is one to which he brings cinematography's eye. What
he films, as opposed to Lumière's context, is a world in which
man has gained control of his environment. The whole set-up
of commercial movie-making is an instance of this state. For
the camera can record any set that man can either discover or
build, and those Hollywood back-lots where frontier towns,
Persian harems, penthouse apartments, jungle clearings and
desert oases stood together are illustrative of the contemporary
power over every location in the world, and over every period
of history. The back-lot is like a mind in which they are all
present, waiting for their turn of attention. Xanadu's enormous
store of *objets d'art*, *bric-à-brac*, and representative pieces from
every culture and period is a perfect equivalent for a big studio's
props department. Kane's inability either to enjoy or discard
the pieces is symptomatic of the modern dilemma whereby the
whole earth is known and yet that body of knowledge over-
whelms. That a childhood sledge should finally outweigh
everything in his collection is proof of Kane's, and Welles's,
surrender to a sense of lost past, of an ambition unworthy of his
powers.

Citizen Kane is a movie to which many stylistic revolutions have been attributed: deep-focus photography, overlapping sound, convoluted flashbacks, expressionism. But they all concentrate in the feeling Welles seems to have had, although unable completely to realize it, about a movie's power of ambiguity over place and person. For *Kane* is Lumière and Méliès in one; the range is from the opening obituary newsreel to the last deluding perspectives of Xanadu. Just as Kane is a man capable of transcending every context he inhabits, of pushing his life to the edge of a reality in which he can himself believe, so Welles is like a man who thought it would be fun to make a movie, and for one time had more licence than any other man in Hollywood has ever had. The result is a particularly contemporary subject for which the film-director and the dictator are both examples: the man who comes to power by control of mass media. When *Kane* was made its application to Hearst must have been obvious; time has extricated those things in the film that apply to Welles himself.

But in 1940 the conjunction of Welles's uninhibited excitement and the acquired professionalism of photographer, Gregg Toland, and art director, Van Nest Polglase, produced a breakthrough in attitudes to setting. Because of the nature of Kane, and the elliptical and fragmentary structure of the film, setting was used so as fully to extend a studio's resources. This extension is comparable with Kane's exercise of every aspect of his power in the way his life is able to realize every wish and fantasy. The lasting power of Xanadu is in its impressions both as fact and fantasy, and these are the very qualities of a film set. Perhaps the most significant revolution aided by *Citizen Kane* was particularly Hollywoodian in that it showed the potential insight into reality that existed in a medium generally thought tied to the most worthless escapism. But it is a matter of the film's impact rather than Welles's own talent. For as Toland's photography, the art direction and Welles's use of dialogue and actors are a culmination of the best of Hollywood in the 'thirties, so the impression made by *Citizen Kane* helped to raise the reputation of directors like Hawks who had long embodied some of the ideas demonstrated in *Kane* without feeling any need, or having any opportunity, to step outside the formula of commercial entertainment to state them.

The technical developments had always been pursued as eagerly in France and Germany, the latter, as Hitler's power extended, supplying Hollywood with *émigré* directors and technicians. In Germany, artificial light and manufactured sets were the tradition, and thus Fritz Lang settled so quickly in America. But in France, the films which today seem most valuable are those in which real settings were used and naturalistic photography was perfected: the work of Jean Renoir. As early as 1931, in *La Chienne*, there is a sequence in which Michel Simon, while shaving, hears and sees a woman singing at a window across the yard. The pull of the focus as it moves to sharpen on the woman, and then back to Simon, is a presentiment of the depth of field Renoir was soon to obtain. For Renoir this technical integration was the necessary expression of his social awareness, not only in the politically co-operative sense of *Le Crime de Monsieur Lange* and *La Marseillaise*, but in the conception of life as a pattern of personalities and principles, all equally justifiable, and all fascinating. *La Chienne, Boudu Sauvé des Eaux, Toni, Partie de Campagne* and *La Règle du Jeu* are perfect examples of it and, because all are concerned with a group and an environment, the use of real locations and cinematography that never deviates from the capacity of the eye are the natural means of rendering it.

So much of *Boudu* is shot in Paris in summer that it is hard to distinguish between the actors and the Parisians. The enjoyment of its making communicates itself as vividly as anything else. The idea of *Boudu* is slight—an opportunity for Michel Simon to indulge both himself and a general anti-bourgeois feeling—but these purposes become enormously sympathetic because one senses their genuineness. For Renoir, as for Hawks, one can often believe that the director and a number of his friends, who happened to be actors and technicians, agreed to make some movie springing directly from their feelings at some particular time and their interest in some particular place. *Boudu*'s last sequence is its complete meaning and *raison d'être*. The tramp has finally slipped the family on whom he has lived for long enough by taking to the river again, from where he was originally rescued. Simon's lazy dog-like swim in the sun ends with a sweeping pan across the river as he lands and settles down to sleep. The pan incorporates the ideals of the film—the sun, the river and freedom to enjoy them—and in its delight at the circle of view, the serene lack of commitment to any particular thing it is, to use Astruc's term, a movement of Boudu's soul. More than that it is the essence of the individuality that exists within the community in Renoir's films. For Renoir does not blur the differences between people or deny self-sufficiency, rather he assumes towards his characters the emotional objectivity of his camera. Any action between them is, he considers, their own affair, which the camera should do no more than record.

Renoir's own function is fulfilled in *La Règle du Jeu* in which he is a constant source of encouragement and organization, hustling guests along corridors, pausing to joke with servants. He is by turns the good friend, worthy of the confidences of all his characters, but finally he is like anyone else, subject to the same rules—though these are not rigid, preordained conditions, but the pattern of various personalities, their deliberate and ironic enactment. What mitigates the sadness in any Renoir film is the complementary and compensatory humour. The downfall of Michel Simon in *La Chienne* is relieved by the superb joke of the ending when, unable to claim it, he watches his own self-portrait being carried away by a wealthy buyer. The sad face that stares back at him from the portrait is Renoir's fatalist comment. Part of the compensation rests in the realization that the world can produce such turns of fortune and in the circle of society and friendship that will be left whatever the passing tragedy. Vital to this circle is its environment, for, just as in Auguste's group studies, the communion and associations are expressed spatially. In *Le Crime de Monsieur Lange* most of the action centres on a courtyard, the people who live round it and their attempt to form a co-operative movement. This directly political theme was stimulated by mid-thirties France, but the sort of atmosphere that supports it features in all Renoir's films. Thus in *Lange* the physical details of life round the courtyard, as often as possible associated by long takes of deep-focused and freely-moving photography, supplies the political ideal much more fluently than any verbal statement. At the moment when Lange kills Batala, the one cynically selfish man in the

courtyard, the action involves a chase through two floors of the
building and the descent of a staircase. It is as if Lange's pursuit gathers the force of the whole building, and when the
camera pans away from him and completes the circle of the
yard before returning to him as he shoots Batala, the movement
not only maintains the spatial ideal, it also underplays the
melodrama of the killing, and, by breaking away from Lange,
implies that the action will by necessity separate him from the
group. The irony affects both characters: Lange's action is so
in keeping with the Wild West heroes he writes about, and when
Batala dies, by a turn of the plot dressed as a priest, he gasps,
'Fetch a priest'.

La Chienne, *Boudu* and *Lange* are all shot in Paris with every
effort made, not only to be faithful to it, but to enjoy the city.
The more intricate the actions of the characters become the
more Renoir is content to adopt the same attitude to them. In
La Règle du Jeu, the spatial relationships that exist within the
house party are so engrossing that, apart from the rigorously
edited shooting sequence, one has the impression of a camera
that is always moving to cover as much as possible. One does
not notice cuts, one delights in a continuity which is often on
the verge of chaos and finally leads to tragedy in the intrusion
of sub-plot into plot, of the theatrical into the real, and of
disaster into balance.

EDITING: MONTAGE OR FLOW

Essentially the camera is capable of recording physical movement so that any movement it cannot cover is intellectually
imposed on the film. This statement brings us to consider the
function of editing.

It is helpful to think of editing as the tool of movement and
to conceive of movement as affecting not only time and place
but the emotions and ideas expressed by the camera. Long
takes, in which the camera runs without interruptions, moving
as needs be to cover the characters or taking a dramatic
course of its own to which the actors conform, can be intoxi-
cating. There is an enormous plastic beauty in such movements
as carried out by Antonioni, Mann, Ophuls and Preminger.

But at times the self-sufficiency of this beauty can obtrude until the formal qualities impress as directorial indulgence. This is least so with Preminger because his movements, like Astruc's, are least noticeable. Whenever movement is sustained beyond its effective limits it seems as fake as the shock-cut. In *Rope* Hitchcock deliberately set out to run the camera to its ten-minute limit and was thus compelled every ten minutes to concentrate on such an image that the joining cut would not be apparent. It is the device, of course, that registers and the moral perplexities of the film that lose their grip.

Hitchcock is by nature a cutter. He itemizes the constituents of a situation by juxtaposition. It is in most cases effective because the tone of his films has convinced us of the necessity for extreme confrontations. At the same time he uses involved camera movements, such as in *Psycho* when the camera cranes up the stairs to the ceiling to look down on Anthony Perkins carrying his mother's body to the cellar. This is a necessary movement as well as being so atmospheric that its elevation is enacted on the audience's fear. With true Hitchcockian irony its necessity is to keep up the source of this fear, to persuade that the mother is alive when she has been dead for years.

The real movement in *Psycho* is psychological, the physical movement only helps to imprint it. Consider two more movements. One in *Battleship Potemkin* of the rebel battleship bombarding Odessa after the massacre. Eisenstein cuts rapidly together shots of statuary to give the effect of a lion being roused by the noise. It is the crudest sort of movement on the same level of nineteenth-century heroic imagery that carved the lions in the first place. The second example is from *Une Vie*. Marquand and Schell spend their wedding night in a field. The act of sexual realization takes place at night. Schell pretends to sleep and Marquand's cut hand is unable to undo the buttons on her dress. He takes out his knife and cuts it open. Next morning there is an exhilarating tracking shot as they roll over together through the corn. Movement here is on various levels. The strained and furtive movements of love are cut into fairly short scenes, the movement of the knife is brutal but human just as the morning's movement is human and ecstatic. Marquand's cut hand constitutes a movement in that we have seen that the wound was incurred in a fight when someone joked about his reputation. The morning tracking shot, in its direction, is a repeat of that slow movement on the jetty when Schell first met Marquand. Eisenstein's movement is what is called 'montage'. Astruc's, I suggest, could be termed 'flow' cinema.

In 1958, Renoir and Rossellini were interviewed together by André Bazin for *France Observateur*.* During the interview Rossellini said:

'I don't know whether, today, *montage* is so essential. I believe we should look at the cinema in a new way, and to start with abandon old myths. The cinema at first was a technical discovery; and everything, even editing, was subordinated to that. Then, in the silent cinema, montage had a precise meaning, because it represented *language*. From the silent cinema we have inherited this myth of *montage*, though it has lost most of its meaning. Consequently, it is in the images themselves that the creative artist can really bring his own observation to bear, his own moral view, his particular vision.'

Rossellini's statement is particularly relevant to the period of about 1958. It came before the work of the young directors in France, before *cinéma-vérité*, before the general recognition of Antonioni. More than anything the remark is a tribute to Rossellini's colleague at the interview, Renoir, and to a number of other directors, many of them veterans. It denies one of the bases of Russian cinema, and of Eisenstein in particular. The particularity of the interview's date is that it was only during the 'fifties that the Russian theories of cinema began to be replaced by the implications of renewed interest in Renoir, the discovery of Mizoguchi and the reappraisal of numerous American directors. One such implication was expressed by Renoir in the same interview: 'I am trying to extend my old ideas, and to establish that the camera finally has only one right—that of recording what happens . . . I don't want the movements of the actor to be determined by the camera, but the movements of the camera to be determined by the actor.' *La Règle du Jeu* demonstrates what these ideas mean for Renoir and, paradoxically, achieves a far subtler theatrical effect than any of the groupings—of characters, décor or emotions—in Eisenstein's work. For Renoir's

* Translated in *Sight and Sound*, Winter 1958-9.

86

theatre is the spontaneous and natural growth of human affairs to a heightened pitch that is still contained within the realistic framework.

The scientific nature of the movie camera obliges movies to be concerned with the relationships between people and places: this is true of Renoir's work, and as true for Lang who deliberately photographs actors in front of sets. The difference is only one of emphasis. That both are successful is because they acknowledge implicitly the validity of the alternative. For both methods the action of the characters is all that exists and both directors might be said to employ 'prose' to record it. The nature of Eisenstein's cinema is essentially poetic, and as such is in opposition to film's nature so that, with television's constant prose, his films seem increasingly pretentious.

At the end of *Strike*, the forces of authority turn on and massacre the strikers. Eisenstein does not simply film this attack, but constructs a *montage* of shots from an abattoir: the men are killed like cattle. Several minutes of film are devoted to this simile and a poetic barrier is erected quite sufficient to lose any feeling of the real event. The result is a contradiction between intention and effect just as dislocating as that in the famous Odessa steps sequence in *Battleship Potemkin*. In both cases the action is of such enormity as to demand Renoir's ideal of a newsreel reliance on the camera, and directly expressive of one of Eisenstein's main themes in the two movies: cruel suppression of those seeking political voice. Inasmuch as the movie camera offers them expression, Eisenstein has denied it by operating the devices by which man controls the camera to the exclusion of its unique powers. The Odessa sequence is so cut that the impact is in the editing rather than the action. The force is as mechanical as a stroboscope to the spectator's eyes, and as authoritarian as the line of advancing soldiers. It is a sequence expressing power, although its intention is to convey injustice. In doing so it establishes a difference of kind between the soldiers and civilians—the one mechanically invincible, the other frail and helpless—that is a denial of photography's ability to show the basic likeness of people however opposed their actions may make them seem. The confusion vitiates much of Eisenstein's work and always derives from his attempt to exert artistic controls over a scientific recording instrument. His sensibility is literary and ideological when it needs to be pragmatic, and his imagination pictorial when it should be visual.

For Eisenstein, the people on the Odessa steps, both soldiers and victims, are without particularity, just as the steps, deprived of their spatial unity by the cutting, are less a location than the setting for a political demonstration which has more importance as a martyrdom in the history books than as an actual event. It is a completely manipulated affair and it breaks down because the effect of the treatment is as autocratic as the soldiers' methods. In *Film Technique*,* Pudovkin said of the ideal director, 'Even when he has to do with real objects in real surroundings he thinks only of their appearance upon the screen. He never considers a real object in the sense of its actual, proper nature, but considers in it only those properties that can be carried over to celluloid.' *Battleship Potemkin* is as much an implementation of this theory as *La Règle du Jeu* is of the statement by Rossellini. There may at one time have been some excuse for finding more value in Eisenstein's method, for saying, as Roger Manvell did in 1944, that the Odessa sequence was 'possibly the most influential six minutes in cinema history'. But the question of influence is now decisive, for it is difficult to see traces of Eisenstein's method in film-making today, even among Russian films. Renoir's ideas, however, are present everywhere even though invariably lacking his inspiration. The increasing use of the image as a direct communication of reality is such that our very sense of reality has shifted from a linguistic to a visual basis. Visual continuity becomes as important as grammatic sequence once was.

Let us consider three demonstrations of the 'flow' principle which themselves describe the evolution in the use of film. In every case, although there is variation in the treatment of visual material, there is no intrusion of an intellectual meaning. The visuals are presented as data and movement is experienced as patterns that emerge freely from the data.

The first case is Tippi Hedren's visit to the Brenner house in *The Birds*. Although ostensibly engaged in a practical joke the visual form indicates a much greater tension, cutting subjec-

* V. I. Pudovkin, translated by Ivor Montagu.

tive forward tracks with reverse tracks in front of Hedren just as Hitchcock does at the climax of *Psycho* when Vera Miles goes up to the house. Hedren plans to leave caged birds in Rod Taylor's house without his knowing who left them. The physical details of the deception and the natural colours of Bodega Bay are shown faithfully enough for one to suspect a totally objective cinema were it not made much more tense by the rhythm of cutting. These cuts are not mechanical and they do not conceal reality; instead they emphasize the association between Hedren and the landscape of her joke. The inequality of tense style and frivolousness shows a sexual impulse on her part and induces extreme alertness in the spectator. This alertness is fulfilled when Hedren comes back to the quay, looks coyly at Taylor who has raced round the bay to meet her, and is bitten on the forehead by a gull, the first bird to attack in the film. There are numerous cuts in this sequence of action but one does not feel that its integrity has been endangered. Rather has the visual treatment conveyed a level of violent excitement to the spectator which is irrational because it comes from only a practical joke which is not vicious for all its undertones of sexual antagonism. The impact is directed at the spectator. The bird that attacks Tippi Hedren is a device that assaults us—an undeserved climax sent by the director to satisfy the desires he has aroused.

Hitchcock's cuts in this sequence are noticeable but essentially cinematic because they increase the spectator's sense of physical actuality. That they are so fundamental to the scene's effect indicates Hitchcock's authoritarianism. By contrast, Preminger's cuts are often 'invisible', being the most efficient way of continuing the visual level without drawing attention to the join. At the beginning of *St Joan*, Richard Widmark, the Dauphin, is seen in bed, unable to sleep. His anxiety is entirely personal and consists of the actor's performance. The camera is removed sufficiently for the tension to be observed rather than contagious. Widmark gets out of bed to be sure that his guards are on duty. The camera describes an arc round his chamber to follow him but keeps his image in the same proportion to the frame throughout so that there is no feeling of sharing in the movement. The arch between the Dauphin's chamber and the ante-chamber is too narrow for the character and the camera to pass through together. For one to follow the other would only make the functionalism ponderous. Preminger cuts from one chamber to the other, matching Widmark's movements perfectly. This is what I mean by an invisible cut—one that is for efficiency's sake and not noticed by the viewer.

This sort of cut is in fact predominant in the commercial cinema: directors like Hitchcock who cut for effect are in the minority, so slight has Eisenstein's influence been. The mechanics of the cut in *St Joan* indicate not only an aesthetic but a commercial sense. Preminger is a director who shoots quickly and this cut would have been envisaged beforehand so that the shooting and set construction could be properly scheduled. At the editing stage the relevant pieces of film would only have had to be trimmed accurately.

Such a convention applies to the putting together of elided action—the ascent of stairs for instance, or any complicated physical action that has to be filmed from several set-ups if the observation of the camera is not to seem overbearing. In Godard's *Pierrot le Fou* there is a sequence which deliberately comments on this convention of film-making and the editorial power it provides. The sequence involves Belmondo and Karina escaping from a flat and driving away in a car. Normally the editor would simply have to put the various stages of the event in their proper order. But Godard has changed the order so that actions are repeated from different viewpoints and the whole process is drawn out beyond its real time-span. Although Godard is making a joke about a cinematic convention the flow of the sequence is not destroyed, instead the film is about Belmondo's and Karina's co-operation with Godard and the characters they are interpreting. The effect is both exciting and mechanical because it makes the spectator question his means of understanding visual data. We seem to have no more knowledge of events than if we were a machine viewing them and being programmed by them. The apparent visual contradictions, instead of disturbing us, merely prove that visual logic does not conform with intellectual logic.

The gaps between Eisenstein, Hitchcock, Preminger and Godard are the development of the cinema and the camera's attitude to people and place. In *Pierrot le Fou* more clearly perhaps than anywhere else the landscape is both place and location at the same time.

The film strip is basic to any film, the editing of it asserts artistic attitude and ambition or, in its absence, affirms the scientific basis of observation which always has a consequent aesthetic justification. Godard's manipulation of sequence is deliberate but the individual items are not interfered with—they record fact, one person jumping from a window, another getting into a car. They involve a sense of place that is more modern than any the cinema has previously known because it rejects personal associations of home or strangeness. It is necessary to consider earlier cinematic treatments of place than Godard's before his establishes its proper position. To do so I shall examine two directors whose films bear out a general social movement of the last hundred years from the frontier community to the city. At the same time the value for a person of the idea of frontier has continued, changing its form in the city to that of an almost political sensibility which is apparent in Godard's work with Lemmy Caution's adventures in *Alphaville*.

THE FRONTIER COMMUNITY: ANTHONY MANN

The sense of frontier, whether it relates to knowledge or a geographical location is particularly American because of a self-conscious observation of their own actions which makes Americans particularly contemporary and particularly cinematic. Just as America's development from pioneer community to atomic society has, in European terms, been compressed, its landscape combines the extremes of open uninhabited prairie and urban complex in greater contrast than any other country. The juxtaposition constitutes a frontier just as the coexistence of ideologies deriving from the two states of living makes a split which can suddenly become critical when a man shoots down the President on main street in the way Billy the Kid shot Sheriff Brady.

American foreign policy and its major domestic issues bear out this theory. For America is a country that has developed its powers to the standards of industrialization but, originally at least, drew back from involvement in two world wars because of its self-imposed heritage of isolation. This still confronts America with feelings of imperialist guilt when it considers itself bound to the defence of insecure states against Communism. While one may make a general comparison between Henry James and Woodrow Wilson in the sense they had of America's being inextricably involved in an older and more cynical Europe, one might relate Kennedy to Hemingway, who described a brutally realistic world but set his own reactions to it against a complicated code of honour—a frontier between the Brett Ashleys and the Robert Cohns.

The Western embodies this idea more satisfactorily than any other period settings Hollywood has celebrated because, at its best, it depends upon an appreciation of the American landscape as fine as Hemingway's in *Big Two-Headed River* and because the society it evokes is one in which opportunity and discipline make a timeless confrontation. The shape taken by a new society is not only fresh in America's past, but relevant to most of the issues it has become involved in since emerging from isolation.

The work of Anthony Mann is unrivalled for its development of the themes in the Western form, combining the visual sensitivity to terrain of a frontier scout with a deliberate but uncontrived sense of morality worked out through the spatial authenticity. In many of his films the frontier is real and, because the law is either non-existent or erratic, the potentially uninhibited action has only the camera's eye as its moral imperative. Thus it is essential that action is clearly observed and that its moral implications arise from it quite naturally. As Godard said in a review of *Man of the West*: 'Avec Anthony Mann, nous avons à chaque plan l'analyse en même temps que la synthèse.'*

Mann's Westerns concentrate on the uncivilized environment and often isolate a few characters in an uninhabited landscape. In *The Naked Spur* the balance between James Stewart's acceptance of a share in the stolen money and his determination to return the outlaw Robert Ryan to justice is all the finer because the five characters are so patently isolated. It is a situation

* *Cahiers du Cinéma*, No. 92.

likely to assist in forming the standards of a future society and what is admirable in the film is not Stewart's resolution but the great difficulty he has in holding to it. The beautifully mountainous country is a source of danger as well as of freedom, and every action has not only the spontaneity of vital movement in a natural environment but serves as definition of every man's nature.

In *Where the River Bends* and *The Far Country* James Stewart becomes involved with pioneering communities and is eventually forced to weigh self-interest against social responsibility. Once again the awareness of the dilemma consists not so much in a self-conscious pondering by Stewart himself but Mann's ability to place every action in perfect physical and moral context at the same time. In *Where the River Bends* Stewart is in charge of a wagon train of supplies for an isolated community beyond Mount Hood. This obligation is all the greater because, although he was once an outlaw, the people of the community have trusted him. Their distant existence is constantly implied by the way the mountain dominates so many scenes. The wagons are stolen from Stewart by Arthur Kennedy, a friend of his outlaw days, and some miners. To recover them he must follow the train and pick off the men one by one. There is a shot in which two men in one of the wagons look back and see miles behind them the pursuing figure of Stewart: the physical and moral aspects are completely integrated. His final fight to the death with Kennedy takes place in the river which winds through the spatial consciousness of the whole film, and when he is helped from the river the rope that pulls him tightens round his neck like the lynch knot he once only just escaped.

Mann has explained, in an interview, how he sees the details of a location shaping the human action:

'Les acteurs atteignent à bien plus de vérité en extérieurs. Dans un studio, tout est calme, tout est construit en prévision de la scène, les lumières sont allumées. Mais si l'acteur doit la jouer au sommet d'une montagne, au bord d'un fleuve ou dans une forêt, il y a le vent, la poussière, la neige, le craquement des branches qui l'interrompent, qui l'obligent à se donner plus: il devient plus vivant.'*

* *Cahiers du Cinéma*, No. 69.

In fact, there is never any sign of improvisation in Mann's films, as this might imply, but a precise realization of action so that the script only becomes fact when the combination of actor and location is exact. There is a mathematical element in his lateral camera movements and infinite perspectives, but this clarity and balance are indications of the elemental newness of the frontier situation. At its best—in *The Far Country*, *The Man from Laramie* and *Man of the West*—the accuracy of the account leads to a moral ambiguity which deepens the significance of action that, as befits a frontier community, is simple and often violent. If one compares these three films with *The Tin Star* it is clear that what stops the tendency to the academic implicit in Mann's meticulous notation of events is a vital involvement of character with location so that the crisis of physical survival always determines the moral issue.

The Tin Star is an academic film. Its enormous visual attractiveness is undermined by the failure to convey the importance for Henry Fonda of his association with Anthony Perkins. The small town, of which Perkins is the new sheriff, is constantly photographed in a depth that relates interior and street so that one has a real sense of the pressures upon the sheriff. But the country beyond, from where Fonda, a bounty-hunter, has come, is not related to the town. It seems not only separate, but lifeless. Perkins is threatened by an unmotivated villain, Neville Brand, who exists, it seems, simply to menace the sheriff. It is an unreasonable situation, and thus the malign force appears much more evil than in a film like *The Far Country* where it is so diffuse that it seems to pass from one character to another. Fonda is too self-sufficient and too respectable to be credible as an adventurer prepared to stop his normal way of life to train a greenhorn. Thus his demonstrations of skill are exhibitionist and the final shoot-out between Perkins and Brand, though realized with ideal travelling shots, is without tension because black villainy and pure good are too obviously opposed.

In Mann's best films one believes that the eventual trial of strength and courage that is obligatory to the Western form will be the vindication of a character, and that it is an issue in doubt. Essential to this doubt is a community in flux and central characters whose lives depend on the form that society takes. It is this criterion that *The Tin Star* ignores because its town is cut off from a sense of vitality and development. The atmosphere is even bourgeois. Contrast this with the setting of *The Far Country*: Skagway in Alaska and Dawson in the Yukon. It is gold-rush time and law and order is in the hands of John McIntire who manipulates his power, arbitrarily but sardonically, towards his own ends. Stewart is an adventurer who has come north with his herd of cattle. He only gets away from Seattle, on the way to Skagway, by a trick after having been accused of killing two men who wanted to back out of their agreement to come on the trip. Stewart's untrusting independence is characteristic of a frontier opportunist. In Skagway he blunders into one of McIntire's hangings and only narrowly escapes death himself in a trial that is farcical but deadly. Instead his herd is confiscated. Without money he agrees to take a supply train to Dawson, but steals back his own herd as he leaves, crossing the border just ahead of McIntire's pursuit.

On the way to Dawson he leads his section of the train on a detour to avoid a pass he considers dangerous. He does not warn the others. They go on and some of them die in an avalanche. By the time he reaches Dawson, therefore, Stewart is identified as a not wholly likeable, but shrewd and tough adventurer as aware of his physical setting as of the free-enterprise prizes to be won in a frontier boom. In this first part of the film McIntire is drawn not as a villain, but as a competitor. Conditions in Dawson force both men to develop their characters: McIntire forms a hardened gang to exploit and cheat the unorganized miners; Stewart attempts to keep out of the conflict and mines his own claim with his partner, Walter Brennan. McIntire attacks Stewart and Brennan as they are leaving with their gold; Brennan is killed and Stewart wounded. There follows a sequence in which Stewart sits alone in the shack drinking coffee with his left hand and flexing his wounded right, looking at his gun in its holster. Brennan's eagerness to buy extra coffee had betrayed the secrecy of their departure and Stewart's awkward efforts to drink are an accompaniment to his lost ability with the gun. For the first time his resolution has become more than self-interest, though there is no doubt that his natural solitariness supplies some of the impulse for revenge. It is perhaps no more than that for Brennan he felt friendship and for McIntire similarity: the wound he has suffered is a revelation of his own nature which he has now deliberately to alter.

The scenes in which Stewart and Brennan are attacked at the river, and Stewart sits alone in the shack, are both exceptionally beautiful. That they contain and hint at such violence is the dramatic tension in Mann's work. For the north-west landscapes have a beauty that depends upon their wildness. Man's efforts to exploit them provoke their natural violence. Thus in *The Far Country* the mountains give up their gold and offer bloodshed and treachery with it; the serene snowscape will erupt into an avalanche that obliterates a supply train. The Korean countryside in *Men in War* has qualities natural to the sun that shines on it, but the long grass that waves in the wind conceals a Communist bayonet.

Mann's attitude to his settings is conveyed in these juxta-positions. The camera reproduces his awe at their beauty and the action shows his respect for their exact nature and a sense of prospective loss that they must be harnessed. Mann's hero regards the country in the same way as his camera but is always confronted with this need to become a part of the organization that is developing the raw land. In this respect Mann alone has been able to relate the Western form to contemporary American life and *Man of the West* shows this more clearly than any other movie. The title suggests archetype, but the hero is Gary Cooper only a few years before his death: a man whose face is lined and anxious, whose movements are taking on the impedi-ments of age. In Mann's unfolding of the Western myth during the 1950s Cooper is a moving climax. Visibly ten years older than Stewart, he is the same character as appeared in *Where the River Bends*: a reformed outlaw living in a developing com-munity. As in the earlier film his loyalty is put to the test.

The conditions of the test are less exciting than tragic. He is charged to take the community's money to a bank. For this he travels to a nearby town to catch a train to the city. The train is held up by bandits and his money stolen. Cooper recognizes the bandits. With two other passengers, Arthur O'Connell and Julie London, he sets off in their pursuit. It is Mann's achieve-

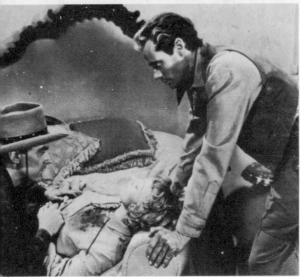

11, 12. The progress of *Rancho Notorious* from rumour's image of Dietrich coloured by her clothes, the bunting and the chuckaluck wheel to the real woman in working clothes. The wound that has killed her repeats the ripped dress of Arthur Kennedy's fiancée.

13. *La Notte*. Jeanne Moreau's provocativeness is quietly ignored by Marcello Mastroianni.

14. *The Miracle Worker*. Anne Bancroft and Patty Duke are beyond our intervention.

15. Intimations of mortality. John Wayne just beaten to the draw by Montgomery Clift in *Red River*.

16. *Anatomy of a Murder*. Lee Remick's ambivalence disturbs James Stewart. Sam Leavitt's 'rough' lighting is utterly objective.

ment that this pursuit manages to suggest dimension in both space and time. Cooper's arrival in the town and his wait for the train have been characterized by a countryman's unease with the bustle of a railway station. But at the robbery this rustic inexperience is replaced by an intelligence that allows him to see the hold-up coming before anyone else and to appreciate its details. Thus as he starts out to recover the money we are aware of an aptitude decreased but not lost. Cooper's walk is so suited to this: gingerly careful, unwilling to stretch his long stride in case it snaps.

The journey takes the three of them out of the prairie and into a deserted landscape of dark, rich colour. There is a shot of them coming on a farmhouse in the hollow of a green meadow, and of their walking towards it, expressive of an isolation that is not entirely geographical. Cooper's walk has become more assured and alert, though it is never likely to share the natural ease of Stewart, who is physically and emotionally fitted to his environment. The Tobin gang are in the farmhouse, led by Lee J. Cobb who was once Cooper's adopted father. The isolation is a just condition of this gang for Tobin is mad and the others at extremes of viciousness and perversion. Theirs is an anachronistic lawlessness and their isolation shows this as much as the reform of Cooper, their erstwhile companion. They have an insane plan to rob a bank in a town several days' journey away.

Cooper is forced to join in this robbery to preserve the safety of O'Connell and London. His respectability is put under test by the gang's attitude to Julie London: the prospect of rape is automatic and they force her to undress in front of them. Cooper is only just able to save her and one senses that his own discipline is cracking. The madness of the Tobin gang is apparent when the town they are planning to raid proves to be a ghost-town in the middle of a desert. Cooper kills Cobb, but not before O'Connell has been murdered and Julie London raped. He rides back with her in a buggy through a field of cactus plants, and this cruel landscape is a perfect image of the difficulty with which Cooper's own rehabilitation has been maintained.

Compared with *The Far Country*, *Man of the West* presents a later stage in the development of a society so that the use of landscape suggests a loss of reason and adaptability in the outlaws where McIntire was on equal terms with Stewart. Because time has moved on and standards have become less violent, the reappearance of violence is all the more disturbing —as disturbing as Aldo Ray's final assumption of command from his officer, Robert Ryan, in *Men in War*, when they attack the Chinese strongpoint with a flame-thrower. The violent beauty of the flame-thrower, the erotic beauty of Julie London undressing before the Tobins and the barren beauty of Cooper's victory in the ghost town all partake of Mann's interrelation of his characters and their surroundings so that the victories and defeats reflect upon the natural settings and all society.

There is, of course, a tragic element in the man who is forced into assisting in the beginnings of an urban society when the open air and untracked territory best express his character and exercise his talents. It is only this that makes Cooper's predicament in *Man of the West* more than conventionally heroic, and the irony of a ghost town as the setting for the catharsis is that it represents Cobb's madness and is also a distorted comment on Cooper's new life. The issue of the adventurer brought to some form of conformity or domesticity is the theme that reacts so well with Mann's photography. The American society in *Cimarron* that moves towards the First World War is one of matriarchal industry and trimming politics. The prairie has been built up.

THE RESTRICTION OF ORGANIZATION: LOSEY

The unease of Mann's heroes when drawn into interiors may be compared with the opposite reaction of characters in Losey's movies. Losey was one of the first American directors to photograph an urban civilization that was recognizably contemporary. His version of *M* has the provable basis of San Francisco, whereas Lang's city in his earlier version is constructed for the movie, the streets as artificial as the interiors. And as in Losey's *M* the steep diagonals of San Francisco are repeated in the interiors in the staircases and ramps against which we see David Wayne, so Losey's world is one in which the shapes and rhythms of the city have formed his characters. Their attempts to escape this influence are so subtly tragic that Losey's movies have a full sense of the intrusion of contemporary urban life. Essentially, the dynamic of Losey's heroes is towards self-determination, but their efforts have obvious political implications because one is made so conscious of the way in which the city serves as microcosm for the whole western capitalist system. There is a revealing comparison to be made between Losey and Capra for both place their heroes in similar positions. The credibility of Losey's response is such as to make one marvel that a film like *Mr Deeds Goes to Town* is only thirty years old. Capra's Deeds manages by his protest to 'stop' the whole corrupt system and reassert, seemingly at a national level, his simple morality. This is a fantasy of harmful proportions assuming a system so feeble that Gary Cooper alone will bring it down in a direct confrontation of system and individual. Both Hawks's *Sergeant York* and *Man of the West* show how much more tragic Cooper's response to social pressure could be.

Losey's hero never experiences his own opposition to certain forces of society as simply as Deeds is made to; symptomatic of this is his preference for living within buildings—the manifestation of society and the symbol of reluctant necessity in so many of Mann's movies. The loss of a sense of ease with exteriors has increased in Losey's films at the same time as his world has witnessed the extension of city into the landscape. Much of *The Dividing Line* is exterior as befits the story of a Mexican youth in a country town. The town has the potential of blending with the country but fails to do so because the people are so organized against the Mexican and the newspaperman who defends him that what might be a richly diffused but co-operative society, as in a Renoir movie, becomes a lynch-mob.

Since Losey's arrival in England exteriors have come to hold an increasingly non-naturalistic value for his characters. In *The Gypsy and the Gentleman*, which is an uncharacteristic venture into period, the real and attractive English countryside is remote from the aristocratic lives. The two gypsies, Mercouri and McGoohan, are obviously more at ease in it, but no more sensitive to its peace. Thus the landscape contributes towards some of the movie's most striking juxtapositions: the savage prize-fight held in a meadow; the island in the middle of a placid lake holding a miniature prison; and the river being made the site of the baroque ending with the lovers kissing each other to death beneath its surface. It is remarkable in this film how, without ever making it his subject, Losey demonstrates the power of the aristocrats in regency England and their dislocation from a rural society. The sunny countryside is a bizarre setting for the gentleman's revels, and this bizarreness turns quickly to tragedy.

That such events take place against such backgrounds is hallucinatory, just as *Time Without Pity*'s ending with Leo Mckern driving round a deserted motor-racing circuit, refusing to stop and talk to Michael Redgrave, is a true image of imminent breakdown and the rich man's frustration with attempts to enjoy his wealth. In *The Criminal* one finds the same experience of exteriors. Those scenes in the out-of-doors are fleeting and unfulfilled: one of Stanley Baker and Margit Saad walking happily in Mayfair is cut off so quickly that they might be escapees risking recapture by going out. This is, of course, exactly the subject of *The Criminal*, which Losey originally intended to set entirely inside the prison. For the prison is a microcosm of society and Stanley Baker is a man who holds back some individuality from his commitment to the society. When freed he robs a racetrack—the filming so abbreviated that it is totally unexciting*—which has been planned in a Sunday-morning conference on Wimbledon Common. This conspiracy sequence is a perfect example of the relationship the characters have with exteriors. They are over-sophisticated figures in a domestic open space, and consequently have an awkwardness not entirely due to their purpose. They sit on the seat at odd, uncommunicative angles and it is only later one realizes how apt an expression this is of the plan that already contains the material of its own betrayal. More than that, the whole setting is contrived as if the robbers felt it necessary to choose an incongruous site for their talk but had only attracted more suspicion because of their own uneasiness with it.

* Losey had not wanted to compete with Kubrick, but his sparse coverage of the robbery is marvellously ordinary.

Baker is returned to prison and has to engineer his release in order to protect the girl he has fallen in love with. Significantly, the means of release are such as to make him the enemy of all the other prisoners, among whom he had been a hero and a leader. By falling in love he has made himself vulnerable. The film ends with him being chased to the field where he had previously buried the race-track money, and being killed by another crook. This death, on a snow-covered field, is truly pitiful because Baker's hopeless inability to deal with the open-air environment is an image of the total restrictedness of his life. The camera rises above the field to show the frantic digging of the criminals to recover the money until they look like insects. It makes an alien and unhelpful wasteland of the countryside because of the insensitivity of people to its nature. Losey also sees a lost world in *The Damned* in which the Dorset seascape has two values: first, as the conventional seaside resort disturbed only beneath the surface by teenage violence and the guarded research establishment; second, after the break of security, which is really equivalent to a nuclear disaster, it is as if contaminated, and there is a poignant sequence in which the children, imprisoned beneath the cliffs, escape to the sunlight and enjoy a few moments' freedom before recapture. *The Damned* ends with the seashore restored to official supervision and the patrolling helicopters that pick off any subversive or contaminated elements. Once again Losey endows the countryside with a heightened unsuitability for his characters, and the success of *The Damned* is partly due to so much of it being set out of doors that the landscape changes from the known Weymouth area of the first part of the film to a cliffside of elemental proportions, the hints of catastrophe making it as much a frontier as any of Mann's.

It is a landscape that completely fulfils the values suggested in the closing sequences of *The Prowler* and *The Criminal* and leads to the stylization of exteriors in *Eve* and *The Servant*, which are both concentrated interior movies, the first moving outside, because of the nature of Rome and Venice, into an extended arcade, and the second having only brief shots out of doors like the snow-covered, deserted park—a caricature of a garden.

The Servant marks the fullest absorption of Losey in his

interior sense; it is remarkable not only in the effects of art direction, but in the way décor supports the idea of people being characterized by the buildings that confine and identify them within the system. The least differentiated picture of this system is the prison in *The Criminal*, but even there distinctions are made. Scout, the eavesdropper and message-carrier, has a cell softened by the rewards of his collaboration.

Before discussing the décor of any films in detail it is important to note the overall attitude of the characters themselves to décor and the way this reflects the undermining influence of system that encourages the potential individualists to take it on directly. Thus in *The Prowler* Van Heflin is a patrol-car policeman in a wealthy Californian suburb who aspires to move from his own dreary lodging and the mobile room of his car into the sort of ease in the houses he guards. It is a calculated attempt by a man not basically evil to attain his ambitions by dishonest means. The same is true of Stanley Baker in *The Criminal* who is always acting outside the law, but within his own code of honour, in an attempt to find a place for himself inside the apparently respectable system. The means by which Heflin breaks the law he guards are integral with his relationship to the homes, and the whole action is set off by a suggestive incident. A wife, Evelyn Keyes, looks out of her window one night and an expression of fear and shock crosses her face. She reports a prowler and Heflin arrives to enquire. Only when Heflin has seduced her and killed her husband does one reflect that the prowler has never been found. Inasmuch as what is not shown on the screen may be said not to exist one feels that there may have been a prior plan between Heflin and Keyes, or that he may have been the prowler himself. At any rate, the presence of the large ornate house is made as much Heflin's target as Evelyn Keyes. Targets abound in his life. His lodging room has a black, bullet-scarred, shooting target on the wall, and in one sequence, as his plans move forward, we see him lying on his bed throwing screwed-up paper balls into the cheap light-bowl.

But, as in *The Criminal*, the success of the immediate plan sets events in motion that lead to disaster. Heflin and Keyes marry but are unable to settle. They attempt to escape but Keyes is pregnant and they find themselves in the middle of the desert, in a desolate ruined shack—the bitter culmination of Heflin's ideal. When the police arrive, Heflin runs away and is forced into the meaningless ascent of a hill that is as much abstract as physical. But he is a target himself now, and is shot down.

The house in which Evelyn Keyes and her husband live is particularized only in its vulgarly romantic Mexican style. But as Losey's career has proceeded such particularities of character have tended to replace the more abstract qualities of the American films—*The Prowler*, *M* and *The Big Night*, especially.* In *Blind Date*, the relatively uninteresting material enabled this aspect to be explored until it became the very subject and provided the characters with an interest that the plot outline had never offered. In every sense *Blind Date* is a set-up film. A young man comes to a Chelsea flat to meet his mistress. She has not yet arrived and he wanders round the flat for several minutes. The police appear and question him in a sequence of growing menace; no crime is named but his guilt is confidently assumed. They then disclose a woman's corpse on a sofa under some coats. The action moves to the police station and the young man, Hardy Kruger, is interrogated by an inspector, Stanley Baker.

For all the circumstantial evidence an intriguing contradiction has already been suggested which is soon to make Baker wary of the justification of his suspicions. The flat we have seen, explored for us by Kruger's wait, is not in keeping with the woman he describes expecting to meet there. Kruger is a young Dutch painter, as flashbacks from the interrogation reveal. He was lonely in London and at the Tate Gallery one day met Micheline Presle, a sophisticated, wealthy woman. They became lovers. The Chelsea rendezvous was one in a succession of meetings. But the flat has a lurid opulence that, we realize on seeing Presle, is not appropriate to her. More than that, one compares the sequence in the flat with those in Kruger's attic studio where he takes her, and as his innocence

---

* This may be due to Losey's having changed design adviser as he crossed the Atlantic. John Hubley helped towards the architectural qualities of *M* and *The Prowler*, Richard Macdonald towards the decorative texture of *Blind Date* and *Eve*.

seems more and more likely a character study is revealed
which fascinates, paradoxically, because of the suppressed
violence it shows. The richness of the sequence in which Kruger
arrives at the flat expands throughout the film. His anxious,
excited movements were tense with sexual charge and an
unconscious doubt about the character of the flat.

For Kruger is dedicated fiercely to his art in a way that is
both sincere and romantic. That he lives, literally, in an attic is
one of Losey's most audacious combinations of the real and the
abstract. When he meets Presle one realizes how much the bare
attic is a retreat from social intercourse for which his awkwardness makes him unsuited, and that his paintings, stark
confrontations with miners, represent a fostering of feelings of
strength and manliness so isolated from experience that they
might lead to homosexuality. There is the same inappropriate-
ness in Presle's declared love for Kruger as between the flat and
Presle's character. When he takes her back to his attic, first to
teach her to paint and then to draw her, there is an ugly
eroticism that conveys the dark, private side of Kruger's
character and the fact that Presle's compliance is less passionate
than arranged. Because this affair is arranged what excitement
she does feel adds a provocativeness that is depraved. The full
irony of the movie is to strip the characters so that the prostitute's flat one first thought unsuited to Presle's social position
has a moral justice, and Kruger's youthful charm, which at first
seemed unlikely to be murderous, proves to have the necessary
underground impulses.

For all its qualities *Blind Date* is limited by the purely
detective-story of the script, and consequently its subtlety is in
two characters and two sets, with Stanley Baker giving a
detailed but almost irrelevant portrayal of a police inspector.
In *The Criminal* Baker is the central character himself and his
ordeal is not an exercise but sufficiently vital to produce a
film of fully universal implication, one in which sets and
characters are various but integrated. Losey combines the real
simplicity of the prison cells with the abstract value of a neutral
background against which character, relationship and process
all become heightened so that a credible hysteria is the level of
prison life.

When Baker is first released from prison he is invited by Sam Wanamaker to a celebration party—to be held in Baker's flat. The party scene involves a large open-plan and multi-level flat. As such it corresponds with the prison sequences in which the community is fully integrated spatially, and thus systematically. It is a wild but joyless party quite without ease or sense of occasion, and although the flat has a brittle surface luxury it is curiously unfinished. In Baker's bedroom a cheap erotic painting barely covers a skylight, and in the living area there seem to be no chairs. When the party breaks up Baker is left alone in his flat, and one immediately feels that for all its defects it is a meaningful place for him and one in which he has a comparative security. He prepares to go to bed and automatically stacks his clothes in prison regulation piles. The blow with which he knocks this pile to the floor is a spontaneous and tragic gesture of the sort, allying idea and action, that distinguishes *The Criminal*. In bed he puts on goggles and prepares to give himself a sunray-lamp tan. But a girl, Margit Saad, is in the bed beside him. As an action that seems in keeping with the mechanical sex at the party and the erotica in his flat the boldness of her presence at first shocks and bewilders Baker; the girl says she simply wanted to find out what it was like to be alone with him. It is possibly this aloneness that disturbs Baker, not only because he has not seen a woman for so long, but because his sexual attitudes are those of the party. Her presence is significantly away from the others—she is an individualist, like Baker. Later in the film, Wanamaker is to suggest he knows her—a suggestion of complicity in a freely interchangeable sexual system—but Saad vigorously denies this.

The love affair between the two individualists is, until the last sequence, confined by interiors, and yet it manages to triumph over them, just as Saad keeps free of Wanamaker's suggestions although Jill Bennett, Baker's former girl-friend, is quite overcome by them, arriving at the party to be seen through a kaleidoscope Wanamaker holds—her image multiplied and disorientated. The first meeting of Baker and Saad is private, a condition not normally allowed in the prison society. The degree to which they are able to break the limitation of this society is shown in one brief sequence in the flat's bathroom. We

have already seen that the door has a blown-up nude photograph on it—the conventional erotic substitute. But Margit
Saad bathing naked is the sexual actuality and when Baker
hauls her out of the bath and carries her into the bedroom the
eroticism is vital and cheerful and its contrast with the lifeless
poster is to the credit of individualism. They are together in the
flat when Baker is arrested and she makes a vain, and significantly unsophisticated, attempt to provide him with an alibi,
though, in fact, she is always absent from the scenes of Baker's
direct criminality.

As soon as Baker is inside prison again, the real attachment
he has made with Saad proves not a consolation, but a danger.
For while he cannot be with her he knows that pressure may be
put on her to discover where he hid the money. When she visits
him in prison there is a sequence that conveys this situation
through the regulations of the occasion. They are not allowed
to touch, but must sit facing each other across a plain table,
every word overheard by a warder. This is a bleak association
of the forces of authority and criminal organizations and their
opposition to Baker, realized so naturally that, for all his care
that Saad should be safe, Baker does not realize the comparison.
Again, one notices the lack of comprehension in Losey's heroes
of the true circumstances, and the consequent preparedness to
attempt to operate within them, thus provoking a more complete destruction.

When Baker's escape is engineered the inevitability of tragedy
is clear if only because he has broken the rule of prison—that
one is given and serves a term. In this sense, the protective
quality of the prison is now denied to him. Saad has in fact been
held a prisoner by Wanamaker and Baker finds them in a barge,
its long narrow cabin as cramped as a prison cell and an
impediment to the bold physical action Baker attempts. It is a
trap he cannot avoid because Saad is the bait and the crowded
close-quarters emphasize the impossibility of further privacy for
them. The barge is also suggestive of the impermanent living
conditions of the criminal class, just as Baker's flat is not convincing as a living place but as a gesture towards one.

Even though Baker and Saad escape his actions have become
so prescribed by the enclosing system and the degree to which

his own nature subscribes to that system that he cannot break out of the situation. His flight to the money, certain to be pursued, is instinctive, as is his death in the field, babbling prayers. Before death he shouts at Saad to get away from him, to save herself from contamination. She does so but leans to one side, clutching at her stomach, in an extraordinary moment which blurs distinctions of acting, directing or chance. The action is suggestive of shared pain from the bullet that is killing Baker, of a frustrated sexual climax, and of the touch that was denied them in prison. It also implies a permanent wound and some sort of absorption of her into the system. The love between them which was sheltered by incongruous urban interiors and tested by separation and the trap, is brought to a tragic and elemental end in the wintry countryside. The memory of Saad persists through the shot of the three men digging wildly and into the last high-angle shot of a prison compound with a circle of prisoners taking their exercise. The exterior, like the field, is deathly, as befits the waste of the prisoners. Life within the prison is deprived but, *The Criminal* suggests, it is the only possible life and it is no different from that existing outside. The last three shots of *The Criminal* illustrate Losey's combination of the physical and the abstract. In Christian Ledieu's words they constitute 'Décor d'une pensée'.*

---

* In *Joseph Losey*, Vol. 11 of Éditions Seghers series 'Cinéma d'Aujourd'-hui'.

5

CHARACTERS AND PEOPLE

The Projection of Personality –
Ontological Status – Acting –
Cary Grant – Marilyn Monroe
and Kim Novak – Personal Freedom

THE PROJECTION OF PERSONALITY

If a film employs a person's presence, appearance, voice,
gestures and movements towards a statement of personality or
the condition of life, what right does the actor have to make his
own contribution to the events that are being used to make a
conclusive statement about him? In other words, the cinema
has brought the epistemological condition of the actor forward
into the universal consciousness. Those Hollywood gossip
romances between people who had to make love in front of the
cameras are not just the sign of an unstable minority but an
advance indication of a society that is uncertain about whether
its individual actions are authentic gestures or artificial poses.

It is impossible, of course, to separate the sense of a person
from the sense of place because the integration of the two is
obligatory to the idea of *mise-en-scène*. But the camera can photograph between two extremes that give a radically different view
of people. There is the long shot that sees people, at a distance,
small, anonymous and in a crowd, and there is the close-up that
sees one person, large, personal and alone. In Lang's work, for
instance, there is the difference between the armies of workers
in *Metropolis* and the increasing close-up of Spencer Tracy in
Fury. The political logic of such a juxtaposition is dictatorship
and its cinematic example occurs in Leni Riefenstahl's *Triumph*

of the Will with the panoramic travelling shots of adoring crowds and megalomaniac close-ups of the orators at Nuremberg.

Triumph of the Will is unusual in the way its camera goes to the two extremes; in most films the area of middle distance and the consequently greater human uncertainties provide the largest part of the visual context. But it is not only the historical political significance of Riefenstahl's film that makes it interesting. The insight it now offers into Nazism is the cinematic image it gives of a relationship between leader and people. The propagandist conviction is certainly conveyed by the style but the mechanics of cinema shadow the certainties with hints at the suppression of freedom involved. As a possible socio-political solution for a modern state film itself disproves the extremes of crowd shot and close-up, suggesting the mindlessness in the one and the monomania in the other. There are few films in which reality and abstraction clash so violently. In terms of place there is the imposition of the classical Nuremberg architecture on Germany of the 30s and in terms of person the close-ups of deranged and often deformed leaders declaiming the ethnic purity of an Aryan race.

Whatever environment is filmed, whether the totally contrived studio interiors of von Sternberg, the country club in Milan, requisitioned by Antonioni for the party in *La Notte*, or the Nuremberg of *Triumph of the Will*, that environment becomes a film set as well as a place, and the people—Dietrich, Monica Vitti, Hitler—become not only contemporaries of those filming them, but film stars, archetypes or myths contemporary for a much greater span of time. It is important to see how influential are the varying production set-ups, the difference between von Sternberg's Hollywood and Antonioni's Italy being an interval of almost twenty years in which the cinema has moved from a mass audience to an *élite*. The artificiality of Sternberg's films complies with the Hollywood archetype for all his personal difficulties with the American production system. His settings are the Shanghai, Morocco, Imperial Russia and Spain only possible on the soundstages and backlots of California, and the plots are as melodramatically separate from ordinary patterns of life as his images are from a Chinese or Spanish reality. As the mass-audience system demanded they are anecdotal, the action having its own dynamic and its own catharsis. The qualities particular to von Sternberg are those that are consistently best in the American cinema: a visual realization such that the simplest morality takes on originality— a process which cracks the cliché open, revealing its original truth—and the development of a star personality into a character that exists for audiences simultaneously as myth and reality. Thus in *Shanghai Express* the array of exotica and the almost intangible light and shadow are emanations from Marlene Dietrich, their consistency with her quite suppressing the literary banality of the script. To conclude that a total emotional artificiality follows from the dreamed-up—but nevertheless realized—environment is equivalent to the belief that Shanghai Lily, the Dietrich character, is conditioned by her reputation as a prostitute to the exclusion of all other possibilities. This is the mistake Clive Brook makes in the movie and it is the trap laid for the audience. What corrects it is the way the world the film presents, and thus finally its scale of values, belongs not to Brook, but to Dietrich. The light is as faithful to Dietrich's nature as to her face, and in the world of diaphanous and dissolving interiors she alone moves with the ease of knowledge. She makes the same demands of trust and acceptance on Brook and the audience.

In Antonioni's case one has a production context that is first European, and subsequently international, and a style that has come out of neo-realism. His qualities of *mise-en-scène* depend upon his awareness of a filmed reality and the subsequently unimpeded plasticity of existence. In *Signora Senza Camelie*, *L'Avventura* and *La Notte*, there are takes of great length and intricacy. But though his backgrounds have remained recognizably Turin, Milan, Taormina or Ravenna, the events have been increasingly influenced by an emotional expressionism that tends to disfigure the photography. In *Le Amiche* there is a high-angle shot of the quayside whereby we discover Madeleine Fischer's suicide, the emotional selection of which is out of keeping with the level and integrated movements of the beach scene which induced the suicide. *L'Avventura* has the stumbling-block of Lea Masari's disappearance which is less ineffective than unnecessary, for a physical deceit is disturbing to the very basis of a movie in which the camera is so all-seeing. In *Il Deserto Rosso* this tendency culminates in a direct interference with materials. To paint apples grey is to be emotionally selective, while maintaining a largely natural environment. Von Sternberg's manipulation is total and, as a result, faithful to the latent meanings of Dietrich's character. This sense of affair between actress and director applies equally to Antonioni's handling of Monica Vitti. The dislocations in Antonioni's world occur through the suggestion of an ideal character he envisages for Vitti. In structural terms this is borne out by his anecdotal pessimism's denial of the documentary aspirations of his camera. The bitterness of his early work has a dejection reminiscent of Carné. The removal of Lea Masari in *L'Avventura* is an oblique indication of this. She could exit through a simple social event— going off with another man—but, because at the anecdotal level Antonioni cannot countenance the implication of such a departure, she goes through a device of expressionism, ceasing to exist for the two main characters. The effect is as much one of mystification as those with which Welles conceals his tycoons. In the same way, in *La Notte*, Monica Vitti breaks off any involvement with Mastroianni when she discovers he is married. This is an instance of the director trying to shape his film to an image he has of Vitti that does not fit a free woman. Whereas Sternberg's films radiate from Dietrich, Antonioni's surround Vitti with suggestions about the sort of person she is.

The need to determine events and to depend upon their physical reality are not consistent with a naturalistic style. Rather do they require the completely selective and authoritarian use of environment such as von Sternberg, Lang or Hitchcock exercise. Godard's movies expose Antonioni's failure more clearly than any others, for he photographs the contemporary French scene with a newsreel lack of diversion, and yet controls his action with the paradoxical idea that it is movie action. Godard is fully aware of the sociological change the cinema has undergone from one sort of audience to another and of the impossibility of making films that are totally modern and yet which do not encapsulate as part of their relationship with an audience the entire history of the movies. More clearly with

Godard than any other director are all movies about movies.

Dietrich is a major figure in this cinematic development and she is today a public figure whose name immediately evokes associations. We have already seen, in *Rancho Notorious*, her effectiveness at suggesting the way this sort of reputation may be quite apart from real character. It is worth examining this idea in more detail and comparing the potential of a Dietrich with that of Monica Vitti, as evident in her work for Antonioni.

As a leading European film actress Vitti could not be unaware of Dietrich's past performances and might even be overawed by them. Yet they represent a tradition of film-making that is not likely to be repeated. In none of her films with Antonioni, apart from dyeing her hair in *La Notte*, has Vitti dressed up. The clothes she wears might be her own, the landscapes against which she moves are ones she knows and the character she plays of a young wealthy woman in contemporary Italy is the very status that being a film-star has brought her.

The parts Dietrich played had no such social base. Indeed, the young German girl brought to America after playing Lola-Lola in von Sternberg's *The Blue Angel* became for six years the focus of his teeming symbolism, his bitter humour and his particular realization of a romantic but psychological mood. For von Sternberg she played Amy Joly, a café-singer in *Morocco*, X27, a prostitute and spy in *Dishonoured*, a prostitute in *Shanghai Express*, a singer and archetypal mother in *Blonde Venus*, Catherine II in *The Scarlet Empress* and 'Concha' Perez in *The Devil Is a Woman*. Just as von Sternberg's world is the epitome of Hollywood falseness and yet an extraordinarily accurate incarnation of human feeling, so Dietrich is the icon in his world, at the same time absurd and profound.

For all von Sternberg's personal skill he is enchanted by Dietrich so that she sometimes dominates the camera in a way that is very modern. The amount that is conveyed by her expression and gestures is considerable, but even more stunning is the time devoted to her meditation. (The comparison with Vitti is particularly close here, for in many sequences Antonioni seems entranced by Vitti's pauses.) There is a moment in *Morocco* when Dietrich after singing in a café is rather patronized by a young woman at one table. Dietrich is dressed for the

number as a man—one of the recurrent themes in her von
Sternberg films is a hieratic sexual ambivalence—and she
gazes at the woman for several seconds before lightly but
sensually kissing her on the lips. The pause while she considers
this gesture is not only one of the cinema's finest suspensions of
the moment but an instance of Dietrich seeming to gain understanding of herself from her own actions. Within the total
artificiality of von Sternberg's films this is an extraordinary
freedom for the actress to retain.

Such unlimited diversity, and the unrestricted stylization of
self that goes with it, is not possible for Monica Vitti. The very
subject of her films with Antonioni is the frustration of freedom
and thus her aimlessness often shapes the films. But whereas the
fantasy of the situation in which von Sternberg set Dietrich was
sufficient to liberate, Antonioni's expressionism confronts the
real Italy uneasily. It is as if he were so conscious of the dangers
to Vitti's personality that he is unwilling to trust her to a full
encounter. The difficulties she experiences in Ravenna in *Il
Deserto Rosso* go so far as to constitute illness, and the sexual
competition in *L'Avventura* is vulgarized by the complete disappearance of one rival and the melodramatic depravity with
which the other rubs the money she has been paid with between
her thighs. The valid personal contribution Vitti makes in her
walk through the hotel at the end of *L'Avventura* and her
experience of the airport in *L'Eclisse* lead on to an epistemological consciousness that is always rejected by the director's
reversion to a simply anecdotal level, even though the ethos of
his films has overcome so simple an interpretation of life.

It is in Godard's work that this consciousness is pursued
and Anna Karina made the most modern of actresses. Although
she does not suggest an intellect equal to Vitti's, she is as much
at the centre of the epistemological issues in her films as
Dietrich is in Sternberg's. The repeated slow stare at the
audience in *Pierrot le Fou* when she says she will be faithful to
Belmondo is a look into her own soul as well as wondering
enquiry about our trust of her. It is not an 'aside'—acknowledging duplicity—but an admission of doubt.

Dietrich is, of course, the most certain of actresses, though
many of her actions are open to various interpretations. With

Karina the cinema has accepted that the problem of interpretation cannot be passed entirely to the audience. The creative ambiguity and range of potential are the subjects and thus the performer is not separated from the person: the two must communicate.

ONTOLOGICAL STATUS

Ontological is a new word. R. D. Laing calls it 'the best adverbial or adjectival derivative of being', thereby suggesting how far changed circumstances have stimulated its use. The development of terminology with which people consider their own existence is only one instance of ontological status. We shall also have to consider the subsequent attitude of film-makers to their actors and their characters. The product of an ontological society will be distinguished in the status people have within the film, particularly their power, or freedom, in relation to the narrative, the camera and the audience's preconception. For only recently, after sixty years of film, has the cinema begun to resolve the difficulty in which it found itself—whether it was a theatrical or a photographic medium.

Lola Montes is in this context a beginning and an end, a period piece embellished with advanced technique, a movie that both evokes nostalgia and disturbs our security of identity. The last film completed by Max Ophuls, it is particularly relevant to its time, 1955, because it is one of the earliest fulfilments of CinemaScope's potential; yet its visual context was not contemporary and urban such as Nicholas Ray described in *Rebel Without a Cause*, the other innovatory wide-screen movie made in the same year. The time, on the contrary, is the nineteenth century and many of the settings are not only cramped but deliberately artificial and decorative. The source of artificiality is the circus performance which provides the film's structure; it is this structure that makes *Lola Montes* a bridge between the earliest and most modern cinema. For the performance is an event in Lola's life and at the same time a recapitulation of that life. The process of her act is likely to lead towards self-awareness just as watching the film will instruct an audience about its own relationship with the movie. It is also a movie in the tradition Truffaut invoked when he called the cinema the art of photographing beautiful women. Martine Carol's Lola Montes has associations with Lillian Gish, Greta Garbo and Marlene Dietrich, as well as with Kim Novak, Jeanne Moreau and Anna Karina. The insights of *Lola Montes* are in the ways it shows people looking at and considering people; its employment of the voyeuristic impulse makes it pre-eminently about the cinema, an autonomous work but an extension of a tradition. *Lola Montes* is not only a mid-nineteenth century courtesan and dancer, but an archetype of the instinctual female and of the malleable female material that every man may shape and infuse as he wishes. Peter Ustinov's ring-master is not only the representation of Ophuls himself, organizing the performance but preserving a relationship of private asides with Lola; he also stands for every other man in the film or watching it. His priority is not absolute because he is as subject to her charms as anyone else; but he knows how impressive Lola is as an act, and how she assumes a personal meaning for every anonymous member of the audience.

The audience in *Lola Montes* is directly addressed even though it is seldom seen. The movie opens with a raised curtain and a series of grandiloquent introductions. The light concentrates on the ring and only the first row of the audience can be seen in the dim shadow. Ustinov makes his announcement that Lola Montes will re-enact scenes from her life. This preparation informs us of the reputation of Lola and its justice, and is like the sort of reputation publicity and performance have given to Elizabeth Taylor. For Lola is presented to us in two ways: as a woman whose reality will be demonstrable, and as a star, a status demonstrated by the whole fact of performance and audience. The voyeurist motive is acknowledged by the real inaccessibility of Lola, who is protected and imprisoned by the limelight. Images of imprisonment are essential to the film, without being necessarily prohibitive. The ring is Lola's prison, but the attraction she holds imprisons the audience. The simple relationship between Lola and the circus audience is made much more complex in the relationship she has with us. For the form of the movie is such that the circus performance is interspersed with flashbacks which either give Lola's 'private' version of the most public events in her life or introduce events which are insignificant to her sensational reputation.

The audience in the circus demands demonstration of its ideas about Lola, but the cinema audience is sufficiently removed in time to be ignorant of the contemporary reputation so that it falls into perspective with the private person in the flashbacks. When the circus audience shouts out questions to her—'How many lovers have you had?' 'Where did you dance naked?'—we appreciate the lack of interest with which she answers even though the provocativeness of the questions intrigues us. We are, as with any movie character, assuming our right to observe and draw conclusions, but at the same time the dangers of this power are demonstrated by the other audience. Just as Lola is earning her living by the act of exposure, and consequently endangering her whole existence, so, as an audience, our vicarious participation questions our nature as onlookers.

Lola's identity is destroyed for her by the moral disapproval of a public which also finds her attractive. So many of the film's images are of imprisonment because Lola's decision to become a dancer was originally an attempt to escape the restrictions of a woman's role in society. By doing so she gradually reaches the state at which she has become a concept, although now it is that of the courtesan, in its way as depersonalized as the ideal of a dutiful wife in respectable society. Ophuls's delight in the decoration of interiors is marvellously controlled in *Lola Montes* by the constant sense of confinement under which Lola lives. The circle of the ring and the claustrophobia of her dressing-room and its surrounding mirrors, are the logical conclusions to the settings in the flashbacks. On the boat from India, on which an adolescent Lola returns to Europe with her mother, she is forced to sleep in an overcrowded dormitory with the other children while her mother is alone in a cabin to entertain any gentlemen friends. On the evening of the dance Lola is sent to bed and wanders past the brightly-lit windows of the deck parlour, through which her mother is seen dancing, and walks to the prow of the ship, so that its restrictions symbolize her situation and her wish to escape assumes the wild, natural qualities of sea and air. When Lola marries she lives in a miserably cold Scottish turret room and her affair with Liszt largely takes place amid the dense furnishings of the interior of his caravan, in which they travel through Europe followed at a discreet distance by Lola's own caravan, the acknowledgement of the inevitable ending of their affair. When it does end, in an inn bedroom, the CinemaScope frame is halved by a stone arch and Lola's bed is surrounded by railings and curtains. All of this is, of course, consistent with our wish that the settings should be accurate to the period of the events, but Ophuls's repeated closing-down of the décor is all the more successful because of the CinemaScope oblong. So often does he block off parts of it that it is reasonable to imagine it representing a deprived opportunity for Lola, or for any woman at that time, and since it is in the circus scenes that its dimensions are most filled one concludes that this life is the fullest expression of her desires.

A further subordination of Ophuls's most natural style is to be seen in the control of camera movements, few of which are not countered or contradicted. When Lola leaves the opera in fury the camera pans back and forth along the tiers of the staircase in reverse of the movements that covered Lola and her mother when they went up to their box. When Liszt and Lola arrive at the country inn in his caravan, the pan from the inn along the road exhilarates as it gathers speed and picks up the caravan and then pans back with it to the inn, the countering movement not dissipating the enjoyment but disciplining it. Lola's introduction to the circus audience consists of her sitting on a revolving throne while the camera tracks a full circle round it in the opposite direction.

The effect of these antithetical movements is to make one especially conscious of the original movement and to add formalization to its spontaneity. This is essentially the method used to present Lola's life in the circus ring: the most notorious events are caricatured with luridly-dressed dwarfs and clowns playing the supporting parts. The film ends with two movements in which the physical sensation is important only in so far as it represents an idea. As a climax to her performance Lola has to climb to the top of the arena and dive into a small pool of water. The ascent is marked off by the caricatures of all her affairs hanging like puppets from the trapeze ropes. As well as offering a summation of her life it is the epitome of her humiliation because, by risking her life in diving, Lola is associating herself with the groundlings' level and denying any prospect of better things. The fact that she is already ill, and that a doctor advises against the dive, are metaphors of how far the degradation has affected her; the possibility that she might be killed is also one of a complete loss of identity, at which stage she would be entirely taken over by the imaginations of the crowd.

Instead, she lives, and wrapped in a towel she sits in a cage, like an animal in a menagerie, with a queue of men before her waiting to pay for a kiss, the money being collected by masked acrobats and tumblers in hollow replicas of Lola's head. The camera tracks back over the heads of the queue, on and on, with Lola in her cage becoming smaller as the queue extends. It is the last shot of the film and by implication the camera might track on over the 'queue' waiting in the cinema auditorium.

The idea of such a movement following on the end of *Lola Montes* links two cultures and two conceptions of narrative that are quite separate even though the interval between them is only a hundred years. The Lola presented in the circus performance is the centre of picaresque events luridly stylized, but the Lola we see off-stage is a much more modern woman. The oppressiveness for this Lola of the performance has reduced her response to an enduring stoicism. It is significant that Martine Carol's performance should not emphasize any of the flamboyant possibilities of period romance—*femme fatale, prima donna,* sentimental *grande dame*—but rather seems withdrawn and close to what, today, we should call neurosis.

Lola seems to have the experience of the years that in fact separate her from us. In the progress of man's view of character they are important years. With the onset of industrialization 'society' itself comes into being as an organization of people in flux over the power and rewards of life. This is in contrast to the long and comparatively static period of aristocracy. The new feeling is twofold: enormous classes of people are for the first time acknowledged as individuals and mankind is split into strata that are not at the extremes of aristocracy and peasantry but are involved in a struggle. Simultaneously man is brought to feel his individuality and his equality.

Not unnaturally the contradiction prompts uncertainty. Previously a man's action had been measurable against two arbitrary standards: the rule of Church or king. The arbitrariness was such that a fatalistic attitude was necessary to endure. But in the nineteenth century man's future becomes viable and an understanding of himself and his organizations seem instruments towards flourishing. Human progress is made a credible concept and given a spiritual ethos above the obvious material and technological changes society is experiencing.

But the knowledge man has sought has come to inhibit actions which earlier would have seemed automatic and natural. The theories of Marx, Darwin and Freud and the acts of Stalin and Eichmann have provided such contradictions of ideal and reality that man believes in a fundamental division between his individual hopes and the inevitable consequences of his organizations. He is less certain of his feelings and actions, more dependent on his knowledge. All his own functioning, which a century before he could believe divine inspiration, can now be explained in mechanical terms. Psychology can provide motivation for his actions and simplify his complexity. He is threatened by machines capable of doing more and more of the things he thought personal. The emotions a man feels are automatically related to his concept of what Man is, and as he can no longer be ignorant of some of the meaning of his behaviour he feels his privacy and autonomy reduced. The feeling of a humanist progress is rivalled by a mechanistic interpretation, particularly when man's whole experience can be terminated as abruptly as one switches off a camera or a projector. R. D. Laing distinguishes the mechanistic and personal attitudes:

'The other as person is seen by me as responsible, as capable of choice, in short, as a self-acting agent. Seen as an organism, all that goes on in that organism can be conceptualized at any level of complexity—atomic, molecular, cellular, systematic, or organismic. Whereas behaviour seen as personal is seen in terms of that person's experience and of his intentions, behaviour seen organismically can only be seen as the contraction or relaxation of certain muscles, etc. Instead of the experience of sequence, one is concerned with a sequence of processes. In man seen as an organism, therefore, there is no place for his desires, fears, hope or despair as such. The ultimates of our explanation are not his intentions to his world but quanta of energy in an energy system.'*

It is a principle of life in Western society that everyone is sane. Being sane allows people to function properly, to compete and to keep up the appearance of an integrated existence. Insanity has not been denied but confined and isolated. This attitude prevails even if its argument has been broken down a little. The social importance of Freud is that he demonstrated that it was not unreasonable to be insane.

He devised a theory from and for the treatment of sick people and thus recognized a basis of health, which if it was not absolute was convenient. The powers that Freud believed his patients lacked were, even if he did not emphasize that consequence of the lack, ones essential to the development of a prosperous and sober middle-class society: reason, truthfulness, moral sensibility and diligence in work and study. For all his awareness of the possible turbulence in individual minds he believed in a body of sanity.

ACTING

If a European intelligentsia shared this feeling at the beginning of the twentieth century then Hollywood was an affront to it. Not only was it the first modern employer to pay beautiful men and women many times more than men who made political decisions, not only did it acquire in the press the reputation of a place where moral promiscuity had been adopted as a standard, but it made and distributed films of negligible literary worth and attracted vast audiences among the lower classes. It was necessary to make it seem frivolous and profiteering, perched on a void.

Theatre was the most 'entertaining' medium still acceptable, having classical antecedence and, as a spectacle, a tradition that maintained class distinction. Its economy was very little

* *The Divided Self*, Tavistock Publications, 1960; Penguin, 1965.

different from that of the Elizabethan theatre and its aspirations were to the greatest Elizabethan dramatist. To match the heightened narrative interpretation the acting in theatres was epic, expressive of universality not simply because the auditorium demanded amplification but because the romantic attitude to man's life coloured the plays, the production and acting. So long as the testing of either heaven or hell was a credible experience so events had to have an enormous dramatic significance, and the characters in plays underwent a form of trial by ordeal. Acting was thought to require inspiration, and under that guise vagueness, imitation and bombast were allowed to pass.

Many early films, perhaps because the absence of speech seemed to indicate an emphasis on mime, reproduced a theatrical form of acting. *Birth of a Nation* has the fluttering arms of the distraught Mae Marsh who always seems near to flight, though at the moment when, pursued to the top of a cliff by a potential rapist, the facility would have been most useful, she drops like a bolster to the piano's plunge and the credit title's arabesques of mourning. Her performance and several of the others are today as laughable as the Forbes Robertson *Hamlet* preserved in the archive.

The archive's preservation of Forbes Robertson should come within the historic, rather than artistic, executive, for it now only affects by reaction. It should go alongside the early newsreel of a royal procession in which Edward VII, when his landau is halted, makes an irritable gesture to the coachman to get on with things, which is a sudden indication of how cinema has altered behaviour. Edward's gesture is, in fact, spontaneous and sympathetic, but it is unimaginable that Elizabeth II should ever be photographed in a similar moment of uninhibitedness. It is a gesture, though, that gives a greater impression of the reality of the times than any of Robertson's flourishes.

Theatrical acting is not yet removed from the movies. The great impersonators—Laurence Olivier, Anna Magnani, Vittorio Gassman, Orson Welles, Peter Sellers—still appear, and for some audiences their appearances have a sense of occasion that constitutes the chief attraction of the cinema. The social *cachet* of the theatre is by no means worn out and it sometimes manifests itself in the oddest places. On a television programme that tried to analyse Lee Strasberg and the Actors' Studio, Strasberg said that those students who went away to Hollywood—and Marlon Brando, James Dean, Paul Newman, Kim Stanley, Julie Harris, Shelley Winters and Karl Malden are a few such examples—returned refreshed, having discovered by contrast what qualities there were in the theatre that were real and genuine. The oddity of this is that as far as one can distinguish a method in Strasberg's work from its results it is one influenced by photographic observation of an actor and the resource to inordinate naturalistic devices to stand up to this observation. Brando's scene in the back of a car with Rod Steiger in *On the Waterfront*, directed by Elia Kazan, at that time Strasberg's colleague, is an impressively virtuoso impersonation of reality, more interesting than Olivier's Archie Rice in *The Entertainer* but not qualitatively different. There is a vast self-consciousness and egotism in both as well as a highly-developed theatrical intelligence. They are treatments of surface and deceit without an admission of artifice in the total presentation; at the moment technique becomes apparent one realizes how condescending and cautious the performances are.

The apparent wealth of detail in one of Brando's, or Olivier's, performances is delusory because it is aggregative. Nothing is allowed to contradict or even to lie oddly in relation to other things. Essentially these are interpretative performances more proper to the theatre. They presuppose a tangible reality like a script rather than a willingness to see what the plastic realization will be. Narrative in the theatre is always demonstrative; consequently the happiest theatre is one that realizes this and prefers abstract rather than realistic movements in its narrative. The cinema's inheritance from theatre is explained by its having to wait thirty years in silence. The fact that speech had to be inserted as titles made words unduly important. The underlining accentuated the movement of simple and conclusive plots and kept characterization at a much more primitive level than the potential of photography promised.

A close-up in, for instance, a Griffith movie was valuable as an item in a narrative, the expressiveness of the performer being focused on a meaning. Thus Griffith would have instructed

Lillian Gish as to the emotional situation and she—with great imagination—would have attempted to imitate it. I would not suggest that all silent cinema is worthless but that every movie made without sound is compelled to ignore the fullest possibilities of the medium. The theatrical content of a silent movie slows and coarsens it. Consider, in contrast, a close-up of Anna Karina in one of Godard's films. The fact that she can speak without altering the level of the film has achieved the cinema's audio-visual reality from which derives a greater reality of character as it seems to us in the audience. There is less impression of the character being presented to us than of a meeting with a stranger in which one notices the physical actions of behaviour without having any idea of what sort of character lies behind them. When we look at Karina we see not an intended meaning but an alert personality. It follows that the most effective actors and actresses in the cinema are those who can achieve such a degree of external and internal relaxation while being filmed that the camera records their nature without defining it. I do not think it is fanciful to claim that to match up to this test is a sign of honesty.

This hypothesis is another way of repeating that the camera's recording powers are paramount in the cinema. It implies that the amount of artifice in a performance is in direct proportion to its failure. When Hitchcock said that 'actors are cattle' I fancy he meant those actors who wanted to act rather than be themselves. 'Actor' is not even a term appropriate to the cinema. The barrier of the screen certainly gives the impression of acting, but what we are seeing in the cinema are people.

The ambiguity of identity is nowhere clearer than in the back-stage formula of which *Lola Montes* is one example. Antonioni's *Signora Senza Camelie* concentrates on more contemporary circumstances: the post-war Italian film world. Lucia Bosé plays a young actress on the verge of stardom. The film is at pains to establish a credible social environment so that the girl seems a free agent formulating her own experience of herself. But this ontological security can be broken down by the conceptualizing status of a film-star and the conflicting abstractions that other people impose on her.

The ontological evanescence is witnessed in one long take

of Bosé preparing and filming a love scene which fuses performance and reality in the way the camera integrates the studio background with the set. Bosé is in costume but the producer thinks it wrong and orders her to change. When she reappears the director rehearses her and Alain Cuny. As the technicians retire behind their own camera Antonioni's closes in from its 'social' stance on to the contrived reality of the bed where the scene is to be played. They sit on the bed. Cuny undoes her blouse, pulls it off Bosé's shoulders and lays her back on the bed. She then rolls Cuny on to his back and they kiss. There are murmurs of approval and cries of 'Censor! Censor!' from the crew. The shooting ends and Cuny stands up, discomposed by the effect it has had on him.

The remainder of *Signora* is forecast in this sequence. Bosé's marriage to a movie financier brings to a head the exploitation of her sex appeal. Her husband considers such work pornography. Instead he will cast her as Joan of Arc. The film flops and the marriage breaks up. Finally Bosé is brought nearer to the image of promiscuity her films have projected. The only work she can get is in 'Slave of the Pyramids', a cheap quickie with a randy leading man. In fact, Antonioni's film is less than an exposition of its own good idea. His pessimism deprives his heroine of a necessary toughness so that the ending is a variation of the 'fate worse than death'.

It follows from Renoir's belief that the camera should serve the person, that the requirement of the cinema is not that a person should perform but that he should be observed, that events should be allowed to happen rather than be designed. The best things in *Signora Senza Camelie* concern the observation of a society. Inasmuch as the art-forms all involve the selection of items from experience and their heightening to a universal abstraction, cinema's dependence on an uninfluential power of observation prescribes it from art. Whereas theatre has a purpose, cinema consists primarily of a means; yet in *Film World*, Ivor Montagu is able to say, 'the art of acting—apart from certain technical considerations . . . does not differ in principle from its art in the theatre'. The difficulty Montagu has in making the distinction is part of his inability to recognize that the classical period of narrative cinema coincides with its fullest commercial success. To select only one example of the best sort of Hollywood acting, Cary Grant, Montagu's mention of him is restricted to the fact that in 1962 he was reported as having earned £270,000.

CARY GRANT

Grant's career is typical of the Hollywood star's relationship with the public. It is impossible to think of any one of his performances in isolation from the others, so that one has less impression of his powers of impersonation than an idea of a contemporary who has grown older with oneself and has changed in appearance and character only in his own terms. Like a public figure he has passed into a popular contemporary mythology: Tony Curtis's brilliant take-off of Grant in *Some Like It Hot* was able to be kept up for half the film without any sort of explanation. Grant has also become identified as the source of a 'type': the handsome, urbane, witty man-of-the-world, and as such is one of the models for many advertisements. This, of course, is part of a mass medium's threat of depersonalization. Grant has never let the threat overcome him; it is his very individuality that constitutes his appeal and yet makes him instantly recognizable. Those stars—Jayne Mansfield for instance—who become a universal archetype but lack the personality to sustain and develop their image, are apt to become part of the waste of fashion. That Mansfield fitted so naturally into Tashlin's parodies of American life was a sign that she was more suited to a particular form and time than to cinema as a whole. Grant's first film, *She Done Him Wrong*, was made with Mae West in 1932 and the slimmer, darker figure does not disguise in his scenes with Mae West exactly those qualities one would expect of him today. To say that is to suggest a lack of surprise in his appearances, but the contrary is true. His most consistent quality is a diffidence or reserve to the events of his movies which gives immediate impression of a real intelligence meeting those events not in a predetermined way but with a flexible novelty of experience. As the attitude attracts our interest, so the completeness of our involvement in the wide potential of his decisions reflects on our interest and thus on what, in the same circumstances, our decision might be. It is Grant's ability to suggest the embodiment of all characteristics simultaneously. The manner and outward 'style' are alert to this range but not necessarily aware of every direction it will take.

Howard Hawks, with whom Grant made *Bringing Up Baby*, *Only Angels Have Wings*, *His Girl Friday*, *I Was a Male War Bride* and *Monkey Business*, has said of him: 'That's the good thing about Grant. 'You say, "Cary, let's try it the opposite way. It will change your dialogue, but don't let it worry you. Say anything you think, and if you can't think of the right thing, I'll write it down for you." But he thinks of the right thing and we go ahead and do it.'*

A great deal of Grant's versatility is apparent from this as well as the inclination, which Hawks abets, to make his own contribution to a part. This talent is reflective of a degree of self-knowledge which partly accounts for the range of Grant's character in his work with Hawks. He fits as easily the self-determining hero of *Only Angels Have Wings* as the humiliated victims of sexual compulsion in *Bringing Up Baby* and *I Was a Male War Bride*. Most important of all, in being at one extreme there are frequent reminders of his ability at the other. In *Bringing Up Baby* Grant gives an impersonation of himself much richer than Tony Curtis's because it does not neglect his more masculine and dominant qualities. Rather are they twisted in another direction: thus the expertise and judgement of *Only Angels Have Wings* become a scientist's knowledge and rationality in *Bringing Up Baby*, to be frustrated by Katherine Hepburn's ability to generate farcical situations and to involve Grant in insane postures in his efforts to solve them. Similarly, at the nadir of his humiliation in *I Was a Male War Bride*, when Grant is forced to dress up as a woman to accompany his new wife, a scene of potentially ultimate degradation when he is questioned on possible female troubles is turned by a flare of masculine wit at the expense of his interrogator as Grant admits to them with feminine frankness. The Grant in *War Bride* and *Bringing Up Baby* is a victim of circumstances who has to suffer every embarrassment to preserve his sanity, even though in

* Interview with Howard Hawks by Peter Bogdanovich, *Movie* 5.

Baby this starts as the childish literalness and subdued sexuality of a caricatured scientist who is led towards a broader attitude by the appearance of Katherine Hepburn, whose behaviour seems to him like that of a new species. Grant's presence in *War Bride* is essential to the comedy of frustration because of the sense he communicates of appreciating the farce and horror of every predicament as well as the audience. The adulthood of Hawks's comedy owes much to Grant because he never allows his awareness to spare him involvement: his rather sceptical reticence is not a front but a relationship with life, a way of looking that infuses his movies.

The hero figure he represents in *Only Angels Have Wings* is an excellent example of the Hawks adventurer: a man of judgement, skill and courage—all of which are, in turn, demonstrated—but conscious of the absurdity of a superman and temperamentally disinclined to be heroic. To this extent Grant's reticence is again important, establishing a coolness between himself and the younger pilots and a sexual belligerence towards Jean Arthur, so that his 'Who's Joe?' comment is not only the adventurer's resignation but a preliminary flirtation with her. The reticence is partly unease with command even though every talent fits him for it. As for John Wayne in *Rio Bravo*, command is justified if those who must obey are convinced of the commander's judgement and have an unbiased relationship with him. In *Rio Bravo*, when Dean Martin feels he has failed, Wayne is prepared to let him go and to have Ricky Nelson's help if it is offered. No one is obliged to assist him by the sort of claims Gary Cooper is made to make on the citizens in *High Noon*. Grant shares this attitude to command even though he often appears authoritarian in *Only Angels*. When he orders Joe to fly it is an insistence on duty and Joe's fatal attempt to re-land is proof of his being not quite good enough. In the same way, though Grant sends Richard Barthelmess on the dangerous plateau flight he does so with the idea of settling the issue of Barthelmess's skill and courage. When Barthelmess succeeds Grant's acceptance of him is complete, and if this standard seems harsh its very arbitrariness may slightly impede Grant's enforcing of it. It is part of the essential fatalistic side of Hawks and it relates to an adventurer's society that is no longer contemporary, but which Hawks's character studies have never allowed to seem unjust. Grant's personality is very sympathetic to the details of its strain for he does not enjoy command but can see it, and his involvement in it, from sufficient distance to gain an aesthetic perspective.

The ambiguity in Grant's simultaneous exercise of and withdrawal from command is typical of the close circles of friendship in Hawks films which flourish when under the greatest pressure. The airfield in *Only Angels Have Wings*, the hotel in *To Have and Have Not* and the sheriff's office in *Rio Bravo* are the sites of the congregation of a few individualists, united by the sense of challenge and friendship rather than a connection of right: thus, even though made in 1944, Bogart in *To Have and Have Not* has only a very general faith in the Free French cause and helps them only when he needs the money. Bogart and Wayne are inheritors of the sort of character that Grant established in *Only Angels* just as they repeat so many of the jokes and pieces of business from the earlier movie. The jokes in Hawks are properly private and a sustenance to the small community. They are usually indicative of the characters' awareness of their danger and the conversion of it with a deadpan wit into nullity. 'Who's Joe?' is, in this sense, a joke, and it is as a deflation of his own nervousness that Bogart cracks so many verbal jokes in *The Big Sleep*. Again, the aesthetic pattern is noticeable. Just as sending Barthelmess on the crucial flight appeals to Grant's sense of irony in *Only Angels*, Bogart takes a highly-strung pleasure in repartee with Gestapo authorities, and in *Rio Bravo* the cut-throat *deguela*, played to overawe the sheriff and his deputies, instead raises their morale and stimulates Dean Martin's complete regeneration.

Grant, Bogart and Wayne are among the outstanding screen personalities, but what distinguishes Grant from the other two is that he has been hero, not only for Hawks, but for Hitchcock, who has a very different attitude to character. *Suspicion*, *Notorious*, *To Catch a Thief* and *North by Northwest* are the films Grant and Hitchcock have made together, and if their tone is more ironic than the director's use of James Stewart, they still

17, 18. *The Far Country*. James Stewart and Walter Brennan succeed as pioneers but not as citizens. They disagree on Stewart's responsibility in the shack Stewart will retreat to when Brennan has been murdered.

19. Hardy Kruger paints Micheline Presle in *Blind Date*, but the activity barely suppresses Kruger's puritan excitement and Presle's calculated sexuality.

20. *The Criminal*. Margit Saad is kept hostage by Sam Wanamaker in the vulgar luxury of a barge. When Stanley Baker arrives the very narrowness seems to converge on his destruction.

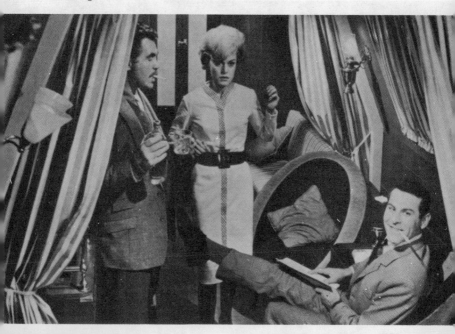

represent a fascinating extension of Grant's personality as shown in his Hawks movies. They do not offer a different person but one in whom the balance has been shifted. One recalls the sequence early in *Notorious* in which the screen is dominated by the back of Grant's head as he stares at Ingrid Bergman and she becomes increasingly put off by his attention. The still, black head emphasizes a darker side of Grant, hinted at in the bitterest jokes of *Only Angels* and his scathing treatment of Ralph Bellamy in *His Girl Friday*. Hitchcock does not attempt to deny the withdrawal in Grant's character but he makes it a source of mystery, not without menace and selfishness.

North by Northwest is the most satisfying exposure of this side of Grant and its accomplishment is especially subtle because in many ways it evokes the idea of masculine elegance and maturity that popularly surrounds Cary Grant. To undermine this reputation is as much Hitchcock's delight as killing off Janet Leigh so early in *Psycho*; both are instances of the ordeals that he makes his characters undergo. When I speak of him exposing another side of Grant, the term is revealing in its comparison with the method of Hawks or Renoir. Even so, Grant's character is too vigorously humorous to suffer completely. The ambiguity of his moral status is at the core of *Suspicion* illustrating Hitchcock's matching of macabre comedy and profound moral dilemma. *Notorious* shows a Grant whose withdrawal is one of the first instances of Hitchcockian voyeurism, a compound of sexual interest, natural aloofness and analytic judgement. But in *North by Northwest* Grant has moved into the most vulnerable category of character in Hitchcock's work: the complacent hero waiting for events to beset him. The mixing in of Grant's own 'advertising' persona is very thorough and demonstrates how far Hitchcock's highly selective camera presents images in which the abstraction is experienced more than reality. The effect of the early scenes in *North by Northwest* is subtly confusing: Grant appears in all his tanned urbanity, he steals other people's taxis, dictates letters walking down the street, jokes about having two ex-wives and a bartender to support. The effect is admirable but the reality is immature. Thus the espionage circuit he becomes involved in can be seen either as hazardous encounter or deserved punishment, and the device that involves him as chance or a deliberating and directing judge.

A comprehension of the more serious purpose behind the conventions of a comedy-thriller is not clarified until the appearance of Eva Marie Saint. To Grant she represents an attractive and sophisticated woman who is so blandly provocative as to startle even his desensitized reactions. She is a version of the female half of an advertising pair and it reflects on Grant that he accepts her sexual advances without any attempt to discover either her real nature or the possible consequences. The complexity of Hitchcock quite transcends the spectator's expectations at this point, for events show how the contrived meeting has a significance for Saint as well as for Grant. She is really an American agent charged with removing him from the spy ring into which he has blundered. The intended means of removal is death and this has an extra implication for her because she is not a professional agent but a woman who in the course of an aimless life became James Mason's mistress, was told that he was a spy and asked by American Security to remain with him as a source of information. Love and betrayal therefore are mingled in her life, and she has now to seduce Grant as a preliminary to planning his death. It is in the long love scene between the two on the train that this dilemma is established. For while it starts as an idealized 'advertised' affair it is persisted with until to stay emotionally and morally withdrawn is impossible. In cinematic terms it consists of a series of close-ups of embraces the visual sensuality of which leads to an unavoidable personal relationship. It is in this way that Hitchcock locates Grant's weakness in his most noticeable characteristic, the cynical isolation being broken down so that his schoolboy involvement in espionage is accompanied by the beginnings of an adult emotional relationship.

But when Grant escapes the trap that Saint had to lay for him his reaction is as single-mindedly vindictive as his first response was immediately receptive to sexual relations. He finds Saint and Mason at an antique auction and so insults her that Mason gathers how deeply they have become involved with each other. Thus Saint's security as a double-agent is endangered. It is to save her that Grant goes to Mason's Mount

Rushmore hide-out when the security forces have told him the full story. The finale has Grant removed from his urban background against a grimly stylized, but 'natural' background of patriotic reference trying to hold Eva Marie Saint from falling to her death. In Hitchcock's terms this is a moral fall, just as Saint's character is that of a fallen woman and Grant's a flippant cynic who is redeemed by his love for her and the efforts this love will induce. In terms of Grant's character the concentration on abstract meanings beneath hectic physical action provides a shrewd appraisal of its full extent. It is additional to his Hawks movies but, one feels, completely in accord with them. For Grant himself it is as if he has demonstrated the range of potential of his own inclinations, and to maintain this balance a real honesty is needed.

Cary Grant's career illustrates the development of movies. He began working soon after sound, and to compare him with a silent-screen actor, like John Gilbert, is to be impressed enormously by Grant's modernity. It is not only that his first movies were in the exceptionally racy company of Mae West but that Grant comes across as a whole being. Instead of being forced into a stylization of gesture or expression his natural reticence is permissible. As a result, he helped to redefine the medium and, with people like Mae West, Bette Davis, Gary Cooper, James Cagney and Humphrey Bogart, he 'dated' John Gilbert, Lillian Gish and Wallace Beery as surely as Groucho Marx dated Buster Keaton and Charlie Chaplin. Grant's popular success began before the Second World War and persists; *North by Northwest* shows the actor's own consciousness of his image. But his independence still seems intact, and his appearance continues to bely his veteran status. Perhaps there is still to come his response to age and approaching debility such as Cooper gave in *Man of the West* and Bogart in his last half-a-dozen movies.

MARILYN MONROE AND KIM NOVAK

Many Hollywood stars have not survived: on seeing *The Glass Key* or *The Blue Dahlia* today it seems extraordinary that Veronica Lake should have been given up by the movies;

Marlon Brando has become victim of his image and his mannerisms; others, like James Dean and Marilyn Monroe, are dead, almost willed so by their public personalities. Monroe is perhaps the archetypal film-star, the holder for the 1950s of the screen's sex-goddess title. Her background was an orphanage, her launch girlie magazines and many of her movies vehicles for her sexuality, and yet she married an American intellectual, had co-starred with Laurence Olivier and had found favour with Edith Sitwell.

The rapidity with which Monroe became an instrument of intellectual self-reproach is proof of the sense of neurosis that surrounded her and fitted the particular period of her fame. Part of this is due to the fact that Monroe's publicity machine, and perhaps she herself, aspired to the position of sex-goddess that Mae West, Jean Harlow and Jane Russell had held previously at a time when the significance of the title was diminishing. Television and the iconography of advertising were competitors that offered a more contemporary version of the archetype, while in the cinema Jayne Mansfield supplied the logic of devastating caricature and Kim Novak introduced an exposed consciousness which Monroe never had. Monroe presented a contradiction between the need for emancipation and a child-like ignorance of the whole context in which it might exist. This may have been touching but it never hinted at completeness or maturity. Her most accomplished 'face' was the wide-eyed innocent, and *Gentlemen Prefer Blondes* is its best example; but it was already out of date, just as the clothes Monroe wore seemed already out of fashion. Even in *Blondes* her most effective scenes are ones in which her sexuality is being exploited without any sign of an intelligence protecting against the exploitation. In terms of style this consists of an impression of performance, rather than existence. Marilyn spoke in 'lines' always, hitting one meaning squarely, and, when given a *double entente*, as in *Some Like It Hot*, ruining both meanings so that any laughter had to be not complicit, but at her expense.

The absence of communication with her audience in the movies was partly made up for by a confessional intimacy off the set. An audience's response to Monroe was to the image which had accumulated ever since her nude calendar pictures, and continually suggested a star of an earlier age: singing to troops in a bubble bath on some wintry Korean plain was a throw-back to Hollywood Canteen; her private life was taken up by gossip columnists with a blend of prurience and puritanism that was wildly inconsistent with American social habits; and, finally, she started fighting with her studio, a relic of the 30s, for by 1960 stars of her importance were independent and it was directors who had fights over the way their movies were cut, something they would not have thought of doing before about 1950.

Comparisons with Jayne Mansfield and Kim Novak help to define Marilyn Monroe's personality. Mansfield was also exploited, particularly in Tashlin's movies, but one notices an awareness of it and a commercial willingness to be exploited with the implied acceptance of a short and lucrative career. Monroe's ignorance is often painful and a number of her films are like stag parties making dirty jokes behind her back. The pain one may feel is not, I think, associated with guilt, it is more a sense of embarrassment at having to watch a performer who is continually made amateur by a lack of understanding of either her own nature or the nature of the medium. Because of this one cannot recall a relaxed Monroe or an impression of her that was not heightened by the strain of having to be a blonde in the movies. Paradoxically she seemed most confident in movies when singing or dancing; at these times she had a routine as well as a script to depend on, and the necessarily stylized gestures represented an ideal of graceful femininity. Thus the 'Black Magic' routine in *Bus Stop* is an accomplished imitation of mannerism. Whenever it was necessary for her to sustain a relationship with another character in a film she experienced such difficulties that she emphasized the Anita Loos sort of character she knew she was competent at. Her long scenes with Robert Mitchum in *River of No Return* have moments of adulthood which veer away into clumsiness as quickly as they are appreciated. No contact is made; the visual richness goes unexplained and the conclusion dawns that Monroe was so out of date that the silent screen might have been a more proper medium for her.

Sadly, there is one piece of film in which she achieves the

complete and intelligent participation of Kim Novak's best movies, and it is in fact silent. It occurs at the end of *Marilyn*, the obituary film Twentieth Century Fox compiled from clips out of most of the films she made for them. It is a test for *Something's Gotta Give*, the film she was fired from immediately before her death; also included in the obituary is the nude scene she did for this movie. It is a vulgar, meretricious nude scene, as artificial and contrived in pose as her calendar photos. Monroe's self-consciousness leads to the most ponderous movements, as if aspiring timidly to a Rubens. The test, on the other hand, although without any context of plot, is very moving. It shows a Monroe who never appeared in movies. The shots in the tests are medium close-up, probably designed as colour guides for the lighting cameraman. Although silent, she is talking, to either the cameraman or the film's director, George Cukor. Her beauty is informed as it had never been before with an intelligence that may derive from the relaxed circumstances and conversational speech. That these conditions fostered one's appearance in movies is a thing that Marilyn Monroe never seems to have realized.

Kim Novak has given evidence of this realization so that her career has surpassed the role of glossy sex symbol she was originally designed for as a replacement for Rita Hayworth; however, the sterility of Hollywood today threatens to withhold parts that might encourage further exploration. Her appearance has significantly altered since her debut in the mid-50s. Starting as a conventional blonde, her face de-characterized by make-up, her own features have gradually emerged; compared with *Jeanne Eagels*, *Pushover* and *The Eddy Duchin Story*, the Novak of *Of Human Bondage* and *Moll Flanders* is a more natural woman, the fullness of her face and body being unconcealed. In this change, *Bell, Book and Candle*, *Strangers When We Meet* and *Vertigo* are vital stages, and it is relevant that all three are especially good colour movies. The accuracy of the medium suggests Novak's comparative modernity, for the colour in most of Monroe's movies was garish. In *Bell, Book and Candle*, in changing from a witch to a normal person, Novak undergoes a process not unlike the emergence she has managed of a rather anxious woman from beneath Hollywood's instant glamour, and after the succession of 'bewitched' shots of her, in hieratic poses, the colour controlled into blue and purple spots, there is a most beautiful moment when she runs into the street after her cat and, unable to find it, cries. To cry is a symptom of unbewitched humanity and the daylight brightness of her face, as it cries, is a proof of radiance. *Strangers When We Meet* is a study in American small-town life and adultery. Novak's marriage is unhappy, and her personality expands in an affair with Kirk Douglas. It is a naturalistic film, capturing the rhythm of small-town life as well as its appearance and Novak is very sensitive to the details of her life. One instance contrasts with Monroe's nude scene: in an attempt to make her cold husband love her Novak undoes her blouse in front of him. It is not a nude scene, but it is much more erotic and much more personal. The shyness and the sensuality are inseparable: it is such a moment as can be experienced only by seeing it.

PERSONAL FREEDOM

Marilyn Monroe's career shows how completely society's casting powers may overawe a personality and restrict a personal exploration of experience to an image of behaviour that conforms with the least intelligent preconceptions. That a woman should be sexually willing, and that she should accept a static position in the sexual and social relationships, is behind the expectation that Monroe should be provocatively voluptuous without herself being able to realize her passion because of the social hypocrisy of censorship. Her sexuality, although so emphasized, takes a course that is not individual and satisfying but disembodied and disappointing.

Censorship of nudity is as much a denial of the medium as the arbitrary prohibition of any visual material. The camera is obliged to record; once Auschwitz had been made fact there could be no question of the camera's right of observation. Censorship is illogical unless it coincides with cinematic criteria, and one would not advocate its practice even on those grounds. To limit the extent of behaviour on the screen indicates a double-standard if a sexual pleasure might be sought in life but only titillated in the movies. A number of recent films have been preoccupied with the sort of pressures they themselves put upon their actresses: thus *Eve, La Notte, Vertigo, Vivre Sa Vie* and *Une Femme Mariée*.

In all these films there is a conflict between self-sufficient existence and abstraction that consists of sequences in which the woman is photographed outside the stimuli of a plot so that her casual actions form the plot of the film, and the attitudes towards her of both the other characters and the iconography in the movies. Jeanne Moreau's wandering through Milan and the party in *La Notte* and James Stewart's observation of Kim Novak in *Vertigo* are such sequences. Godard's films are in part pretexts for detailed visual accounts of Anna Karina and Macha Meril. The reaction of the various women to imposition differs considerably. Moreau in *La Notte* and Meril are emancipated and able to survey their range of social opportunity. Moreau is dissatisfied with the alternatives of marital and adulterous love and likely to entertain both without being fulfilled. Meril, on the other hand, takes pleasure in both and some delight in her own duality. The attempts of the two men to prescribe her potential provide the epistemological interest in her life but the baby growing inside her hints at the delicacy of the balance. Novak and Karina are much more the victims of design. In *Vertigo* Novak's complicity in deception results in the real love she feels for Stewart being distorted by his original conception of her. When he attempts to recast her appearance and character as they first attracted him Stewart is ironically undermining her real personality to the point of breakdown. Karina's context is much less authoritarian than Novak's. She is so economically restricted that she becomes a prostitute. But this experience leads to an awareness of her own soul. Hers, for all its sudden death, is a freer, more hopeful life.

We can directly associate the sense of life in Godard's films with the imperative of his camera. Thus when Karina writes a letter of application to a brothel the degradation of the idea of what she is doing is nullified because the constant observation of her writing guarantees that she does not surrender individuality. The prostitute has always been one of the main abstractions of woman in society. *Vivre Sa Vie* and Losey's *Eve* are assertions of its meaninglessness as a categorization. Those scenes in *Eve* of Moreau undressing and bathing describe an animal female whose treatment of Stanley Baker becomes increasingly reasonable and decreasingly vicious as the survey of behaviour goes on. A mechanically moving image of a woman moves also emotionally and ideologically. The intrusion of design on this movement, whether it is Stanley Baker's wish that Moreau should be his mistress alone—or that he should be hers, for the power structure is finally reversed in *Eve*—Meril's husband's and lover's hopes that she should be faithful to them or James Stewart's that the second Kim Novak should revert to the first, is equivalent to freezing the image, to imprisoning animation.

Such a personal direction of events to comply with an individual's wish is not only the autocracy in human relationships but the equivalent of the artist's manipulation of his own material towards a desired end. The camera's ability to present events in something other than a literary or artistic form introduces qualities of the unknown or incomprehensible. The richest 'meaning' of sequences like Dietrich kissing the woman in *Morocco*, the camera tracking away from the imprisoned Lola Montes or of Cary Grant asking 'Who's Joe?' in *Only Angels*, is to reduce certainty and to increase divergence beyond a point at which it can be contained by words.

This can be the saving enigma for a person subjected to the pressure of film and it is more likely to occur when the person is aware of the superiority of behaviour as a possible relationship with the camera. This chance of equality did not occur in the cinema without sound because only then was the medium fully compatible with the way people behave. It may have seemed in the late 1920s that sound enabled narrative to be speeded up, whereas in fact this speed took it into a new area of relationships with its audience. Consider *Morocco* again, made in 1930 and with only speech and natural effects on its sound-track. *Morocco*, reduced to paper, is a comically romantic plot in which a café singer follows a legionnaire into the desert simply to be with him. But the romance is undercut by the fact that this gesture is unnecessary because Cooper and Dietrich admit to loving each other. He could have deserted and gone away with her. As such it would have been a romance with a happy ending, the characters masters of their own fate. But in the dissolving figurations of light and shade in von Sternberg's world they do not have that power. Consequently the free actions they take tend to imprison them further. Dietrich's kiss, for instance, is a brilliant imaginative action that increases her notoriety and the aura of amorality that surrounds her. There is another sequence involving the suspension of a moment. Cooper and Dietrich have agreed to go away. He remains in her dressing-room while she goes into the café to sing. While we hear the music he wanders round the dressing-room aimlessly. He finds a necklace that Adolphe Menjou has given Dietrich and he tries on her black top hat. Then he writes, 'I changed my mind. Good Luck', on the mirror and goes back to the desert. There is much more to the sequence, of course, but none of it is conclusive. Cooper's reason might be anger at seeing the necklace, a sense of interior confinement, an aroused distrust of women, a passing fancy or the thought that all love is lived through and forgotten. He may not have any reason—the freedom is shocking in its destructiveness.

6

NARRATIVE PERSONALITY

Eventful: Fritz Lang – Anecdotal:
Renoir – Moralist: Hitchcock –
Behaviourist: Hawks – Romantic:
Demy and Rivette – Consensus:
Preminger

When the Hollywood studios were at their most productive one
wing or one floor would accommodate the writers. They would
sit all day in offices and write stories and treatments for the
movies. A good movie, it was said, needed a good story, told
straightforwardly. But another, more cynical version was also
to be heard: there are only half a dozen stories in the world;
every movie is a variation on one of them.

How important was the story? When Howard Hawks made
The Big Sleep for Warners he not only had Raymond Chandler's
novel but Jules Furthman, Leigh Brackett and William
Faulkner to adapt it. Even then he and Humphrey Bogart
made up some things as they went along, and even then they
didn't understand the story. When the film was over they asked
Chandler to explain one particularly tortuous point, but he
didn't understand it either!

For *The Big Sleep* and many other great Hollywood movies
one has a clearer recollection of the images than of the plot.
The comparison that television made with the cinema indicated
how far the most satisfying effects of moving film were audio-
visual rather than narrative. On the one hand the television
series emphasized the script-writer's difficulties in reworking the
same old stories. At the same time, the enormous amount of
live film shown on television asserted the camera's own power
by integrating meaning and image. Newsreel coverage could be

actual, unrehearsed and random as it covered the major news stories, but, as when Kennedy and Oswald were shot, it might suddenly break into a more recognizably narrative form. There have been many attempts to explain the killing of Kennedy as if it should be an item in a narrative of international conspiracy. It is difficult to believe that the actions were human, separate and unreasonable. The camera had seen them happen and placed them in a known context but it could not connect them with the context. The images remained. The cameras went on to record Kennedy's successor and new moments of particular drama.

Our familiarity through newsreel film with even the limits of our world—whether they are the Vietnam jungle, the orbit paths of space capsules or the intestinal tracts—has broken the associations between feature film and narrative. It is necessary now for a film to seem to be aware that the parameters of its screen, its plot and characterization are not definitive but only arbitrary. The specific test of this sort of modernity is in how we may define the personality of the film's narrative. We might consider the following possibilities: anecdotal, moral, behaviourist, romantic, democratic and divergent. Examples from all can be found today but, nevertheless, taken in this order they will illustrate the progress of what I consider the main stream of cinema, even though the stages have no sequence of increasing superiority. Frequently they may overlap and it is only useful to distinguish them in order to clarify film in terms that have been largely neglected.

EVENTFUL: FRITZ LANG

It is appropriate to place Lang first in this series because his narrative method has the simplicity of the earliest cinema, even to the extent of misleading some critics into considering as melodrama the most refined abstraction. Paradoxically, between 1920 and 1960 Lang has purified even his own simplicity while treating an increasingly complicated human condition. It is as if Lang had reduced language to mathematics or, as Jacques Rivette wrote, to 'l'aspect d'épure ou plutôt d'exposé, que prend aussitôt le déroulement des images: comme si ce à quoi nous assistions était moins la mise en scène d'un scénario que la simple lecture de ce scénario.'*

It should not be thought that this indicates a literary cinema, but that it is one devoid of interior psychological realism. Lang's characters are not people but characters. His action is not a representation of reality but cinematic events. The eventfulness constitutes perhaps the most formally beautiful cinema of all, without the beauty ever being more than exactness. Framing is perfectly composed but restrained by its own balance, just as the editing separates events without allowing sensation to colour them. This grace is the nearest cinematic approximation to mythology, and the urban characters in Lang's American films are no different from those in the legendary *Die Niebelungen* and *Der müde Tod*. The quality of dream is not altered by the circumstances being those of death, violence and poverty. Its consistency indicates the facts of observation and creation involved in film-making and its objectivity allows the created characters to seem uninhibited by the observation. This is a constant and critical preoccupation in the cinema and Lang's serene solution to it ensures his modernity for all the apparent naïveté of his movies.

His world opposes good and evil, as it does light and darkness. They become confused because only appearance exists as evidence and Lang disallows the least subjective interpretation. As if observing an organism or an insect he can discern life from death with events as the movement from one to another. The furious rate of dangerous events is his logic of ordeal and it is equivalent to the great journeys and trials of Aeneas and Galahad. As if the narrative were centuries old it has forgotten the ordinary and stimulated the fantastic: thus the extraordinary profusion of event in films like *Dr Mabuse*, *Der Spieler*, *The Ministry of Fear*, *Moonfleet* and the two Indian films, all of which are epic in the calmness with which they recount fantastic excitement. The characters do not encounter events emotionally or intellectually but with their whole physical being, every gesture of which denotes a metaphysical generalization. Thus, in the way of the earliest movies, love, hate and fear are in a glance. Eventfulness and activity are the only signs of life and

* *Cahiers du Cinéma*, No. 76.

the degrees of animation and vigour are spiritual indices. The monotonous and uniform movements of the workers in *Metropolis* and the remorseless movement the factory clock imposes on the man who must move the clock's hands to every flashing bulb illustrate the protagonist energy and the Mabusian ideal of destruction. And yet as we have seen, in *Fury* and *Rancho Notorious*, the energy may lead good intentions into vicious means.

Physically it is an expressionist world without going to the lengths of distortion. The sets have been constructed out of theatrical materials; the costumes and furnishings are brandnew; and, most fundamental of all, the light transcends the idea of real light sources—like sun, streetlight, interior lights—and emphasizes the cinematic method of illuminating relevance. The light is the very landscape in the way that terrain is for Mann and interior décor for Losey. It is also a motif, like the brooch in *Rancho Notorious*, that moves fluidly. Thus, although *Metropolis* has an oppressed individual striving to reach the light from a dark cell, the moment of murder in *The Woman in the Window*, the explosion in *The Big Heat*, and the hotel and tailor's shop in *The Ministry of Fear* are all shot in brilliant high-key, and the scenes of love and hiding in *You Only Live Once* and *The Ministry of Fear* are surrounded by shadow.

The action of *The Ministry of Fear* is headlong. Ray Milland leaves an asylum in the middle of war having been committed there for the mercy-killing of his wife; immediately, at a country fête, he wins a cake that contains microfilm of military plans. Milland becomes involved in an espionage plot that is nominally between Nazis and British just as supposedly it is set in London and the English countryside. But the war is no more specific than it is in *Hangmen Also Die*; instead it is only one example of the Mabusian oppression of humanity. The background of the asylum—in Greene's novel a titbit of guilt—in the film particularizes the individual's vulnerability so that his claims of conspiracy seem insane to the forces of authority.

The problem of convincing people is not a moral one, such as Hitchcock poses to Cary Grant in *North by Northwest*, but a perpetual condition of Lang's world. Insanity surrounds the protagonist in the confusion between reality and illusion which the visual style does nothing to settle. Indeed, as one of Milland's several tormentors says to him in *Ministry of Fear*, 'You are most attractive when lying.' The forces of authority are particularly ambiguous and an indication of how Lang uses the war as a means to explore mythology rather than the actually embattled country we see in Jennings's films. The organization that authority makes has been recognizably a substitute for the forces of disorder since *Mabuse* and *M*, and in *The Ministry of Fear* the policeman is a figure of menace. He appears first when Milland recovers consciousness after an explosion. Milland sees a figure wearing a black suit and a black hat sitting with his back turned in the corner of a room in a chair which he has rocked at an angle on to its back legs: a shadow of the figure is on the wall in front of him. The visual presentation is so cryptic and the context of the film so hallucinatory that one is prepared to believe the policeman a spy and this Scotland Yard a fake. Even when the policeman helps Milland it is in a manner so forbidding that the scene at a bomb-crater in the countryside where they search for the microfilm is like an approach to hell. Even at the climax of the movie when the dark figure of the policeman climbs a narrow brightly-lit staircase to rescue Milland he is like an executioner ascending the scaffold. The 'happy end' is always visually pessimistic because, as separate films have proved, Mabuse cannot be killed and the light that seems to welcome a hero is so unreliable as to expose rather than reward him.

ANECDOTAL: RENOIR

In Jean Renoir's biography of his father there is a glowing sense of family. In both Auguste's paintings and Jean's films this ambience is broadened to embrace servants, friends, acquaintances and passers-by. The society achieved is felt to be counterbalancing and thus there is a great generosity towards individual action. It is not a censorious society and we have seen how the equivalent of Auguste's busy crowd scenes is the depth of Jean's focus and the movement of his camera so as to connect people and associate their motives. A conclusive narrative is alien to such feelings, but the passing anecdote is perfectly suited to it. For in a circle of friends stories and jokes will be told about chance events without any extrusion of possible implications or verdicts. The fact of society will always outweigh incidents that seem to betray its unity.

The consciousness of the narrator must be found within this society and the only detachment from events that it exhibits is one of tolerance. As in Guy de Maupassant's work the story-teller is often a participant, for even though Renoir's movies are never first-person the camera is so closely identified with the characters that it conveys the same enjoyment in the fortuitousness or irony of events as Maupassant's stories. In both there is more sense of the inevitable human conclusions to human affairs than the assertion of destiny or government. The society is free but equal; its members can enjoy the same things and make the same mistakes.

In his concentration on brief interludes in human life that carry no more meaning than their own action and in his tendency to the precise description of a visual experience of an event, Maupassant is a writer whose work preludes the invention of cinema. The conclusion of *Cemetery Walkers*, for instance, in which the story-teller, while strolling in a cemetery, sees a repetition of the seduction once practised on him is very like the plasticity and spatial relationship of a scene from a Renoir movie. Every visual event has charm, beauty or distinctiveness that generates response before an intellectual judgement can be worked out. Thus the first intrusion of Boudu into the bourgeois household of the bookseller Lestingois is a panning shot with him as seen through a telescope from the house. At first Lestingois is moving the telescope idly to look at girls' legs but it takes on intention and excitement to cover Boudu's progress. Lestingois's opinion 'He is magnificent' is at one level an emotionally paternal gesture from the bourgeois but it is also an immediate reaction to a visual event that persuades him to go to Boudu's aid when he sees him jumping into the Seine.

Part of the irony of *Boudu* comes from the prompt humanity of this action. Boudu is taken in to the household, dressed in Lestingois's clothes and fed at his table. He brings chaos. His table manners are appalling: told to sprinkle salt on spilled wine he pours wine on spilled salt. He overthrows the social system of the household by interrupting Lestingois's access to the maid's room and seducing his wife. One quiet afternoon Lestingois's wife wants Boudu to renew his attentions and in his embarrassed struggle they fall through a doorway to discover Lestingois and the maid enjoying each others' attentions. The odd conclusion to this is that Boudu shall marry the maid, a palatable fate for her because she likes him and because he has won first prize in the lottery on a ticket Lestingois gave him. The wedding party is rowed down the Seine. Boudu sees a flower and reaches for it. The boat overturns and he is away.

There is no suggestion that this is a deliberate action on Boudu's part. Just as he was content to live where he woke up to find himself, he swims ashore and resumes the tramp's life, not returning to his wife and his money because of the complication and because he goes where events take him, which is the sole discipline, of course, of Renoir's camera. There is no meaning to Boudu, he is an animal of the human species. The camera observes his behaviour. Thus that original panning shot, his habit of sitting jammed between doorposts, his behaviour at table and his unconnected strolls through the odd spatial arrangement of the Lestingois household. This is why earlier I described the final pan as a movement of Boudu's soul, for the whole identity of the narrative is closer to Boudu than to any other character. Even so, the others are seen in the round. Lestingois is generous, his wife, though neurotic, is passionate, and the maid is good-humoured.

Boudu's intrusion has disrupted their system but has not brought them under the eye of eternity. The humour of the blundering of one adulterous couple on another is sustained by this equal treatment of people and by the photographic acceptance of human behaviour. Its effect makes a striking contrast with that moment in *La Notte* when the two couples come face to face, and an interesting foresight of the conclusion of *La Règle du Jeu* when suspicions of adultery held by the house-party guests and the servants mingle and a tragedy occurs out of proportion to the circumstances but still credible and, in part, funny.

Repeated viewings of *La Règle* confirm the impression of integrity in the film and its perfect embodiment, Renoir's own presence. Detailed significance—audio-visual events that in a narrative sequence become evidence of meaning—continues to accumulate without ever disturbing the film's unique sense of disorganization. The apparent source of stability, Octave, is himself finally entangled by events, even playing a main but unwitting part in the tragedy; and this is a metaphor of Renoir's admission that the director, supposedly the authoritative and manipulating figure, is as much victim as originator of circumstances.

Sequences are joined not by an exclusive narrative bond, as limiting as a spotlight, but by means that accommodate an expanding social and physical contingency. The voice of the commentator at the airport is cut to the same voice on the radio in Norah Gregor's bedroom. We later discover Dalio listening to the radio and at the house-party several guests refer to Jurieu's outburst. The story does not advance with the addition of characters; instead, possible relationships are uncovered. The chaos of the confused chase at the end of the film is thus a parody of physical action that represents an impossibly huge totality of relationships that occur and subside with great rapidity under the increasing pressure.

The Feydeau-like sexual pursuit emerges from the masquerade, an attempt by the characters to put an elegant gloss on their lives. That the butler is called Corneille and that he nimbly arranges the disposal of fainting bodies maintains the theatrical self-consciousness during the collision of coincidences. And yet finally the butler's finger snap that commands a minion is replaced by the nervous run of a middle-aged man as he goes to bring in Jurieu's corpse. The instant of physical shock seems to answer the previous balletic flow of chase. The comparison of people with Dalio's mechanical toys has been made consciously by Renoir, but not to the extent that every instance is planned.

That there is a small stage within the house, the rehearsed sketches of which are overrun by the spontaneous and dangerous farce, is a deliberate image of the confusion between conceptions of life and the intractable reality. There is detail to support the enactment of this idea: the toy birds on the floor that recall the game birds shot down; Octave walking across the terrace to find

Jurieu's body being photographed in exactly the same way as when he impersonated the performance of Norah Gregor's father. As in *Boudu* the doorway is made a means of discovery and yet, though in *Portrait of a Lady* Isabel's view through a doorway is carefully selected for us by James, in *La Règle* there are so many doorways revealing so many things that one is not conscious of arrangement. It even seems possible that the characters have been let loose. The illusion of reality is complete enough to carry over to our attitudes towards the character, as well as the presence, of people, and to convince us of the illusoriness of universal meaning. Renoir has reproduced our experience of life by making his subject the individual means of understanding within a massive, disordered society. The images in *La Règle* are of an infinity within which 'tout le monde a ses raisons' and the preference is 'pour que chacun les expose librement'.

Renoir takes a major step of withdrawal in allowing the spectator to come to terms with the material in the way that he has done himself. But this permissiveness is still part of an invocation to enjoyment and fulfilment that is a complete philosophy for all: that we be tolerant. For Renoir the camera remains a tool to be used in the description of life, whereas for Godard it is an expansion of communication and life itself. Renoir is a classical example of the humanistic, social culture, like Mozart or Bonnard. Distinctive of this classicism is the sense we have of the unity of man and subject so that neither choice nor calculation seems to have taken place. The events themselves are so entire as to be inscrutable: as Pascal said, 'where one expected to discover a style, one finds a man'. The supreme stylistic quality is a natural ease so commanding that it can accomplish the credible enactment of considerable stylization. Thus Mozart makes opera a realistic form, Bonnard adopts a harmony of colour unknown in nature and Renoir conspires towards the beguiling balance of spontaneity and theatre. In all these cases the work is non-reasoning, content to continue the manifestation of integration, accepting it as calmly as seasonal renewal and the movement of the stars. Art is not a proper description: such work is reality itself.

The movement from *Boudu* to *La Règle du Jeu* is one of

evolution for Renoir. For in *La Règle* the theatrical level of spontaneous events is much more conscious and his own presence indicates the dawning of the idea that a social circle has directors, just like films. Since the war the theatrical reflection in his films has increased—as in *Le Carrosse d'Or* and *French Can-Can*—as has the emphasis on a producer who simultaneously organizes and becomes involved in events. Like Lang's this is a reduction of the actual that carries the cinema from a concern with verisimilitude to an awareness of epistemology.

Renoir's American films, influenced no doubt by the more schematic scenarios and the more precise camera-work in Hollywood, have a far less involved style than that of *La Règle* and a much more direct statement of philosophical issues. The didactic ambiguity of *The Woman on the Beach* and the abstract sparseness of characterization are such as even recall Lang. With Renoir's return to Europe the philosophical consciousness is retained but the unpredictability is regained to achieve the exquisite late masterpieces: *The River, Le Carrosse d'Or, French Can-Can* and *Elena et les Hommes*.

Carrosse d'Or and *Can-Can* are primarily concerned with performance and the metaphor it makes of a human relationship. The opening shot of *Carrosse d'Or* is a track forward across the proscenium arch of a theatre, at which moment the set magically becomes reality. Metamorphosis proliferates: every character is observed as a performer and it is the accredited actress, Anna Magnani, who is most able to live without affectation; the children and clowns of the *commedia dell' arte* troupe make the most mundane actions balletic, ushering on the other players like Corneille in *La Règle*; the action of the film is a succession of masquerades and dissimulations which thrust dramatic roles on the characters. Even the seemingly ordinary events are shaped to conform to a pattern of theatre: thus the clothes of aristocrat, soldier and bullfighter are as much costume as any on the stage and bystanders make compositions from Goya, Velazquez and Picasso, spontaneously and yet as formally as the troupe.

At the centre is Anna Magnani, the only one of the players who moves from theatre to life, as shown by the way she changes her costume for normal clothes. Like a character in the play she is loved by three men and, although successful as an actress—which in her terms means winning the audience, and thus the three men—she only manages to embarrass their affairs, as if the magical qualities of an actress could not settle to ordinariness. At the end of the film she is alone on the stage and speaks to the lovers she has lost, admitting that she cries a little. This moment is the complement of that in *French Can-Can* when Jean Gabin rebukes the women he has loved and produced by saying that the theatre is his love and that he will continue to look at people for their aptitude in it. This is not a hardened show-business attitude but an allegory of life sustained by the interchangeability of *Carrosse d'Or*. The acceptance of performance and the enthusiasm for it, and the realization that style is character just as appearance is nature is, in Renoir's eyes, a fitness for the illusoriness of life. It involves an acceptance of human weakness and delusion that is asked of his audience by Renoir in the quotation from Beaumarchais in the prologue to *La Règle*: 'Si l'amour porte des ailes, N'est-ce pas pour voltiger?'*

MORALIST: HITCHCOCK

Hitchcock is a commercial genius: *Psycho* has one of the best profit/cost ratios in the history of the cinema. Very few directors can offer a body of work so imaginatively disturbing. In watching Hitchcock films one becomes conscious of issues of freedom, not only to the extent that the characters in the film enjoy it but in how far the spectator in the cinema is deprived of it.

Hitchcock is a contemporary of the commercial cinema. He was born in 1899, only a few years after Lumière's first show at the Regent Polytechnic; *The Great Train Robbery* or *Rescued by Rover* might have been the first films he saw. He began as a film publicist and turned to script-writing before aspiring to directing. In 1921 he completed *Always Tell Your Wife* at the Islington Studios after the director had fallen ill. He continued to work as assistant director and set designer at a time when film-making was largely unorganized by trade unions. Before sound broke into the middle of *Blackmail* he had directed ten

* *The Marriage of Figaro*, Act IV, Scene x.

silent movies, and did fourteen more sound pictures before going to America to make *Rebecca*. It is a life constantly involved with the cinema and it has produced an attitude perfectly in keeping with the ideals of the film industry. Talking about *Psycho* he invoked the standards of popular, unsophisticated entertainment: 'To me it's a *fun* picture. The processes through which we take the audience, you see, it's rather like taking them through the haunted house at the fairground or the roller-coaster.'* And in 1959, when asked 'Quelle est alors la logique profonde de vos films?' he answered, 'Faire souffrir le spectateur.'†

Essential to every Hitchcock film is this awareness the director has of his spectator. It conceives of the spectator as an economic generalization and there is an element of sadism in the devices inflicted. In one way Hitchcock's films are un-cinematic: his images are most effective when most contrived. At the same time his work defines the nature of cinema more than any other director's. The chief contribution to this definition is the similarity of treatment he offers to his audience and to the characters in his films. And if Hitchcock evokes the voyeur in one it is, I think, because he regards his own characters in this way.

Speaking about his confessed inclination to torture his characters, Hitchcock said, 'That scene in *Vertigo* where James Stewart forces Miss Kim Novak to alter her whole personality by altering her lipstick, hairstyle, even hair-tint—for me it has the compulsion of a striptease in reverse. The woman is made insecure by being forced to make up, not take-off.'‡

The setting of *Vertigo* is San Francisco and Hitchcock emphasizes the sheerness of that city. This is clearly relevant to vertigo—the complaint of the private detective played by James Stewart—but it is an image Hitchcock has already made us familiar with: the cliff-top and the staircase of Manderley in *Rebecca*; the steep streets of Quebec in *I Confess*; the staircase, guarded by a dog, that Farley Granger ascends in *Strangers on a*

* *Movie* 6, interview with Ian Cameron and V. F. Perkins.
† *Cahiers du Cinéma*, No. 102, interview with Jean Domarchi and Jean Douchet.
‡ *Evening Standard*, 24th March, 1965. Interview with Alexander Walker.

Train. More than specific instances of steepness there is Hitchcock's use of high-angle camerawork at moments of crisis and judgement. At the conclusion of the court proceedings in *The Paradine Case*, for example, the camera towers above Gregory Peck. Height is a metaphysical symbol for Hitchcock just as the fact that so many of his characters have 'fallen' is a sign of their moral condition.

In *Vertigo* Stewart is hired by a friend, Tom Helmore, to keep a watch on his wife, Kim Novak. There is a long sequence in which he trails her through San Francisco and into the Californian countryside as she visits places associated with her Spanish grandmother. The grandmother committed suicide and Helmore has told Stewart that he fears his wife's own depression may be leading to this end. Ostensibly, the terms on which the film opens are those of a thriller, and the method of narration transmits these terms to the audience. But Hitchcock is not content that Stewart should be simply the ingenious and heroic detective of tradition or that we should be allowed to enjoy the thrills unaffected. Both Stewart and the spectator follow Novak in the same degree of ignorance, and when Stewart's interest grows into sympathy and love it is an expression of what many of the spectators may feel. Stewart rescues Novak from an attempt to drown herself and the pattern of pursuit changes to their travelling together. It is a love affair, but blighted by Novak's remoteness and the emphasis this gives to Stewart's original role as detective and watcher. When they visit the monastery where the grandmother died a distraught Novak runs away from Stewart up the bell tower. When he tries to follow vertigo disables him. He reaches the top only to see Novak's body in the courtyard below. Stewart is quietly condemned for negligence at the inquest and he has a breakdown.

Several months later, when his recovery seems good, he sees a girl in the street who resembles Kim Novak. At this point the difficulty of distinguishing the two Kim Novaks from the two characters she is playing is such that I must divulge the device behind the film. Hitchcock himself waits a little longer but still reveals it half an hour before the end of what started as a thriller, the twist of which one might have expected would be reserved for the last minute. The throwaway shows how little the 'detective story' interests him compared with the moral psychology. The two Kim Novaks are, as our eyes tell us, one. More than that, Novak has not been Helmore's wife, but only part of a conspiracy with him to accomplish the killing of his real wife. She had not been an unknowing object of pursuit but a decoy. Helmore had been waiting at the top of the tower with his unconscious wife whom he had thrown down; he had hidden with Novak and escaped when Stewart collapsed. To impersonate the wife Novak had been blonde, now she is a brunette.

Just as Helmore has deceived Stewart, so Hitchcock has misled the spectator by ensuring that he gains information in exactly the same way as Stewart. Stewart's assignment to follow and the subsequent attraction he feels towards his object are the equivalents of the cinematic method. Because the central character is a detective and because the movie's main purpose seems to be the solution of a mystery, which on the available evidence presupposes a supernatural intervention in man's affairs, *Vertigo* progresses by what appears to be a factual gathering. The facts can be related to the ideal of pure cinema: what a person looks like, what she does, the manner of her gestures. It is in these terms that Stewart watches Novak and the entire visual material is directed to this information; cuts separate fact from fact rather than allowing them to elide with each other so that their certainty might be undermined by context. And, of course, Novak is behaving to the order of this method through her conspiracy with Helmore, which is the equivalent of her co-operation with her director.

The appearance of the second Novak is a crucial indication of *Vertigo*'s real nature, for Stewart's obsession with the Novak face and the associations of guilt he has with it override the detective in him. He attempts, as Hitchcock indicated in his interview, to recreate the appearance she had as Helmore's wife. When the transformation is complete and the second Novak stands in a sexually-charged and quite non-naturalistic green light, the exact image of her earlier self, and the camera tracks a full circle of vortex round them while they kiss, we can see how deranged Stewart is. He notices only that his dream has been reincarnated and that it is possible for him now to exercise the desire he had felt earlier but which had been suppressed by the nature of his job. For Novak the position is ontologically precarious. She has herself fallen in love, but while in her first character the mechanism of deceit kept her from being frank, she now recognizes how far Stewart is obsessed. Finally she confesses to the trick. Furiously Stewart takes her back to the monastery and chases her to the top of the tower. Novak is startled at the top by the sudden appearance of a nun—black robes appearing from black shadow—and falls to her death. This death is accident, punishment and suicide of remorse and identification, so involved have the layers of duplicity become. For Stewart, left at the top of the tower, there is no prospect but madness. Hitchcock has even intimated that he expects Stewart might throw himself down. Vertigo has been made the symptom of delusion, indecision, guilt, sexual obsession and, finally, chaos.

I have found it more necessary to detail the sequence of events in *Vertigo* than in any other film.* As in *Psycho* the movement of plot hypnotizes; at the same time the overtly narrative aspect is a pretext for Hitchcock to uncover spiritual responses. The height of his plots is when the mystery is most inexplicable, so that the rational processes the characters have been following break into psychological fantasy. Cary Grant, stranded in a mid-West desert in *North by Northwest* is in such a position; the whole idea of *The Birds* is perhaps Hitchcock's boldest juxtaposition of the real and the abstract. It is this talent that enables him to appeal more than any other director to the most general and most exclusive of film audiences. The cynical use of *doubles ententes* is the director's own awareness of his width of appeal. When Anthony Perkins remarks to Janet Leigh in *Psycho* that taxidermy is his hobby, the horrible pun is a dare to the audience: how can such artifice coexist with a tension so compulsive? Why, in fact, do the most old-fashioned plots work in his hands?

Basically, the effectiveness lies in the paradox that Hitchcock's films purport to be a sequence of factual statements, but that these 'facts' are subsequently revealed to be false. Because the method filters a continuum of experience into discrete items, the real source of disorientation is the insinuation

* An excellent and more comprehensive analysis of *Vertigo* is to be found in *Hitchcock's Films* by Robin Wood, Zwemmer, 1965.

of the film's form with the natural processes of watching a movie, particularly a movie from Hollywood in a circuit cinema. While Hitchcock seems the most penetrative talent the cinema has offered, his method is already stranded by events that have separated the film process from the commercial structure that originally fostered it. In some ways Hitchcock, more than many of his contemporaries, adheres to an old-fashioned cinematic concept. His reliance on the conclusive 'story' form is such that he has concentrated on making all its connections plausible, so that the story has become more and more isolated from a spectator's sense of external reality. The photographic images have consequently moved further towards the abstract and Hitchcock's most striking achievements have occurred when the counterpoint between reality and the abstract has been most disarming. Only a great talent could have done this and only a supreme showman could have continued doing it in Hollywood. As a result he has come to occupy the position of creative artist, and it is this that makes an anachronism. His films are concentrated on intention, and their elements have to be meaningful, whether the meaning is conveyed directly or by contradiction.

I said in Chapter 3 that Hitchcock utilized back-projection more successfully than most directors and this is because the relationship between person and background in his films is conceptual rather than real. The isolated Cary Grant in the prairie in *North by Northwest* is as much a figure projected against a background as Stewart struggling to climb the vertiginous face of San Francisco or Anthony Perkins playing out his fantasies in the Gothic set of *Psycho*. All these situations are convergent on meaning and the result of calculation. Hitchcock has admitted just how important the process of planning and conception is: 'Je ne regarde jamais dans le viseur. Je prends un crayon, et je dessine le plan suivant pour le chef-operateur lorsqu'il y a une difficulté. Mon film est terminé avant le tournage. C'est pourquoi j'ai mis un an à écrire *North by Northwest*. Si je vais aux rushes après, c'est pour voir si les cheveux et le visage d'Eva Marie Saint sont comme il faut. Je sais tout.'*

* *Cahiers du Cinéma*, No. 102.

The truly creative process then is one of solitary imagination and it is literary in the sense that much of it can be set down in a shooting script. It seems to me that Hitchcock conceives of his event and his way of presenting it simultaneously. That is the power of his best movies, but it is what today makes their meaningfulness increasingly claustrophobic. 'Je sais tout' is an aspiration to sublimity that is sustained by enough of his movies even though it is a denial of the camera's potential.

BEHAVIOURIST: HAWKS

'Mon film est terminé avant le tournage' is a comment that would please those people in the film industry who look on the movies simply as products. It would enable them to forecast production schedules exactly. But even in Hollywood there are many directors for whom it would represent an impossibility. Howard Hawks is only three years older than Hitchcock and he also started directing during the 20s; Hawks and Hitchcock are the supreme Hollywood directors still functioning. They are very different, though, and while time has concentrated on the abstraction in Hitchcock's work, it has given more freedom to the behaviourism in Hawks's movies.

As noted earlier, Cary Grant is common to both directors' films, and both have tended to repeat characters and situations; but their attitudes to this repetition differ. Hawks indulges his own pleasures by duplicating a small circle of friendly expertise and private jokes with the circle of characters in his films. Grant is there, because, like Bogart or Wayne, he is a friend of Hawks. For Hitchcock, on the other hand, he is an ideal figure for the performance of a ritual; his character and reactions are entirely preconceived. Hitchcock's devising fusion of action and shot often leads to subjective photography, his camera taking up positions that are more emotionally or atmospherically apt than Hawks's strictly recording machine. Speaking of the early influence of German trick-photography, Hawks said: 'I don't like tricks. I only tried that one time. I've always been rather mechanically-minded so I tried a whole lot of mechanical things, and then gave them up completely—most of the time my camera stays on eye level now. Once in a while, I'll move the camera as if a man were walking and seeing something. And it pulls back or it moves in for emphasis when you don't want to make a cut. But, outside of that, I just use the simplest camera in the world.'*

The desire to entertain on Hawks's part, to share certain jokes, activities and people, is quite unalloyed by the sort of purpose Hitchcock's films contain. Hawks places much less reliance on the effects of the camera than Hitchcock, who deliberately uses it to create emotional response. Because of the nature of his friends Hawks's films are as recognizable as Hitchcock's but Hawks himself is anonymous compared with the presence of Hitchcock one feels and, once ritually in every film, actually notices—a visual grotesque passing across the screen. If Hawks were to appear in his own films he would not stand out because the activities he records are his own. Hitchcock's physique compels him to meditation, but Hawks has been active. Before movies he built and raced cars and planes. He was brought up not in a city as dense as London, but in Goshen, Indiana, the sort of country Nick Adams grew up in. The associations with Hemingway emerge in a respect for professionalism and personality and in a documentary celebration of some of man's most vigorous activities: flying planes in *Dawn Patrol*, *Only Angels* and *Air Force*; driving a herd of cattle in *Red River*; hunting big game in *Hatari!*, and in *To Have and Have Not* and *The Big Sleep* sitting out a tight spot and keeping the hand steady.

It is important to notice in Hawks how professionalism modifies heroism: Hemingway's knowledge that every man is afraid all the time but that some are still able to do their job is very close to Hawks's attitude. None of his heroic figures are ever isolated by adulation; instead, their prowess is either knowingly slighted by companions or set off by an inability to deal with less dramatic, more personal affairs. In that scene in *Rio Bravo* where John Wayne is held up outside the Hotel Alamo, he and Ricky Nelson may extricate themselves with ingenuity, skill and courage but not without Angie Dickinson throwing a flower-pot through a window to provide an initial distraction. And when Wayne has arranged with the under-

* *Movie* 5, interview with Peter Bogdanovich.

taker for the disposal of the bodies he still has to deal with Angie who is angry at having been so frightened, proud of having been so helpful and rapidly getting drunk on the whisky Nelson offers to settle her nerves. Personality is what attracts Hawks; a job he considers obligatory. How plot can be created out of these two is often in some doubt and very rarely is its development felt to be important. It is a commercial necessity that Hawks has done his best to conform with, but sometimes, as with *The Big Sleep*, frankly given up.

Rio Bravo has a plot that is in one sense a parody of *High Noon*: the sheriff with little support against a band of outlaws. But rather than adopt the minute-by-minute account of the Kramer-Zinnemann movie, and its unsubtle social self-righteousness, Hawks makes the plot almost incidental to the character studies. The contention with the outlaws is provoked by a brief spasm of violence in the first few minutes of the film. After that, there is no real movement for over two hours, but under the pressure of the set-up the characters of the sheriff and his friend develop. As so often, friendship is Hawks's subject and the small circle draws together under pressure, preferring to disguise its real personal links with jokes, private games and apparent disrespect. More than that, the private examination ironically exposes the heroism we see in the direct encounters with the outlaws. Dean Martin has been a drunk ever since a girl walked out on him, and now John Wayne, who is trying to nurse him out of the drunkenness, is getting tied up with Angie Dickinson. Their encounters are a succession of misunderstandings and bristling displays of independence. But they are accurately enough presented to reduce the external events to insignificance.

A lot of the jokes and characters in *Rio Bravo* refer back to *Red River*, *The Big Sleep*, *To Have and Have Not* and *Only Angels Have Wings*. For all the pressure that exists in these movies, they are Utopian. They describe a Hawksian ideal of comradeship that is private inasmuch as it refers behaviour to a code as exclusive and autocratic as *aficion*. One would not expect a contemporary urban film from Hawks because he does not have a social mind. Thus *The Big Heat* is a study of metropolitan organization in which the characters are protagonists, while

The Big Sleep is less about a city even than Chandler's Los Angeles: it is about Humphrey Bogart and Lauren Bacall, and about their friendship and association with the Hawks circle. What stops the Hawksian view from the potential fascism of a heroic form is the sense of reluctance with which power is exercised and the constant balance of bravery and character. There still emerges a cinematic pitch of excellence in which character and performance are combined, as when Bogart says to Bacall near the end of *The Big Sleep*, 'You looked good when you were doing that.' *The Big Sleep* is blatantly self-indulgent: Bogart cracking joke after joke; Dorothy Malone popping up for a mid-afternoon affair; Bacall singing a song—as gratuitous as Angie Dickinson showing her legs at the end of *Rio Bravo*; several sequences of cross-talk between Bogart and Bacall. The circumstances of the movie are not the plot's, but simply the year, 1946, and Hawks and some friends getting together to make a film, the thread of which—since financial guarantors approve of threads—is Chandler's thriller. After that, improvisation: 'The main idea was to make every scene fun to look at. A place where Bogey has to walk into a book store I said, "This is an awfully ordinary scene. Can't you think of something to do?" And he just pushed up his hat brim, put on glasses and got a little effeminate. The moment he did that, I said, "O.K. Come on, we're off, I'll write some new dialogue when we're inside." '*

Hawks's Utopia is one of freedom, its cinematic success reflects how often the director has rightly judged his friends worthy of a free camera. The sadness is always that the film should end. Any conclusion to a Hawks film is one of convenience: Wayne and Dickinson will go on arguing; Bogart and Bacall are destined for many more tight scrapes; Grant will have to go on flying beat-up aeroplanes. No Hollywood films are more divergent than Hawks's, seeming to blend with documentary. The freedom is not entirely unconstrained, though. Failure is always admitted as a possibility and in many cases the exercise of freedom brings painful results: Joe dies; Clift takes Wayne's herd from him in *Red River*; and in every movie there are the old men, most eminently Walter Brennan

* *Movie* 5.

in *Rio Bravo*. Or even John Wayne. In *Hatari!*, shot in 1961–2, Wayne captures his own rhinoceros: the camera proves it. But he is heavier than he was in *Red River*, the film in which age caught up with him and his adopted son took over his authority. Within two years of *Hatari!* Wayne was in hospital with cancer. Wayne, Hawks and Grant are in their sixties. Bogart is dead already. Death is as common as happiness in the Hawks world, and the latter is sharpest when the former is approached most closely. 'The simplest camera in the world' can record all the subtleties of that approach.

ROMANTIC: DEMY AND RIVETTE

It is a sign of how far the cinema has declined from its commercial heights that the romantic film is seen so seldom today. Yet though the cinema was once thought of in respectable circles as a haven of romantic delusion the term needs closer definition because one of the screen's foremost romantics, Josef von Sternberg, has had such difficulties in obtaining work in Hollywood even during the heyday of the romantic cinema. A movie is romantic when its effectiveness is due fundamentally to the conviction its atmosphere carries. The atmosphere is an image of the quality of belief of everyone existing in the film. Consequently it has to surpass the factual nature of film and elevate it to a spiritual reflection: whether of religious faith, erotic love or paranoid fear. It depends upon the heightening of the image by colour, light or by mystification.

There is, as we have noted, a sense in which all cinema is romantic because every image will combine a factual level and imaginative implications. The Hollywood genres of Western, woman's picture and costume piece are the forms of romanticism and the great stars are photographed faces and icons. But these genres and stars are almost defunct and the truest romanticism in photography is to be found in advertising, particularly that of fashion where the recollections of Hollywood between 1930 and 1950 are still vivid.

In his revival of the musical and of images from favourite movies Jacques Demy is a contemporary romantic and his own additions to the form denote not a repetition, but an exploration, of its possibilities. Thus in *Baie des Anges* he so formalizes absurdity that it assumes the quality of ritual. Money loses its competitive satisfaction and acquires a spiritual value. The means of transposition is the roulette wheel where enormous sums may be won or lost in a minute, making an elegant parody of the honest efforts of conventional society. Like *Lola*, *Baie des Anges* is a religious film celebrating the faith that the characters have in each other. Both are formal films to the point of artificiality and the celebration derives from the fact that the most elaborate composition of relationships does not inhibit the individual's faith. Freedom of belief is Demy's subject, and even if the structure of his films is ordered and ordained, and the visual context a glorification of the everyday, there is still a religious sense of the possibility of failure of faith. The beauty of the people in Demy's films represents their faith just as the radiance indicates saintliness in pre-Renaissance religious paintings. *Baie des Anges* is his most subtle movie because Jeanne Moreau's performance combines the beatitude of joy with a much more modern awareness of despair. The rapid movement from one to the other is the film's tension and religious suspension. Compared with *Baie des Anges*, *Lola* is a more closed and more perfect film and Anouk Aimée's Lola a monotone of delight.

Baie des Anges offers a world of freedom to Claude Mann, a young Parisian bank clerk who lives with his father. He is drawn to it by a small success at the Deauville casino. His father disapproves of gambling so that Mann's departure for Nice is a family break and the father's vow to offer no help when he loses his money is a provocation to the son's pride. In the South he meets Jeanne Moreau whom he has seen evicted from the Deauville casino for cheating. They meet at the tables. Moreau bets on 17 and notices Mann when he does likewise; 35 comes up. Mann bets on 3 and Moreau joins him: 3 wins. It is a statement of love. They sit together during an afternoon of unblemished success. Factually-minded spectators may cavil at their luck, those who accept it are party to the sort of faith Demy is concerned with.

Their love is complete even though unsupported. As Mann discovers more about Moreau he appreciates how their love will

21. Cary Grant as Charley's Aunt. *I Was a Male War Bride.*

22, 23. Strangers on a train. The meeting arranged but the consequence unsuspected. The killing is fake but its significance is real. The extras in a Hitchcock movie are powerless, a gesture towards society. Grant and Saint are on a separate plane. *North by Northwest.*

24. Peter Ustinov presents Martine Carol as *Lola Montes*. But between announcements he whispers asides to Lola.

25. Jeanne Moreau as *Eve*. The personality grows in solitude to self-sufficiency.

26. Macha Meril in her bathroom in *Une Femme Mariée* makes herself an object and thus acquires an object's privacy.

be tested and how his comprehension of Nice has to change from that of a Parisian for the first time in the south to that of a believer on the Bay of Angels. This is not especially difficult because it is already indicated in the visual context which elicits the grace it knows exists in everything. Sunlight is the photographic means to radiance. The range of whites is so great that the fewer blacks impress on it with the effect of deliberate complement. The sky is white, the pebbles on the beach, the walls of hotel rooms, the uniforms of American sailors on the promenade, the sports car bought with winnings, the sunlight into the lens; and Jeanne Moreau is white: her hair, her suit, her shoes, her underclothes, her skin—only her eyes are black. The city suit Mann wears from Paris is black, so is his hair, and the casino is a series of blacks: furniture, cloths, croupiers' suits, curtains and cool shadow. The casino itself shares the transforming generosity Demy brings to the cabaret in *Lola*. Both might be affected by viciousness, but the cabaret is less a brothel than a place of sentimental happiness, and the casino is not a gambling hall but a church. Its darkness is like a cathedral, its dimensions are deliberately extended and the muttered voices of croupiers speak the liturgy. When Mann and Moreau finally leave the casino together, recognizing their mutual need, they are photographed arm-in-arm going into the white through a black arch: it is a married couple leaving the church and entering paradise.

A clearly-defined hierarchy exists in *Baie des Anges* between paradise and despair. Jeanne Moreau's life must lead to one or the other. She is the image of freedom from the conventional, hard-working respectability that Claude Mann is trying to escape. In *Lola*, when he is fired from his job, Roland explains this instinct:

'Alors, vous me comprenez certainement. Une phrase m'a frappé. On dit, page 55: "Il n'y a pas de dignité possible, pas de vie réelle pour un homme qui travaille douze heures par jour sans savoir pourquoi il travaille." En fait, c'est vrai, je ne sais pas pourquoi je travaille.'*

Moreau knows why she gambles: her ability to survive loss and enjoy victory are integral to her ontological security. If,

* *L'Avant-Scène*, No. 4.

in workaday Parisian terms, to live from one casino to another is a dream, then Moreau's life is a fulfilled dream. The dream is a form close to Demy, particularly its tendency to coincidence and the opportunities for pattern this offers. Thus *Lola* is an exploration of the streets of Nantes, where Demy himself was a boy, and of chance meetings and necessary farewells which combine in a graceful structure of romance, the images of which have already reappeared in his two subsequent films. The exteriors of Nantes are in fact ordinary, as are those of Cherbourg or even Nice. But their mundane quality does not deny that dreams may flourish in them. Lola has been left with a child by Michel but she has faith that he will return, and, so long as her belief endures, her faithfulness is not broken by her sleeping with the American sailors who come to the cabaret. Anyway, the one she likes best looks like Michel. After the magical seven years Michel does return rich enough to own a white sports car. He has been in Matareva, an island in the Pacific. Previously Roland has seen a film set in Matareva which starred Gary Cooper, tall and blond as Michel. The film: 'C'était beau, les gens avaient l'air heureux.' Roland loves Lola and when Michel returns he leaves Nantes reappearing in *Les Parapluies de Cherbourg* to marry Catherine Deneuve after she has been left pregnant.

It is a situation common to Demy's films that, while the setting remains the French provinces, the hopes of the characters aspire outwards so lyrically that the aura of places like Matareva is drawn in until Nantes and Nice become locations in divine geography. Demy's faith is inextricably mixed in the cinematic and the religious. The ritual of situation and character in the American films he might have watched as a boy is not contradicted by his intense photographic sensitivity, which is always controlled by the natural movement and gesture of people and never by values of composition or artifice. The artificiality that Demy does employ is most obvious in *Les Parapluies de Cherbourg* in which the dialogue is all sung and the sets and costumes are like a rainbow, a fantastic richness ordered by a mathematical system of comparison which, with the song, establishes the convention of fairy-tale without ever upsetting visual naturalism.

Everyone in Demy's films is capable of being happy because

no one can escape the pattern that underlies society. The moments of unhappiness that do occur are due to a loss of faith: Marc Michel's melancholy departure from Nantes in *Lola* is compared with the serene exit of the American sailor. Nino Castonuelvo returns to Cherbourg to find he has lost Catherine Deneuve, but after a period of depression his faith reasserts itself. Just as the light pervades all of *Lola* and *Baie des Anges*, and song and colour all of *Parapluies*, the paradise is inevitable and the freedom from worldly cares that Moreau enjoys in *Baie des Anges* is only preliminary to an obsession with roulette, the index to her faith, that imprisons her in a lonely physical freedom. Thus the last shot of *Baie des Anges* is the solution to the first in which the camera tracks rapidly away from Moreau as she walks along the promenade at Nice early in the morning. Relationships are the proper destination of every character in Demy, and their short periods of loneliness are symptomatic of spiritual isolation and difficulty. Meetings and love are everything because they add impetus to the coincidences of character and relationship that already exist. Roland's meeting with Lola in the passage Pommeraye is more apt because he has just met an adolescent girl who reminded him of the younger Lola, while the girl has met the American sailor who slept with Lola the previous night and who is the same blond image as Gary Cooper and like one of Donen's sailors in *On the Town*.

The beautiful people in Demy's films have the apparently disparate antecedents of religious painting and Hollywood movies that make his photographic sense of faith so uniquely and unabashedly vulgar. The music Michel Legrand composes for Demy is nostalgic of the sentimental background scores that Tiomkin, Rozsa, Steiner and Victor Young have composed in Hollywood. But like Bresson's music it signals the pitch of emotional tension and communicates the stages of the ceremony to the spectator. The soaring piano in *Baie des Anges* that occurs with the montage at the roulette wheel accompanies a spirit thriving most freely during the discipline of the game. This paradox constitutes Demy's conception of grace and Jeanne Moreau's elation at victory is one of the most remarkable contemporary religious images. When she parades into the bridal suite of the hotel at Monte Carlo and turns against the white sun behind the balcony and asks 'Quel luxe?' the moment is luminous with assurance.

The Bay of Angels is Moreau's and Nantes is Lola's, but it is in an ironic sense that Jacques Rivette's film is called *Paris Nous Appartient*. The photography in *Paris Nous Appartient* is always obviously Paris, the lighting is as natural as possible, the camera angles are uncommitted. Once again the ideal that the camera should record is adhered to. What it records is as reflective of the people working on the film as a Renoir movie. Rivette wanted to make a feature: he had a group of young actors and technicians but little money. They could not afford to move outside Paris; they had to use their own apartments and the public places. They filmed in summer when people were free and the light was good. The immediate subject is similarly a group of young people rehearsing *Pericles*. Because the development of plot is much less important than the creation of atmosphere many of the images might be interchangeable with a contemporary documentary of the lives of the people making the film.

The gulf between modern Paris and the classically remote settings of *Pericles* is one that adds to our idea of the condition of the young people at the centre of the film. They are members of an advanced contemporary society but they are young people with ambitions and ideals that relate them to the play's heroic context. Why should Paris not belong to them, in the summer, while they are independent? To rehearse *Pericles* is an indulgence in a commercial theatrical world, but the wish is sustained by the hopes and at first the incongruity is itself a sign of youthful energy and idealism. Paris in the early 1960s, inhabited by young intellectuals and artists, is not only its subject but its ideal.

But the aptness of *Pericles* is sinister. For the play is itself surrounded by chaos: it was not included in the First Folio; very little of it is academically attributed to Shakespeare; its origin is Rome of the fifth or sixth century A.D.—the onset of the Dark Ages. The text itself is unclear, marred by omissions and subject to rapid changes of style and quality. Finally, the story of *Pericles* moves with frantic disregard for sequence, and the impulse that starts this movement is fear. The opening of

Pericles is almost certainly not Shakespeare's work, but in its situation and implications it has a disturbing power that is similar to the effect of Rivette's film. Pericles comes to Antioch to win Antiochus's daughter in marriage. To do so he must answer Antiochus's riddle; if he fails he will die. The riddle alludes to the secret incest between Antiochus and his daughter. Pericles guesses this and Antiochus, guessing Pericles's suspicions, delays giving his answer so that Pericles may escape to Tyre. Pericles's flight begins the series of journeys which propel the play forward. Antiochus does not appear again; a report comes later that he and his daughter have been shrivelled by fire.

Fear, a riddle, and unnatural evil are elements in *Paris Nous Appartient* that seem to conspire against the young people. None of them is easily demonstrated, and all the camera sees of them is the trace and sign: but by the end of the movie their influence has gathered so strongly that, although the images are still undistorted, one might be seeing Paris after a great disaster. Clearly the Bomb is a relevant symbol. Nobody will ever be able to film it explode; instead one can only sit afraid and wait. It is the supreme symbol because of its power, but it is not the only one. Power is felt in much more ordinary human and social terms. The Paris theatre is such that the production of *Pericles* may be taken over by a more commercial producer. A love affair can be betrayed by one's lover loving someone else, and in the close circle of Parisian life which the film observes this cannot be ignored. An organization may exist, of which every manifestation of power is the imagined instrument. Its aims may be total control and, like Mabuse's, the chance to destroy everything. Rivette's introduction of a sequence from Lang's *Metropolis* is as important as his use of *Pericles*. The sequence shows the Tower of Babel, in which depersonalized humanity labours against a background of formal stylization. It is a captivity as complete as Auschwitz.

The inhibition of fear grows through the film like a cancer. Significantly, no form of authority is ever seen, and in that sense the Paris depicted is a site of freedom. But the withdrawal of recognizable authority also takes away a sense of order, and in the consequent speculation there is no reason why the American expatriate's warnings of a secret malevolent organization should not be justified. There is thus no reason why the characters should not join the American's own organization to oppose it. The conflicts of human ambitions and sexual rivalry merge with the inclination to form fundamental groupings in which emotion and politics balance uneasily. The inducement to this is a growing awareness of the totalitarian nature of society and the simultaneous mistrust of visual information. Another riddle is composed: who can be trusted? Who is on my side? What side is it I am on? Originally, the idea of a riddle is connected with the production of *Pericles*. Juan is supposed to have written a score for the play, but he is dead: he may have killed himself, he may have been killed. The search for this score, by Gianni Esposito the producer, and Betty Schneider, the young girl who is drawn into the circle, is at the centre of the action; but by the time a tape is found—it may be Juan's, it may not—the original simplicity has been confused. The tape itself is of a guitar: as formless and instinctive as the circumstances that surround it: not a solution but another riddle.

CONSENSUS: PREMINGER

To say that Otto Preminger is concerned with a consensus is to associate him with the current state of society in Western democracies. Consensus is a cumbersome ideal whereby every action has the agreement of every member of the state. It can be a cowardly retreat from responsibility, but that possibility should not hide the fact that it is a solution offered to the most searching contradiction within a free society. Some people have criticized Preminger's movies for their moral equivocation but his method remains one of the most plausible solutions to the cinematic problem whereby an item of characterization that supports an interpretation also restricts all the others that the natural recording device implies exist. In *The Cardinal* Tom Tryon says that 'facts are not truth', thus describing the gap between films and the literary art. Preminger's political sense has none of the moral traditions that the great novels of the nineteenth century constructed. Instead it particularizes the problem of the system: that action and decisions must be taken even though doubt may be the condition of the authority.

Advise and Consent brings out the way in which political life is complicated by the democratic predicament of the politicians, and uses the camera to stand for the imperative of representation. The effect of Preminger's film is, significantly, to create a sense of pattern with the various personalities in a hypothetical situation. The policies are not of intrinsic importance. It is Preminger's achievement to convince one of the social and visual verisimilitude of the Washington life he shows without having recourse to the Republican or Democrat labels. The value of the human incidents in the film—Henry Fonda's lying to the Senate Committee, Don Murray's suicide, Walter Pidgeon's love-affair with Gene Tierney—is for the individuals alone. The treatment of often highly-charged relationships imposes the camera's objectivity on the spectator and establishes the relationships as expressions of personal freedom, but at the same time social acts so embedded in peoples' lives that they cannot be looked at in isolation. The faculty of judgement is not approved of by Preminger and the intricate but self-effacing movements of his camera are devoted to so complete a picture that it will not be attempted. It is a vital condition of that society that the ambitions and behaviour of its members balance. Failure is the worst that can happen to his characters and is typified by rejection of the society. Thus Don Murray is a failure in *Advise and Consent* because he feels unable to face the homosexual incident in his past. Henry Fonda's failure is one he realizes and his lie is expressed as a practical, rather than a moral, error. Momentarily his judgement failed and his ambition overwhelmed him. He subsequently recognizes that he is bound to withdraw because his lie is likely to upset the balance.

Doubt is the inevitable reaction to the debate of ideas in Preminger's movies and yet action is the necessary response. Freedom of expression is permitted in *Advise and Consent* without prejudice, but it is placed under a criterion of honour that does not relate to conscience but to the standards of society. George Grizzard's efforts to blackmail Murray are appreciated by the other senators and although no official expulsion is possible he is an outcast from their confidence. This confidence unites political opponents, like Walter Pidgeon and Charles Laughton, so that for both of them the functioning of the system is superior to the fulfilment of partisan policy. Pidgeon is the most mature of Preminger's heroes—though 'hero' is less apt than ideal protagonist. For an audience he is not so much admirable as reasonable and reliable. The reliance is stronger because we are led to identify him with the system of government and, its perfect expression, the system of the film. Mechanics of government interest him and the personal freedom that his skill and knowledge support is ironically put to organizational rather than personal use. One does not recall his name in the film but remembers he was the Majority Leader. When various human opinions meet in discussion an impersonal voice is obtained which is democratic decision. The richest patterns in *Advise and Consent* are those created between the freedom of personality and the rules to which the people commit themselves. Thus Vice-President Lew Ayres succeeds the dead President Franchot Tone as automatically as a Kleenex tissue. And though he is overawed by his new office the immediate response of the Senate is of such trust that he is correspondingly heartened.

Advise and Consent illustrates a trend in Preminger's work: it is a thoroughly practical film about an abstract subject. The quality of justice in *Anatomy of a Murder*, the saintliness of *St Joan*, the nature of faith in *The Cardinal* and the validity of nationalism in *Exodus* all share this paradox. In contrast to the definition of romanticism, Preminger is one of the most unatmospheric directors. So intent is he on the shifting movements of the characters that his Israel in *Exodus* and his small town in *Anatomy* seem as neutral as if in a newsreel. That sweeping pan over the landscape of Cyprus at the beginning of *Exodus* is not a pastoral movement; significantly it ends on Eva Marie Saint's eyes. The human perception and understanding of an event are more important to Preminger than the event itself. Thus his St Joan is not a saint but a girl some think a saint and others scorn. Her miracles are accomplished not with dramatic cuts or effects but during level and controlled shots. Similarly, the cynical are no more condemned than the charitable are elevated. Even though the Archbishop in *St Joan* mouths many of Shaw's sharpest comments on faith, Joan kneels before him and the camera rises above him in a complementary and ambivalent movement.

Shaw's play is, I think, equivocal about the nature of Joan. It is the attempt of an incredulous man to make himself believe. Consequently it is a miracle without passion. Such an absence is genuinely proper to Preminger because he thinks of Joan's life not as a miracle but as an event. Whereas Shaw was socially and politically aligned, the essence of Preminger's position is to be neutral to faith and faithful to his camera. He is at pains to reduce any prejudicial association. Early in *Anatomy* the judge, Joseph Welch, has to rebuke the court for their laughter at the mention of panties. Panties, he says, play a great part in the case and will be mentioned frequently. Laugh now and be done with it. Just as the audience is given a juridical duty this advice is directed to them as well as to the court. Preminger's purpose is to raise the political sense of his audience.

7

THE VISUAL SOCIETY

Documentary – Synthesis – Voyeurism – The Decline of Art

DOCUMENTARY

In the previous chapter I said that Otto Preminger was an unatmospheric director but that in *Advise and Consent* he presented a Washington that was utterly convincing. The atmosphere of activity is certainly conveyed by the film but this is as concrete as the space between people. There is no sense of the urban personality of Washington such as Rivette conjures out of Paris and Demy from Nice. The treatment is not subjective but documentary: Only when a film is most specifically about an object, rather than a subject, will it present facts, rather than one version of the truth, about it. Documentary does not follow upon an attitude to material but from a conception of the camera.

The description 'documentary' originated in the 1930s with the films of Grierson, Anstey, Elton and others, and the publication of Paul Rotha's *Documentary Film*. It was largely a reaction against the monopoly, in the absence of television, that the entertainment movie had on the uses of film. For Grierson and the others documentary was a value word to hold up like a shield of sincerity and commitment against 'the shimsham mechanics of the studio and the lily-fingered interpretation of the metropolitan actor'. Real people, real problems were the subject, 'the creative treatment of actuality' the hope.

The accumulation of a theory of documentary in Britain, as opposed to the idea of feature, was always more conscious of political and sociological reasons for its being than any further fulfilment of the film process. Significantly its chief subjects were the primitive natural existence in remote parts of the world and the degradation of some aspects of city life. Its indignation may have been justified, but the movement seems to have remained disapproving of advancing times. Furthermore its function was to bring to the general attention certain unnoticed peoples' lives. Today the level of television's reporting would make such a crusade unnecessary.

Grierson's distaste for the artificiality of Hollywood, and his sense of the unknown, unphotographed areas of English life inspired his own films. But by the standards film had already achieved this was a reactionary ideal only permitted by the imminence of war and the consequent demand for patriotic film. It was as if the English documentary-makers had not realized that in any film there is inevitably a level of documentary which derives from the process but which does not deny a liberation of fantasy. Film's nature is so reflexive that realism and surrealism are always capable of being held in balance. To suppose that some people have greater ontological integrity than others because they are more dependent on their own labour is often accompanied by supposing them worthy of being photographed because they are so unphotogenic. Both judgements expose a simplist subjectivity of political and aesthetic conviction that dismisses the nature of man revealed in the means of the film process. Their certainty is convergent, their poetry will be evoked rather than spontaneous.

A succession of visual facts does not necessarily constitute meaning, just as behaviour does not tend to explanation. In the way that Nicholas Ray once defended the discreteness of a film and its script, any person might say, 'If I understood myself, why should I continue to live?' Fact indicates personality in that it is open to unlimited interpretation. No event exists without the process by which it is apprehended and understood. It is irrelevant and impossible to refer it to an absolute standard like realism because the means of measurement cannot be extricated from the observation. The relationship between the real and the surreal is not distinct but blurred. The rational cannot be transgressed; it waits to be superseded.

The conjunction in Luis Bunuel's career of *L'Âge d'Or* and

Las Hurdes, the one ostensibly feature and the other documentary, demonstrates how far the personal use of film makes
distributors' categorizations meaningless. The images of *L'Âge
d'Or*, of Gaston Modot making love with Lya Lys in the mud
in the middle of a ceremony founding the Roman Empire, are
no less real or more fantastic than those in *Las Hurdes* of the
children putting poison herbs on their non-poisonous snake-
bites. Bunuel does not distinguish between interior and exterior
realities. The visual facts of the world bear witness to every
fantasy, and every dream is detailed by fact. Modot hurling a
pine tree, a harvesting machine, an archbishop, a giraffe and
feathers from a window is as reliable as the shots of piled bodies
in *Nuit et Brouillard*, while the last shot of *L'Âge d'Or*—a cross
draped with women's hair—is weirdly prophetic of the rooms
full of cut hair in Resnais's film.

To say that *Las Hurdes* is not a story film, and that *L'Âge d'Or*
is, is to illustrate the literary fallacy. In fact a film's subject is
to be found not in its script, or even in the director's account of
his intentions, but in the film-strip itself. The idea of a subject
may be so tenuous that it cannot be discovered or described.
As a result film permits man to discover a range of subjects
previously unknown and to take an attitude to them that would
have been impossible before the cinema. Among the films being
made today that fit the old description of documentary there are
some that so exercise this modernity that they frequently
confuse any spectator who still wishes to keep the categories
rigidly separate.

The documentary film-maker is less noticeable today. He
may also be an anthropologist, a journalist, a doctor or any
man on holiday with his 8-mm. camera. The description has to
be as wide as the uses of film, wide enough to embrace spacemen
as well as Chris Marker, who himself catches the tone of the
private traveller. *Lettre de Sibérie* begins: 'Je vous écris d'un
pays lointain', like a family letter.

The characteristic of Marker's films is not the subservience
of everything he has seen to an opinion about them, but a
deliberate combination of various methods of meaning and
information that constitutes an interior dialogue between
opinions. He is conscious of taking his camera to places that

though largely unknown are still the objects of many attributions of meaning: Siberia, China, Cuba and Israel. He is also aware of the power of the recording instruments he takes and of the epistemological traps involved in their use: he repeats the same strip of film about Iakoutsk in Siberia, giving three different impressions by using a Russian commentary, an American and his own comparatively detached synthesis.

The scenes from Iakoutsk that Marker chooses seem perfectly mundane: a car driving down a street, workmen making a road, a passer-by looking at the camera. But because he senses their flexibility they begin to reverberate with implication as the commentary adds the possibilities. This dual sense of existence, which ideally should charge all films, is particularly at the centre of the documentaries that have been called *cinéma-vérité*: the integration of the commonplace and the theatrical.

To the extent that these new films attempt to escape the older traditions of documentary and the conclusiveness of feature film they are scientific. Strangely enough, though unwilling to dictate their own course, they often repeat the situations that are familiar from the ostensibly contrived feature films. In Jean Rouch's *Chronique d'un Été* there is a sequence in which the people who have been interviewed during the film sit round a table together. The camera and tape record whatever direction their conversation takes. An African Negro asks a girl why she has numbers written on her arm: she is a Jewess and the numbers were printed on her at a concentration camp. There is potential in this incident for the most heightened dramatic movie. As it is, though, the question is asked, the answer given and the questioner stunned by the tactlessness of his ignorance. As in Resnais's *Muriel* the events seem withdrawn from us by their privacy and diverging into the universal as our imagination fills them. Rouch's people never submit to a total, dehumanizing conceptualization. They are like people we meet on the street, at the same time remote and yet images of ourselves. It is as if we were experimenting with them without ever harming their potential.

'*Cinéma-vérité*' is only one more category, but the films generally classified as such do have common factors in their production that are indicative of the state film has reached with the decline of the commercial feature. They are no longer the work of 'film directors' and wealthy production companies designed for circuit showing. Marker is a traveller, Jean Rouch is an anthropologist and the American films made by Drew Associates are sponsored by *Time-Life*. They employ fewer people and much simpler instruments than the large studios. Hand-held cameras and tape-recorders are able to capture events simultaneously and can be managed by only two people. The meticulous image achieved by a dozen highly-skilled technicians is jettisoned in favour of a more rapidly obtained 'snap'. These films have been criticized as being a form of emotional espionage, although what one is seeing is not a person being spied on but the fusion of camera and person. Even so, the morality of journalistic enquiry dominates the American films particularly. The subjects of the Drew-Leacock movies are usually celebrities quite used to being filmed, as in most of *Primary*—an account of the Kennedy-Hubert Humphrey election in Wisconsin in 1960—oblivious of any particular camera. In others, like *Jane*, *Eddie* and *The Chair*, there are public and private scenes, but even in the private scenes no direct link is made between the photographer and the subject. These are journalistic movies in that they are focused on an event—Jane Fonda's opening on Broadway in 'The Fun Couple', Eddie Sachs's attempt to win the Indianapolis 500, the moves to have Paul Crump's death sentence repealed. Consequently, their visual material has to be specific to the moment and the photographic quality is so impersonal that the spectator is led to judge not the morality, but the reality, of the event.

The main theme in the Drew-Leacock films is success; the idea they convey of emotional happiness being related to this success has perhaps been fed by Hollywood's genre of success stories. Thus Jane Fonda is having a love affair with her producer which flourishes while the play seems to be shaping well. But after the first-night failure their relationship is depressed, Jane stares into her dressing-room mirror and says, 'The script has to be better.' The producer, speaking to no one in particular, says, 'I know it has no story. The characters interest me.' One is convinced of the spontaneity of these lines, and yet they might also be the improvisation of intelligent actors or even unwitting comments on the philosophy of *cinéma-vérité*. The situation is reminiscent of Hollywood back-stage films, but the visual texture is rough and spontaneous, emphasizing its momentary nature. It is tempting to see Jane's 'dropping' of the producer as cynical until one appreciates that the potential of context that the method conveys is so much greater than the feature allows, that such an imposition would be thoroughly unjustified interference. Similarly, in *The Chair*, the camera concentrates more on the defence lawyer, Don Moore, than on Crump himself.

In one sequence Moore is in his office waiting to hear whether Cardinal Cantwell will support the appeal for Crump. When he hears the good news, Moore says: 'He will? Oh, thank God, thank God! If you regard this as impertinent I wish you'd tell me, but will you read me the statement.' He writes it down and raises his fist in triumph. 'That's marvellous. Words fail me, Father. This is such a good thing to do. You're in my prayers, Father.' He puts out a cigarette, leans back in his chair and for a long time can only shuffle in his seat. He puts his hands over his eyes and cries. 'I don't even believe in God. That's it. That's it. That's a ball-game.'

One's reactions are contradictory. The sense of actuality excites; Moore's emotion slightly repels. Perhaps Moore is just an ambitious man, and yet he helps save Crump's life, a worthy humanitarian end. Such speculation only demonstrates how little value the supply of motivation has for the people in this sort of film. You are shown Don Moore and Jane Fonda. Possibly both 'act' for their cameraman in a few instances, even if subconsciously. One might argue that Jane Fonda had been so exhausted by the confidential camera in the fortnight before opening night that her stage performance was depleted. But such a reading is an attempt to solve the material one has seen, and implies an inheritance from feature film and the classical novel that there is a complex or riddle, like 'Rosebud' in *Kane*, waiting to be solved. The value of these films is the degree to which they multiply response, increasing one's awareness of the means of film so that one is as uncertain as Jane Fonda about which of her actions are more artificial or more sincere than the others.

Richard Leacock has denied being a sociologist and admitted the excitement of watching people. He admits his need for a subject that is intent enough on its intrinsic narrative not to be upset, and yet there are startlingly rich images that strike one because of what they seem to crystallize: Moore, after the commutation, at the races, watching a horse win embodies the social drive for success just as the close-up of Jane Fonda as she reads Walter Kerr's review—'Oh God, it's really like needles'—presents a personal sorrow. The success and the sorrow are subject to the same test of reality so that even allowing for Leacock's lack of ambition his films offer unique insights into the values of a society.

Rouch's *Chronique d'un Été*, although the product of a sociologically trained man, is less socially interesting. It removes the pressure of real life and substitutes that of the camera. Some of the most interesting moments in the Drew-Leacock films are when people are doing nothing except looking at things—the interval between words when Moore puts down the phone and simply allows himself to pause accentuates the sense of phenomenon. There are many such moments in *Chronique d'un Été* which takes ordinary, non-famous people and begins by asking them 'Are you happy?' Each person is interviewed twice, at the beginning and end of the summer. Afterwards, all the characters gather in a cinema and see the assembled material. The material is amorphous, shooting being terminated arbitrarily but without any attempt to inject completeness. It is open-ended, and it does not claim to be reliable; in the discussion some of the people say they were acting. All have been conscious of the machinery of the film, and exposed by its unwillingness to direct them. The moving images record them; the flat screen makes theatre of them. The sort of complexity that has been revealed in their lives and the difficulties they have in securing a basis of reality against which to reassure themselves make the original question irrelevant, even though it pertains to an ideal that is commonly held.

By concentrating so completely on its own interviews, *Chronique d'un Été* gives the impression of being a series of exercises among a group of actors. It makes the separation of meaning and existence we have noted earlier, and just as we sense a reality surrounding each character that would extend infinitely as we attempted to fasten on a piece of 'evidence', so the characters themselves perhaps realize the way in which they are understood. In his attitude to material Rouch has limited his own intrusion as far as he is able. He wants his subjects to lay down the terms with which they may be measured: these terms are communicative, for the film makes a connection of the sort that the oldest documentary-makers intended. We note identity with these people, but not at a simply economic, social or national level. As if they were our children we sense that they are an extension of us and we of them.

It is in the broadest cultural connections that Marker's and Rouch's films are so successful. Marker's work is almost entirely that of a traveller encountering foreign cultures and Rouch's introduction of Negro to White reaches a magnificent climax in *Lion Hunt*, which concerns the ritual of a primitive and remote West African tribe. Shot over a period of seven years, the final version is, as always with Rouch, a compromise with the time-limits of exhibition; ideally one would see all the footage. But, although cut down, one feels the great time and effort contributed by the Africans to the killing of the lion and the cultural role it plays for them. The camera does not seem an intrusion; indeed, Rouch's Parisians are much more embarrassed by it. At the same time, for the Parisians and the Africans it serves as an analog of their experience. For the Parisians it is the constant eye of existence around which their complexities revolve, and for the Africans it is the straight, narrative line of time recording the details of past hunts like memory for an illiterate culture. *Lion Hunt* begins and ends with the story of the hunt being told round the camp fire to children of the tribe. It is Rouch's achievement that while this is a primitive ritual he convinces us that it is the same sort of experience as his Parisians have. In both cases he has gone so directly to the cultural life of the two groups of people that we do not feel the need of an 'artistic' version of it. The Africans' faith in the simplicity of events and the Parisians' in their ferment both undermine any imposed balance. If it does occur it will be by chance.

SYNTHESIS

Just as Rouch's *Lion Hunt* impresses as an epic adventure and as a factual account, so all Godard's films are not only the events of their plots and characters but documentaries on the making of a film. Godard's interest in the cinema is such that his work can have no other subject. He is at the same time the last great artistic director—because of the prestige he has—and the first great new film-maker in that he synthesizes the two categories of cinema, the film director and the scientist, the artist and the layman. With synthesis there comes dissolution of previous terminology. Every person rediscovers his infinite capacity. In *Bande à Part* two of the central characters are travelling in the Metro. They look at a man and imagine two reasons for his presence: he is transporting a bomb; he is visiting his child in hospital. Benovolence and malevolence are supported equally by the man's bland face. There is no meaning in the world, only supposition and its food, fact.

If one tries to discuss Godard's characters, in the way one talks of Hitchcock's or Renoir's, one notices immediately how they straddle the worlds of the film and the film-makers, not in the idyllic sense of Renoir, but because of an insecurity of identity deriving from a contemporary inability to discern reality from fantasy. People are isolated and their attempts at communication are only the sending of conflicting signals. The audio-visual society is such that words are no longer the perfect Jamesian instrument of intention. *Vivre Sa Vie* opens with Nana in a café, about to end an affair with Paul:

'PAUL: Ce type, il t'intéresse vraiment?

NANA: Tu sais . . . je ne sais pas, je me demande à quoi je pense.

PAUL: Il a plus d'argent que moi?

NANA: Qu'est-ce que ça peut te faire? Qu'est-ce que ça peut te faire? . . . Qu'est-ce que ça peut te faire? Qu'est-ce que ça peut te faire?

PAUL: Ca ne va pas . . . non?

NANA: Non . . . rien . . . je voulais dire cette phrase avec une
idée précise . . . et je savais pas quelle était la meilleure
façon d'exprimer cette idée, ou plutôt, je le savais, mais
maintenant je ne le sais plus . . . alors que justement je
devrais le savoir.'*

Nana can be no more confident of social criteria than she
can of understanding between people. Godard shoots the scene
with such disregard for cinematic convention that Nana and
Paul sit with their backs to the camera. The absence of an
attempt to make a connection of understanding with the
audience predicts the course of the rest of the film in which
Nana becomes a prostitute, falls in love with a young man, but
is killed as one pimp double-crosses another. These events are
not experienced as narrative because Nana encounters them
without purpose. In all of Godard's films there exists a state of
spiritual boredom which is the complement of an awe of discovery. Macha Meril in *Une Femme Mariée* is shocked by nothing
because she knows anything can happen. Like Anna Karina in
Vivre Sa Vie she measures her reactions and attempts to define
her position. The social obstacles to being a prostitute or to
loving two men at the same time are irrelevant. Attempts to
understand life, to finalize its complexities are useless but they
cannot be avoided because the human intelligence has reached
the stage of evolution when every event is interrogatory.

In a conversation with Nana, the philosopher, Brice Parain,
tells a story about Porthos from *The Three Musketeers*. Porthos
has planted a bomb. As he walks away he looks at his feet and
wonders how they move. He stops. The bomb explodes, and
as Parain says, 'La première fois qu'il a pensé, il en est mort.'
This tragic joke forebodes the frailty of intellect, and when
Nana finds someone to love they read Edgar Allan Poe's story,
The Oval Mirror, in which a young man paints (or renders
into Art) the woman he loves.

'Et, pendant un moment, le peinture se tint en extase devant
le travail qu'il avait travaillé . . . mais une minute après, comme
l contemplait encore, il tremblait et il fut frappé d'effroi. Il

* *Vivre Sa Vie, L'Avant-Scène*, No. 19.

criant d'une voix éclante: "En vérité, c'est la vie elle-même!"
Il se retourna brusquement pour regarder sa bien-aimée . . .
elle était morte.'*

The literary allusiveness is typical of Godard's work because
his men in particular are representatives of a literary culture
having landed on a new planet seeing the situations of literature occur haphazardly instead of purposefully. In *Le Petit
Soldat* the end of Cocteau's *Thomas l'Imposteur* is quoted: 'Une
balle, se dit-il, je suis perdu si je ne fais pas semblant d'être
mort. Mais, en lui, la fiction et la réalité ne formaient qu'un.
Guillaume Thomas était mort.' The sort of consciousness that
witnesses its own death is exactly that of the actress watching
herself die on the screen, and Godard's usual actress is Anna
Karina, his wife and ex-wife. This personal association is of
great importance in Godard's movies in that there exists a
tension between the cinematic enjoyment of Karina and the
literary understanding of her. This tension is strongest in *Pierrot
le Fou* in which Belmondo plays a writer who runs away from a
political maelstrom with Karina. Their love is constantly
threatened by his intellectuality and the contrast it makes with
her intuitiveness. Thus Godard associates the woman, either
Karina or Macha Meril, most closely with the nature of film,
while the man has the greater difficulty in conforming with the
novel conditions of the visual society. All moral and authoritative criteria have vanished and in their place there exist
equivalents of the camera's rules: life must move on; from one
instant to another anything can happen; one cannot judge by
appearances.

The logical consequence of these new rules is a society
towards which Godard's films have been gradually evolving.
It embodies the view that people are so effectively isolated by
loneliness and subjectivity that they are like machines and that
the only possible way to continue to live without breaking down
is as a machine. Godard has thus turned Cocteau's romantic
flourish at the end of *Thomas* to an image of a machine recording
its own cessation. The ending of *Pierrot le Fou* in which Belmondo
wraps his head round with dynamite, lights the fuse and is
unable to extinguish it in time, is an experiment and an accident

* *L'Avant-Scène.*

because life has reached a stage when every action is an experiment and when every consequence can be experienced as an accident.

It is the complete dissolution of the humanist tradition. The conscience of the computer rather than that of the most sensitive artist is required to measure events. A perfect example of this is the return of the two soldiers, Ulysse and Michel-Ange, from the war in *Les Carabiniers*. They bring back postcards as symbols of their plunder. In a long, monotonous shot they put one after another on the table, their dull voices itemizing their titles. Cities, art treasures, beautiful women, wonders of the world. The fantastic contained by the commonplace. Godard's style is utterly photographic and non-interpretative. There is no question of how accurately the camera is recording an event. No more distinction exists between the two than between Rouch's tribesmen and their lion.

People cannot understand each other but neither can they avoid each other. The spatial relationship is the only language of human relationships. The hands that come together across a sheet at the beginning and part at the end of *Une Femme Mariée* are attempts at a relationship. They are very personal emblems of sexuality representing the nakedness of the rest of the body. The images of hands, thighs, knees, shoulders and faces are cut together, creating an effect of serene eroticism. But this serenity is not romantic; it is the response of detachment. The hands are not only the private means of touch and caress but signs of identity—the rings indicating married status, smoothness female and hair male. They are at the same time intimate and impersonal. Their actions are independent to the point of being mechanical and consequently their intentions are interchangeable. The emotion in these sequences is by necessity generalized because Macha Meril senses the fallibility of depending upon personalization. This reflective automatization of private behaviour is very typical of Godard and it constitutes what one might call a bathroom apprehension of life. Allowing that in the bathroom the most personal acts are carried out with the least self-consciousness, the torture scene in *Le Petit Soldat* and the analysis of prostitution in *Vivre Sa Vie* provide further examples of the way in which emotional involvement to the extent of degradation is absolved by a cold, factual account. Anna Karina lying with customer after customer and washing her hands between sessions—like the couples in *Une Femme Mariée*—paradoxically discovers her soul through a consciousness of her precarious withdrawal. She might say like Meril: 'Je sais pas c'qui arrive . . . Ca m'empêche de devenir folle.'

The face of Macha Meril is a sign of human existence and human mortality: its elements are its own means of observation —eyes, ears, nose and mouth. Almost as if we were looking at the face of an insect we reject attributions of our own meaning and ideas that we might apply to it. We realize the anthropomorphism of such ideas. Looking at her face is like looking at a camera.

The means by which the apparatus of the film observes the characters is equally mechanical. No attempt is made to make them items in a construct or to make incidents pregnant with the evidence they contribute towards a construct. The sequence of events is perfectly compatible with the camera, rather than with the intellect. Godard's characters are in a position of affluence that is typical of the Western potential. They are cut off from the simple pastoral reality that supports life and from the possibility of finite relationships; they face the capacity of a mechanized society. The 'social' and 'economic' pressures on character of the novel have been removed and no profounder sequence is looked for than that of time. The variations of outer form in the different films are all random, even in *Vivre Sa Vie* which is divided into chapters, but where there is such a contrast between the literary structure and the inconsequent, unmotivated events that we realize that the idea of Karina's life that the chapters convey does not exclude all others from her consciousness. Her discovery of her own soul is not a religious experience or the artistic climax of self-knowledge like Lear's 'I am a very foolish, fond old man', but her description for herself of a consciousness, a method of treating chaos without being overcome by it.

Godard's people move and act, often, as if by random selection, pleased to be free from choice. In *Pierrot le Fou* Belmondo runs away with Karina on impulse without questioning the corpse in her room. He is a writer and he has recollections of a literary culture—when he falls in love with her he cries. They move south into an image of the primaeval forest, living alone on an island with a fox and a parrot. In this unaccompanied existence man is not a social being but a species characterizing his surroundings with his imaginative projections. The removal of the signs of society fulfils the consciousness they have already reached. For the idea of society has existed long enough in the abstract without a practical example and now must be given up. Like language it is not absolute but is effective only for as long as people respect it, like the rules of a game. The actions are private, their immediacy of execution overcoming doubts about explanation just as their physical contiguity obliterates the idea of emotional communication. The great actions in Godard's films—Karina dancing and writing a letter in *Vivre Sa Vie*; the moment's silence in *Bande à Part*; Macha Meril being chased by her husband through their house in *Une Femme Mariée*, and Belmondo and Karina crossing a river in *Pierrot*—are not indications of character and meaning, but revelations of total cinema in the sense that the cinematic method is providing a complete replica of human experience. The equality Godard's work realizes is a chilling one: that every person, every event is equally worth watching, that choice and selection, the distinctions of the artist, are tyrannous and deluding. *Pierrot le Fou* is perhaps the first film that does not aspire to or need to be a masterpiece. It is a freedom won with more difficulty than its flawless autonomy suggests, for *Alphaville* does need to be a great work. In consequence it is Godard's dullest film. The primitive adoption of forces of good and evil has reverted to a tension of narrative and philosophical banality even though some of the particularization—Caution's arrival at the hotel, for instance—are brilliant metaphors of our present degradation. *Alphaville*'s intellectual pessimism makes it the sort of film Belmondo in *Pierrot* might have made. In it the savagery of life is focused sharply on its contemporary examples. The feminine imperturbability of *Pierrot* absolves the savagery and observes the events. Godard's greatest admission is his humility before Karina, who was his wife when they made *Vivre Sa Vie*, but who had left him when they made *Pierrot le Fou*.

VOYEURISM

Godard's is as yet the only demonstration of a visual society to have emerged from the feature film that is convincingly complete in that the fact of authorship does not seem to intrude on our experience of it. Many will argue against even the likelihood of a visual society, indicating the enormous disparity between an advanced European intellectual and Afro-Asian peasants. But Rouch's *Lion Hunt* has demonstrated how easily such primitive societies may grasp the workings of a visual culture, missing out altogether the literary stage.

The visual society reacts upon itself until it produces a visible society. The camera's verdict that although everyone looks different they are subject to the same general conditions is an analogy of the political state of democracy, and the difficulty with which Godard reaches a totally non-authoritarian directorship is the equivalent of the problem of the political leader in a democracy that Preminger has observed, that out of a proper doubt and dissension must come decision which, however much a compromise or consensus, must offend some members of the democracy as sharply as if it were the act of an acknowledged dictator.

For the member of a visual society democracy is one alternative to inertia. We first see Jean-Paul Belmondo in *Pierrot le Fou* in his bath reading Fauré on Velazquez to his daughter and then at a party where conversation has become formalized into the exaggerations of advertising. His experiment with Karina is a reaction against the impossibility of either the domestic or the social life. But, again, like a democrat, Belmondo in his adventure has to balance the unreasonableness and the unavoidability of acting. He is a contemplative being forced into motion. Thus even his frequent attempts to write a novel are activated by the camera panning with his writing hand in big close-up so that the words and the colour of the ink assume, like Johns's letters, iconographic meanings beyond their linguistic function. His name is Ferdinand but Karina keeps calling him 'Pierrot le Fou', a mythical gangster, and leading him towards the activity of Pierrot. There is no better cinematic equivalent of a Heisenbergian uncertainty in the *mise-en-scène* which overcomes not only Belmondo's conceptualization but sixty years of cinematic tradition. The adventure into the south in *Pierrot* is into a world of such spontaneity as to constitute a parody of the manipulative power of a script, a director or an artist.

If we compare the relationship between a leader and the members of society with that which exists between people in a film and the film's *mise-en-scène* we are comparing not parts of the systems of government and cinema but the mutual communication that is, in both cases, the whole thing of which every item—whether, say, the cutting in the film, or the confidence in the state—is an expression. Only with a leader can the diverse individuals conceive of a focus to the ordering of their events and only with the confidence that some of the figures seen on a screen are the film's characters can the audience begin to perceive information out of the mass of fact. Just as such an identification limits the characters so the acclamation as leader impedes the function of leadership. The leader is the apex of political systems in whom the abstract ideals of the state and society may be made concrete. The more totalitarian the leader the greater the gap between the natural state of chaos and the version of organization that is offered to the people.

A more democratic conception is also more adventurous because, even if minimally, it encourages a greater acceptance of the chaos of human divergence. The leader needs increasingly to be seen, not at the demand of the visual society, but because the idea of a visual society is gaining currency irrespective of supporting evidence. Thus there is a general belief that Kennedy won the presidency because he outshone Nixon in television debates, that Home was forced out of office and leadership because of his inability in front of the camera and that Lecanuet reordered French political alignment because he took advantage of television. This level of belief directly stimulates subsequent politicians to a visual consciousness without necessarily attempting to verify the hypothesis.

This idea contains an affront to the moral literary conscience, like that of film-stars being paid more than politicians, because it seems to suppose that people may be elected on grounds other than fitness for office and that demagogy is being invited into politics. In fact, the visual apparatus itself is more penetrative of the idea of dissimulation than any other safeguard of liberties could hope to be because it allows us to appreciate that truthfulness is not a quality men can reliably recognize. Even if reproducing the doubt of personal contact it still offers a remarkable substitute for the communal involvement that democrats deplore as vanishing from society. The remedy is to advance the amount of coverage as rapidly as possible. But although Senator Kennedy took pains to attract every camera during his campaign, and attempted to open his administration to the cameras more than any previous president had done, it is still unthinkable that he would have allowed cameras to observe his councils during the Cuban crisis of October 1962 even though he had gained knowledge of the concentration of missiles in Cuba through the medium of photography. This contradiction is part of what seems the necessary privacy of democracy, but it can only be rationalized as an obstacle between people and leaders, the very relationship that democracy is supposed to represent. The most totalitarian governments are also those least visually manifested and nothing is more likely to disperse the unequal authority of leadership than a perpetual observation of it. *Point of Order*, the film of the Army versus McCarthy hearings, demonstrates the dislocations that can result when the process of observation is introduced during, rather than before, an event. When shown in England, twelve years after the hearings, *Point of Order* was called a modern morality in which Joseph Welch routed the villainous Senator McCarthy and Roy Cohn. Perhaps it needed Preminger's use of Welch in *Anatomy of a Murder* to show how rhetorical he is in *Point of Order*. McCarthy on the other hand appears as an unsophisticated visual performer, a politician who functioned through the means of politics and not the villain that Welch makes him out to be. The conclusion to be drawn from *Point of Order* is the necessity of observation. For Welch has the sophistication of self-knowledge and if McCarthy was a bigot he was so unconsciously, perhaps because he never had the opportunity to see how he appeared to others. His '*mise-en-scène*' of the hearings is, compared with Welch's, primitive and thus he appears in the wrong. He seems spied upon, and to Welch's skill he can only offer the dignity of the simpleton.

The issue of privacy in an advanced and liberal democracy is critical. Concomitant with the ideal that justice should be seen to be done is the legal requirement that a passer-by witnessing crime is bound to intervene. The status of the individual in a visual society has somehow to tolerate the demands of spectators, and has to be willing to be seen. The only way this can be achieved and the society still be advanced is if the spectators have a tolerant intelligence that is in many respects alien to the organization necessary to make society function. I would suggest that we need to redefine the word 'voyeur' in order to be able to describe this status properly.

The current understanding of voyeur is much broader than the dictionary provides for. This is largely because it is a word that has passed very quickly into common usage. It does not even occur in the third revised edition of the *Shorter Oxford English Dictionary*, published in 1955, and *Webster's Third New International Dictionary*, published in 1961, gives as primary meaning, 'one whose sexual desire is concentrated upon seeing sex organs and sexual acts'. We are certainly highly conscious of the sexual content of imagery and I think sex has always been one of the primary means of understanding film just as it influences the way people communicate with each other. But to the extent that much of this sexuality is subconscious we can define voyeurism more broadly. It can even be taken to mean the inclination to interpret people for oneself by looking at them that springs naturally from an urban existence that makes human contact commonplace and communication rare. Voyeurism is the interpretation of other people in one's own terms; a declaration of love is its climax. Clearly it focuses the issue of privacy sharply in that it provides a means of social realization and at the same time threatens interference.

Rear Window is a classic voyeurist movie in many ways analogous with the whole process of cinema, and it is worth considering it and another, Lang's *The Woman in the Window*, for their treatment of visual curiosity in modern society. The setting for *Rear Window* is exactly that of *Le Crime de Monsieur*

Lange: the well of a block of flats and the windows that look out on it. But whereas Renoir is concerned with the communal integration of this setting, Hitchcock, who never seems entirely to have lost the sensibility of a London suburbanite, isolates each inhabitant behind his window. The spectator's sense of a narrative derives from the camera being sited in James Stewart's room, where Stewart lies with a broken leg in plaster, with nothing to do but look out of the window. As such, his presence is not consistent with the habits of the other people in the block who at different times go out to work and come home again. Neither is his eye especially sympathetic to their lives, because he is a press photographer who leads a wandering and dangerous life. His apartment is not a home but a base. Visual events need to be not only exciting for him, they must reveal a meaning that constitutes news. Stewart's technical equipment of binoculars and telephoto viewfinders is advanced, but his sensitivity is crudely biased towards sensation rather than human involvement. He allows Grace Kelly, a girl who loves him, to come to his apartment every night with his dinner and to sit in his lap and kiss him, but he rejects the idea of marrying her.

Marriage is a relationship he can observe through his window. One husband is henpecked, taken less notice of than the dog; another, Raymond Burr, has an invalid wife, whose meals he cooks only for her to throw them on the floor. The fact that Stewart has seldom had to live in his apartment for long is implicit in the effect of intrusion his observation makes on these domestic lives. A similar change in routine occurs at the outset of *Woman in the Window*. Edward G. Robinson is a successful middle-aged businessman with a wife and children. It is summer and his family are going on holiday leaving him to follow them later; temporarily, he is able to assume something of the status of a bachelor. Just as Stewart's convalescence forces him into contact with the mundane, so Robinson's freedom admits the chance of encountering the exotic. One night at his club Robinson is joking with his friends about how he might exercise his summer freedom: the suggestions are the fantasies of respectable men. Robinson is left in an enveloping arm-chair taking an after-dinner sleep before going home.

Sleep for James Stewart is not a matter of routine. Unable to take exercise he sits all day and all night long in his wheelchair. He sleeps for an hour or two at a time when his boredom can find no alternative, an irregular pattern compared with the lives of the other people in the block. One stormy night he is awake often enough to become suspicious of what Raymond Burr is doing. There has been an angry argument with his wife and then several times during the night, despite torrential rain, Burr goes out carrying a heavy suitcase. In the morning the blinds are down in the wife's bedroom. Stewart believes that Burr has murdered her.

Robinson wakes from his sleep and leaves the club. He stops outside to look at the portrait of a woman in an art gallery window which has caught his attention earlier in the evening. The screen's frame at this point is a rich black save for the sharply outlined Robinson and the softer light on the portrait in the window. As Robinson is looking, Joan Bennett, the woman in the picture, walks into the darkness and stands next to him. She is charming to him and they go off together for a drink. When he takes her home to her apartment she invites him in. Her protector finds them there and attacks Robinson. A pair of scissors are to hand and Robinson kills to preserve his own life.

The predicaments in the two films are complementary and their relationship is increased by the fact that in neither film is the central character participating in events as is usual in film narrative. To that extent both movies are commentaries on film's sublimatory means of narration. Stewart is removed from the physical action until the end of *Rear Window* while Robinson's entire experience of *Woman in the Window* is really a dream from which he is awakened, still sitting in his chair at the club, at the end of the movie. By identifying the two characters with their audiences Lang and Hitchcock are commenting upon the cinema spectator's preconception that the visual events shown him should constitute a narrative.

The events in *Rear Window* slowly confirm Stewart's suspicions. He convinces Grace Kelly, Thelma Ritter, the nurse who visits him every day, and even Wendell Corey, his sceptical policeman friend. He continues his observation of Burr from the shadowy recesses of his own room. To gain more evidence he even telephones Burr to ask what he did with the head. Burr only discovers Stewart's whereabouts through another trick to gather proof. He finds Grace Kelly searching the apartment for the wife's wedding ring, which Stewart supposes she would be wearing if in fact she were on holiday. Kelly finds the ring and is only saved from Burr by the arrival of the police, called by Stewart. She gestures across the courtyard to Stewart with the ring she has put on her own finger. (Perhaps a fortuitous allusion to the marital intentions she has on Stewart—but perhaps Hitch's intimation of how their marriage might end.) Burr follows the direction of the gesture and looks into the camera. Stewart, alone and defenceless, prepares for Burr to come to his apartment with the only weapon he has to hand—flashbulbs.

But when Burr arrives the effect of menace is ambiguous. The real nature of the relationship between the two men is only revealed in their first physical confrontation. Burr opens the door and looks into the dark apartment, his head outlined against the light in the corridor. He asks, 'What do you want with me?' The figure of Stewart, scarcely discernible against the darkness of the room, does not answer. What, indeed, does he want with Burr? He wanted no involvement which might require understanding of motive and character. Burr has previously seemed to us a single-minded killer because we have seen him through Stewart's apparatus of inspection. But as he stands at the door he is a big, slightly awkward man, puzzled, frightened and, above all, tired. We remember perhaps that when he cooked the meals his wife rejected he tied an apron round his big waist.

Burr does at last advance ponderously on Stewart, blinded by the flashbulbs : at each explosion he takes off his thick-lensed spectacles and rubs at his eyes like a child. They struggle and Stewart falls out of the window. But he only breaks his other leg ; Burr is taken away.

Robinson's survival of the events of *Woman in the Window* is even less troubled. He blinks his eyes clear of sleep and his mind of dreams and goes home. But Robinson's dream has been the surfacing of his own fantasies, and the relentless progress of his original crime has led him to contemplate another murder and his own suicide. The setting of his dream does not differ from the setting of the rest of the film. As always, Lang's sets and lighting are stylized, not to the extent of expressionism but to a point at which one experiences both the fact and the moral implication of the events. Robinson's public life aspires to a degree of respectability which runs counter to the life he dreams about, but his own responses are as appropriate in either.

Similarly, the real impact of *Rear Window* is to point out the interference of Stewart's curiosity which would only be justified by moral criteria he does not seem to hold himself. His voyeurism is a symptom of social isolation and its method is not properly related to inflexible judgements. It is as much a sign of character as Robinson's dream is the admission of a suppressed side of his life. In both cases the implication is that character cannot be as arbitrarily and conveniently split as the people would like.

The cinema has nothing to do with the camera being unable to lie. It goes beyond lies or truth in any absolute sense, recognizing only the event and the observer, depending upon the quality of the process of observation and taking its moral direction by the consequences of the observation. Alain Resnais's *Nuit et Brouillard* has an apparently simple pattern of spectator and filmed event which, if entered into, imposes a dilemma on the spectator as severe as the film's subject: Auschwitz. Auschwitz is presented on two levels: original German or Allied newsreel of the camp and Resnais's own camera at the site of Auschwitz on a summer day ten years after the camp was entered by Allied troops. The act of presentation is enforced by the commentary which calmly notes a succession of facts about the camp: how the Jews were collected from the various occupied cities of Europe; their transportation to the camp; conditions of accommodation; their extermination; the use of by-products—hair, teeth fillings, skin; the figures involved. The commentary's precision and calm are those of industrial documentary. In the same way there is no sensationalism in the visual treatment. It has that remoteness of old newsreel. The spectator's difficulty in keeping his gaze directed at the screen is eased by the methodical commentary, the objectivity of the camera and the resignation of prisoners and guards. Any sign of protest would bring emotion rapidly and overpoweringly to the surface. But a strange new norm is achieved and one of the world's great traumatic experiences becomes a process. It is the calm that allows one to watch. The longer one watches the more one realizes that we are seeing people, the prisoners and the guards, like ourselves. There is not a wall of evil or madness separating us from Auschwitz. It has to be admitted for we are seeing the proof.

The climax of the commentary moves away from fact to responsibility. The conclusion it comes to, that we are all responsible, is no more than the implication of our own looking and admitting. The newsreel singles no one out as the responsible evil genius—there is, if you like, no Mabuse. We see the camp worked by people. We must share the responsibility once we have looked. It is with this thought that the film's form becomes significant. We had supposed the newsreel to be intercut with shots taken after 1945. But they could as well have been taken before the Nazi camp, and hence before a new concentration and solution.

THE DECLINE OF ART

When one writes a book about film it becomes necessary to describe what one has seen. Consequently the act of writing is likely to be as informative about the nature of writing as about the nature of cinema. The degree to which the account of moving images is an absurd attempt at an impossible duplication makes one aware of the gaps between a literary and a visual sensibility and between what we think of as art and what impresses as actuality.

I take up my pen to write that it is raining and in the middle of the sentence the sun comes out. The linear narrative was always an inexact representation of change, reducing the phenomenon to a proposition that might be informed with irony, melancholy or joy, but which was as restricted by the current range of human reference as by the number of words that could be used to describe it. Literature is, like acting, an

27. Jean Renoir's presence in *La Règle du Jeu* is an encouragement to his friends who are also his actors.

28. There are some situations one has to sit out, keeping steady and seeing the funny side of things. Bogart and Bacall in *The Big Sleep*.

29, 30. *Vertigo.* James Stewart and the two Kim Novaks. In both scenes Stewart looms menacingly above her. In the first she ignores him and thus increases his attraction, but in the second she recoils from it.

imitation. Its progress has been towards realism and the emotional density of Henry James is its apotheosis. But as well as the fullest implementation of a literary possibility James is an example of a mind ineradicably shaped by the literary culture. The systems of literature made concrete a moral and artistic establishment that required as subject the convention of London society and the more unique nature of Mrs Brookenham's circle. Even as his novels are dazzling in their skill and insight they are depressing in the servitude they reveal.

Even Ernest Hemingway, whose best prose moves into the very narrow straits modernity allows, hoped that some things he had written might last beside the work of the masters he had had his education from. In the book in which he was most conscious of the disparity between written account and an event, *Death in the Afternoon*, he was forced to allow that bull-fighting was an impermanent art and that the past masters, Belmonte and Joselito, would not again be equalled. The respect for the monumental in art that we find in Hemingway is, of course, the conservation of the literary culture and it is a profound reaction to the conditions of social, let alone scientific, evolution. If persisted in, today, in the face of such rapid change, it is very difficult for this faith not to find itself associated with the forces of political and social reaction and for the aspirations towards aristocracy in a writer like Hemingway to be made plain. The sense of Wolfean loss that is in Hemingway's 'Pamplona now is changed; they have built apartment buildings out over all the sweep of plain that ran to the edge of the plateau; so now you cannot see the mountain' is as much an aristocratic melancholy as old Touchett's slow release of life on the English lawn at the opening of *The Portrait of a Lady*.

Touchett looks fearfully forward to 1916, during which year Henry James died and the Somme was fought, and Hemingway's sadness over Pamplona to the great cities he so carefully avoided and to Auschwitz and Hiroshima, respectively the parody and the destruction of the idea of a city. Such immense demonstrations of the cruel, senseless and unenlightened aspects of humanity fulfil James's sense of irrational evil and demolish Hemingway's defence of an honourable way of life. What both would have denied has been accomplished: the individual's validity is only one in a collection of different coloured spheres like the parts of models of molecular structures. Those things Hemingway found impermanent because of their mutability have come closer to the rhythm of the times.

It would seem that the onus of art had moved towards the camera, and, indeed, during the 1920s and 1930s particularly and still in some places today, the Art of the Film is believed in. But has not the onus of art vanished entirely? The idea of film as a director's medium necessarily involved an emphasis on editing, the means by which the director could inflict his personality upon the film strip. Today we are beginning to recognize the mechanical nature of the medium and to avoid the sterility of the artistic cinema. The cinema affords the first mechanical, rather than human, means of reconstructing events and as such it allows a novel impersonality of approach because the recognition of chaos is only possible if there exists a preconception of order. Thus the liberal withdrawal from the state of chaos may be replaced by what is merely a factual observation of it.

Art will decline as meaning subsides. The novel is the classical expression of meaning and in the cinema Hitchcock is the greatest elucidator of meaning. To note the failure of both James and Hitchcock is to step outside their own terms, something that time accomplished during their own lifetimes. Let us compare two classical works: *What Maisie Knew* and *Psycho*. The most striking characteristic they share is that of being so highly wrought. It is possible to take details from either and see them as microcosmic of the general effect. Both are brimming with intelligence and purpose and utterly sparse of incidents that do not assist this purpose.

What Maisie Knew has one idea to which James was stimulated by a newspaper report of divorce proceedings. Maisie is a child who must live six months of the year with her mother and six months with her father. Both parents remarry and both subsequently indulge in further adultery. Significantly this action is symmetrical and noticeably James feels it as an expression of a human selfishness and irresponsibility that is close to evil. Maisie is supposed by her elders to be open to corruption simply by 'knowing about' what is going on around her but, in fact, though she may notice events she does not know them for the evil that the participants, and James, consider them.

The elaboration of syntax supports an irony which is frequently accurate to a minute point and which comes from the detached moral consciousness of the author. But at times that detachment is felt by the reader to be a gap between life and the moral consciousness and at those times the efforts of the prose to report every nuance of the situation reflect a protocol and etiquette that are strangling the society. The whole predicament of Maisie allows James to revel in the levels of hierarchy in the name of a child's naïve observation. Too often one is struck not by her ignorant innocence but by the author's skill in establishing that infancy at the same time as giving an 'adult' narrative of the events.

The effect of *Maisie* depends on James's confidence in reality and the reference of people and events to a morality enforced by the confidence; it followed that literary perfection might be contained in an effect that was artistic because of its balance. Thus in *Maisie* there is an ironic balance between Maisie's knowledge and her elders' expectations of her. Childish purity and adult wickedness were credible extremes of behaviour for James between which it might be possible to achieve a life that was adult and morally responsible. Such a hope is not private to James, it is the faith of liberals everywhere. But it is only possible for as long as the conceptions of purity and wickedness remain valid and for as long as the author's manipulation of his own characters does not seem interfering.

There is in James all the subtle dogmatism of a sensitive moral conscience living off private means at the centre of an Empire. Time has added a further irony to his own in under-lining those intimations of the twentieth century that he had. It now seems less reprehensible of Maisie's parents and step-parents and thus it appears that in the novel they are given so little chance. The novelist's design has excluded them from our sympathy so exclusively that they now insinuate themselves despite the total apparatus of the book. The true irony of Maisie's predicament seems to have escaped James himself. Thus when Mrs Wix says to her, 'What I did lose patience at this morning was at how it was that without your seeming to condemn—for you didn't, you remember!—you yet did seem to *know*', James is unwittingly predicting the ethic of the camera in the way that that 'shot' from *The Portrait of a Lady* is a clue to its sensitivity.

In that *Maisie* is about society's disguise of the sordid and *Psycho* is about its violent irruption into life the works share a sense of restriction that applies not only to the characters but to the spectators. *Psycho*'s images are of people menaced by physical objects, the menace being extracted from a continuum by some of Hitchcock's most calculated measures. As one sees the film one sees the skeleton of that intention fleshed out perfectly. The film's claustrophobia springs not just from confined space but financial circumstances, parental influence and the simple act of looking. Obsession crowds out reason and preconception sight.

Hitchcock's advancing camera takes us towards the façade of a skyscraper in Phoenix City that has emerged from Saul Bass's credit titles of disintegrating and re-forming skyscrapers. It picks out one window, open six inches with the blind down. The gap is narrow and excitingly dark. The camera slides through, sucking in its audience. The interior is a rented room. Janet Leigh and John Gavin are on the bed making unachieved love in the half-light. She still wears her brassière and a slip. These details may seem titillatory, and that is their very significance. For Janet Leigh is presented as provocatively as a lingerie advertisement, the textual contrast between the nylon underclothes and her glistening midriff much more disturbing to the audience and to Gavin than nakedness would be. The sequence is contraceptive to passion and encouraging pornography. They are secretive, meeting only in lunch-hours, because they want no one to know, illicit because they cannot yet afford to marry. The frustration makes them irritable. The room is not only a sign of their condition but a cause of their further dissatisfaction. Later, in her office, Janet Leigh has the chance to steal a lot of money deposited by a client. Her boss trusts her to bank it. On the excuse of a headache she goes back to her apartment. Her debate about taking the money is not dramatized. We simply see the bag holding the money on the bed while she changes her clothes so relentless is its compulsion. For the second time we see her undressed, though this time her actions are so purposeful that the effect is functional as well as erotic.

As she is driving out of Phoenix her boss sees her, looking down at her, and at the camera, through the window of her car. He looks puzzled because he would have expected her to be at the bank. She drives on and halts at a garage and used-car lot. Afraid of being traced she trades in her car for another, so anxious that she takes an absurd loss on the deal. Then she drives on into the night and the rain, with the money and a growing panic at what she has done. As the accumulated frustration overcame her in stealing the money, fear and the impetus of her own action stop her turning back. In the car that takes her on there is the illusion of security and her own control.

The first night she sleeps in the car, but as darkness descends on the second night and her increasingly worried face is illuminated only by the headlights of passing cars, she sees the sign of a motel and stops. She can have little accurate idea of her position and less of her own intentions. Her dilemma is constricting her freedom, and the choice she makes in stopping is, of course, fatal. The motel has no guests. Its owner, Anthony Perkins, had forgotten to turn the light off. The invitation is a trap. It is natural that with a car she should stop at a motel, but less natural, one feels, on learning that her destination, the town where Gavin lives, is only a few miles farther on. There is a similar delayed questioning of why the motel sign should be alight. Perkins claims to have forgotten to turn it off. But this implies it has burnt all through the day. Would he not have forgotten only to turn it on?

The car has taken control of her, mastering the pusillanimous vacuum left by the shock of her crime, and while she drove this fear began to work on her. Her drive has not been the experience of landscape or journey but the oppression of guilt. She hears the evidence accumulated against her so that her emotional flight into the night is countered by a growing rational desire to turn back. The change is illustrated by the rain that falls. In Phoenix it had been hot and dry, essentially a town in the middle of the desert. The rain now streams down the windows of the car, picking up every passing light, making visibility worse, but not touching, only surrounding, Leigh. To drive in these conditions, and at the same time to realize her mistake in taking the money and leaving Phoenix, is an ordeal; what Francis Fergusson in an essay on *Oedipus Rex* calls, 'the suffering and perceiving part of the tragic rhythm'.*

In stopping at the providential motel, she surrenders not only to the conditions on the road, but subconsciously to the feeling that her whole action is wrong. At this point, about thirty minutes into the film, it is possible to conceive the ending of Janet Leigh returning next day to Phoenix, restoring the money and perhaps reordering her life. This 'short-story' form is even what she intends. But the weight of attention makes a solution of greater conclusiveness inevitable. Hitchcock is not as concerned with her moral difficulty as we may have been led to believe. He goes on to eliminate Janet Leigh in a way that, by the terms of her story, is harsh but, judged by the way she has been presented to us, is eminently logical and takes the film deeper than its introductory level of anecdote.

The motel itself, its office and the chalets, are as modern in design as one would expect. There is a larger house on a rise above the motel, much older in style, its design more vertical and pointed than the low horizontals of the chalets. Although its height reminds us of the building in which we first discovered Leigh and Gavin, that we see it first in the dark rising above us like some dark house of horror is the introduction of an item from Gothic melodrama into a film so far completely contemporary with its hard lines of building, car, and object, and its morally indeterminate attitude towards the characters.

The change is made even more closely in the next sequence. The young man who runs the motel, Anthony Perkins, takes Leigh into the room next to the office and gives her milk and sandwiches. The office is bare and functional, but the room is much more in keeping with the style of the house. The furniture is old and heavy and the walls are covered with period prints and the stuffed bodies of birds; taxidermy is the young man's

* Francis Fergusson, *The Idea of a Theater*, Doubleday Anchor Books and Princeton University Press, 1949.

hobby. He lives in the house with his mother. And when he goes to fetch the sandwiches from the house we hear her talking to her son about Leigh, angry that he should have let her stay. The conversation that follows between Leigh and Perkins begins as commonplace. He seems a nice young man, if a little awkward. But when she questions his relations with his mother the awkwardness seems more ugly. Perkins appears to be kept prisoner from experience by his mother. The birds on the wall are made to assume menacing positions by dramatically subjective camera angles. The threat that now surrounds Leigh comes from the young man: his attitude to his mother constricts his awareness of Leigh's attractiveness. Thus the malevolence is still focused on Janet Leigh. One realizes that the whole film has had her under a succession of oppressively frustrating and threatening situations to which she has reacted, not sensibly, but instinctively as a bird—the creature to which Perkins likens her.

One may also realize that Leigh has been under pressure from the audience. For just as Hitchcock has been isolating and observing her, and the characters in the film have been staring at her, so we have been watching her anxiety and suffering. And with what feelings? An identifying process, certainly, as her attempt to escape enlists our sympathies; at the same time, with a detached excitement that is sadistic and voyeuristic. Her sexual attractiveness is shown and repeated, its lack of fulfilment disappoints us as well as her, so that there is some part in us that enjoys her ordeal, and joins Hitchcock in tightening the screws.

Whatever element of voyeurism we have experienced, it is now shared in the film by Perkins. For when Leigh goes to the chalet next to his office, he makes use of a peephole in the adjoining wall. His staring eye is ours if only because he sees what we see; Leigh, again in her underwear, taking off her brassière. Our view of this is curtailed by a cut, exact to the frame, which has the brassière unfastened and in her hands, the instant prior to removal—a stage, one may realize, that could not be achieved without its creating enough momentum to bare the breasts.

The killing that follows is a ritual sex-murder and the climactic rite in the drawn-out ceremony between film and audience. Leigh undresses to take a shower in the small bathroom adjoining her bedroom. This closet is in white tile, lit to the brightness of a furnace. It is also the most confined space in which we have seen her. Under the shower of water she seems like a praying angel in a Renaissance religious painting. This is immediately prior to her death and establishes her role as a martyr to the film's final purpose, an examination of Perkins; even so it is, to some extent, a gratuitous visual detail provided by Hitchcock's fertile imagination that is experienced as invention rather than spontaneity. The water falling on her is not only the fulfilment of the rain that beat against her car but the first visible sign of things affecting her conventionally groomed quality. Her hair, which has previously been crisply still, darkens and clings to her head: an image of the remote effect the audience's libido is beginning to have on her. Death and achievement follow. The figure of an old woman appears, blurred through the plastic shower curtains—like the original appearance of the motel through the windscreen. The curtain is drawn back and a cruel, phallic knife strikes repeatedly. Her blood mingles with the shower water that runs away through the plughole. The killer, of course, is Perkins himself, dressed up as his mother: his mother stuffed, with all the conflicting implications of one personality crowding out another.

A similar process has occurred in Hitchcock's scheme to suppress the spectator's intelligence. It is not the ingenuity or motivation of the murder that is the point of the film but the series of devices by which it is offered to and withdrawn from us. The voyeuristic impulse is worked by the most careful taunts. The actual story becomes less important as the spectator is drawn into the film more completely. The murder of Janet Leigh is made an expression of our reactions towards her as the first section of the film has aroused them. Perkins, Hitchcock's eventual subject, is by common definition a madman. The director's irony is to make his first fully mad act the expression of the audience's suppressed desires.

The final claustrophobia of *Psycho* is in its authoritarianism. Even in that scene between Leigh and Perkins in which her aberration is equated with his permanent illness the point is made through deliberate dialogue and sustained only by the psychic tension that has been accumulated. In a cooler visual context the comparison would be fanciful; such a moral equation is unthinkable in *Pierrot* because of the greater tolerance of the movie. Hitchcock's imperatives are as strict as his every shot is telling. The law-abiding morality is almost frigidly rigorous in Hitchcock and is more like the obedience demanded by a totalitarian state than, say, James's expansive exploration of moral limits. If one thinks of the film director as the technician-artist Hitchcock must be considered supreme, but already the disparity between his skill and the potential of his instruments has been made so obvious that what in *Vertigo* and *North by Northwest* is credibly a moral conscience is in *Psycho* a force of self-abusing cruelty.

In *The Cinema as Art*,* Ralph Stephenson and Jean Debrix quote approvingly from Henry James to describe the Art of cinema of showing 'the true essence of things': 'life is all inclusion and confusion, while art is all discrimination and selection.' Such a feeling is a true watershed between the literary, or artistic, culture and the cinematic, or scientific, culture. The cinema elides this division in the way it carries on the narrative tradition and yet redefines narrative in a way that recasts our estimate of all previous literature. Godard's films comply with no academy; they are not efforts to define mankind but research into the nature of the means by which every man may make his own attempt.

Pierrot is as simple and phenomenal as Jasper Johns's flags. Once the realization has been made, that a film can be made thus or a flag painted thus, the painter or director, without claiming to be an artist, has penetrated the ambiguity of illusion and reality and of experience and consciousness. They have turned on their sneering critics who said anyone can do that and demonstrated that such action is not infantile pretension but the fulfilment of a real freedom. Those paths of communication that had fallen into the hands of minorities have been given a general vindication. Godard's cinematic method is that of the snapshot; he may convince us that our own snapshots have factual and imaginative implications as

* Penguin, 1966.

rich as those of a classical painting, like Velazquez's *Las Meninas*, or a classical novel, like *What Maisie Knew*. It is a greater potential equality than those of economics or politics because it offers people the opportunity to see themselves as extraordinary.

FILM AND CIVILIZATION

Renoir and Godard – Commer-
cialism – Amateurism – Futurism

If movie man does exist as a useful generalization, able to
make and view films and to appear in them, and able to apply
this variety of roles to his whole life, is it enough to hope that
he may be able to see himself as more extraordinary? Is such a
man to be a reflective information machine, or will he ever
regret the lost powers of ignorance and the fantasy they encouraged? Are the paths of communication to enrich mankind or
merely to exercise him?

RENOIR AND GODARD

One of the cinematic disappointments of 1966 was that the
plans for Jean Renoir's new movie were abandoned. In the
July edition of *Cahiers du Cinéma* he said: 'Alors, maintenant
je sais que j'ai l'espoir d'un sens, pour ce film, l'espoir qu'il
signifiera quelque chose, et peut-être même quelque chose
d'intéressant.' Characteristically, he would say little more:
'Je crois absolument que le véritable sens d'un film ne se
découvre qu'en le tournant.' The film was not realized. There
was a plan: five episodes concerning people who instigated
revolutions, large or small, in their lives. But, said Renoir, he
distrusted plans. They were the curse of civilization. His own
plans collapsed. The film was to have been called *C'est La
Révolution* and in the same interview Renoir recalled how,
when a young man in the cavalry, this phrase had habitually
recognized any small insubordination. In France in 1966

neither Renoir's frustration nor the suppression of Rivette's *La Religieuse* prompted a revolution. Such disappointments are usual in our civilization.

Instead Renoir gave us a novel, his first, *Les Cahiers du Capitaine Georges*. It is a novel that recalls the style and mood of Maupassant, as one would expect, but it is also too exciting and moving to seem dated. Georges is the son of a good family at the time of the *belle époque*. As an adolescent he is introduced by his father to Gilberte, an accomplished and sophisticated courtesan, so that he shall lose his virginity and develop some manners. It is a successful experience and the pleasures Georges shares with Gilberte go towards making him a humane, humorous, tender but robust, vital but mortal man. The consciousness of this provokes him, in later life, to this thought: 'I find myself wondering, in the light of all that has happened, whether if Hitler had spent a few years in Gilberte's school, in that atmosphere of genuine civilization, he might not have been transformed.'*

When Renoir imagines the effect of a proper sexual and emotional education on Hitler he is acknowledging Hitler as the evil man of history and as a phenomenon which we all have to explain and absorb if we are to proceed without being haunted. My own suggestion that Hitler could not have occurred in an age of television is only another attempt to bring the rogue to heel and—in likening Hitler to a disease which might be prevented by a vaccine—an indication of how far we dehumanize Hitler, or assume that he was not human. And yet Hitler triumphantly expressed himself in his rise from lowly origins to dictatorial power. We feel bound to disapprove of him, but the spectacle of this man breaking through the machinery of state and society is not unlike that of an anarchist and existentialist hero. Whatever else he did, Hitler raised everyone's pulse and, by his example, forced a reappraisal of the civilized values we felt he endangered.

He exposed the liberal complacency that allowed one to disagree with what he said but persuaded one to defend to the death his right to say it. The ideal of tolerance had eventually to give way to mobilization and the most complete of wars.

* *The Notebooks of Captain Georges*, Jean Renoir, Collins, 1966.

Whereas the first war had seemed to end civilization by insisting on brutality, by carrying off the young of a generation and by coinciding with the overthrow of aristocracy, the second war transformed civilization. It was not only the British experience that national participation had never been greater. The civilians were not exempt: they were bombed and, through radio, made more conversant with the details of the war— though clearly not to the extent that we are now with the Vietnam war. The war also advanced the mechanization of society and its technology: the Maginôt line—the battle situation which had endured throughout the first war—was quickly outflanked. The intensity of bombing stimulated the production of a bomb which made any military preparations, other than an effective means for its delivery, irrelevant.

It was also a war in which we were unable to escape the compromise of politics. We were made to ally with the Russians and, in doing so, to reflect on what the war was about. As well as a war between Hitler and Churchill, between the axis and the allied powers, it was a struggle between fascism and communism, in which doctrines we felt uninvolved. Hitler, Stalin, and later Khrushchev, taught those who hoped for the peace of the world to be strong and to be ready. We had been too clever for ourselves in making the bomb. Under its eye our doctrines were equally self-interested and equally absurd. For all that men like Oppenheimer regretted what they had done, they did not notice that they had controlled man. There might be squabbles still over the new small countries—Cuba, Korea, Vietnam—but they were destructive games of ingenious cruelty which we tolerated: a theatrical performance that demonstrated how we had been neutralized and exposed our neglect of creative civilization.

There was nothing left but to develop, to become more prosperous, more relaxed, more free and, inevitably, more crowded. But how could we relax with the future yet so foreboding? By 1975 our roads would be jammed; by 2000 we should starve. Such awesome social problems confront us that the individual must be stoical. He cannot hope to understand, but he may be knowledgeable; knowledge is the currency of the age: half of the scientists who have ever lived are alive today.

Man knows himself; the computer mimics his brain as children in a zoo imitate the monkeys.

Godard's films are vibrant with the menace of this civilization: it is only thus that he is able to transform the reality of Paris into Alphaville, lost in the infinity of space, the manifestation of Éluard's capital of pain. There is no need to catalogue the aggravations of this civilization; it is enough to note how they coincide with its benefits. In *Pierrot* the clothes and cosmetics that enable people to look attractive and not to smell have become narcissistic fetishes, and in *Made in U.S.A.* the planes that allow travel bring constant noise in the air. When Belmondo's wife, in *Pierrot*, explains the ingenuity of her lingerie, he comments that this is 'le civilisation du cul'.

Although a reactionary, Belmondo revolts. He pursues what Karina recognizes as an implacably straight line to destruction, or, in the words of Céline (one of Godard's favourite authors), 'au bout de la nuit'. He argues that he is free; he can turn the wheel of the car in which he and Karina flee this way or that. A spin and they are off the road, in the sea, only to walk in another straight line along the water's edge. But Godard does not permit these contrary impulses, of directness and circularity, to stay unambiguous. In *Alphaville*, the imposed straight line becomes the expression of freedom. The condemned man, before he walks the plank into a swimming pool inhabited by Bondian huntresses, says: 'In order to create life it is merely necessary to advance in a straight line towards all that we love . . . The truth is that there is nothing true in man except love and faith, courage and tenderness, generosity and sacrifice; everything else is but the artifice created by the progress of your own blind ignorance.'*

But if a man observes his own direction as intently as Porthos did his own feet, the ambiguity may enchant him. The outward signs of the world become inscrutable. Authority is indistinguishable from a variety of organizations, and true love cannot be discerned from treachery. The suicide which Pierrot tries out like a new game comes near to being a statement of artistic self-denial: the pan that moves towards the sun, from the ragged column of smoke in which Belmondo

* *Alphaville*, Lorrimer Films, 1966.

has immolated himself, threatens the plausibility of making any more films.

Godard has already made three more films, however. In only one of these, *Made in U.S.A.*, does he retain Anna Karina. It is possible that in time it may appear as an experiment or as an act of exorcism but, at the moment, it does not communicate.

Godard's difficulty, quite apart from that dramatized in *Pierrot*, is symptomatic. He is now an established figure whose films are taken up by art-house circuits which, in Britain and America, reach an audience unsympathetic to the Hollywood traditions Godard is devoted to. Thus a reference to Bogart or Widmark is for Godard a homage; for his audience, it is the password of a cult. Despairing of a mass audience Godard may make films for his friends or, like Andy Warhol, for his own amusement. While in *Pierrot* his relationship with Karina had enriched the film, in *Made in U.S.A.* she is allowed no emotional or sexual relationship with anyone in the film. Like the Natasha von Braun in *Alphaville* she is reduced to an image of beauty in a complex political situation. She has become Godard's mouthpiece, speaking—at length, and with little interest—those thoughts which Belmondo in *Pierrot* puts in his notebook. The accusation Karina made to Belmondo, that he spoke to her in words when she looked at him with feelings, still seems accurate. Its tragedy is not evaded by imposing a sensibility on Karina; instead, Godard comes close to self-pity.

Increasingly, Godard's preoccupation has become factual: a concern for his own evolution, contemporary political events and the everyday objects and encounters which make his films so life-like. It may be that the feature form is something he has to transcend. It is an indication of his difficulty that, after *Made in U.S.A.*, it seems so hopeless, and of his commitment to the camera—to see only what it sees—that one does not eliminate the possibility of his finding a new form for film, cinematic or otherwise.

COMMERCIALISM

Since the main part of this book was written there has been a dramatic change in the terms of sale of old movies to television.

The figures in Chapter 3 were true for the 1965–6 winter. In the Spring 1965 *Sight and Sound* a Twentieth Century-Fox executive was reported as describing a buyers' market in which deals were done at £5,000 a picture. However, in November 1966 The *Evening Standard* carried a story that the share-value of companies like United Artists had risen considerably, chiefly because television companies were becoming increasingly interested in old movies: it was estimated that each film might be worth £170,000.

Even if these films are ones that were more successful in the cinemas, it is an extraordinary change. Significantly, it is only since the film companies have had such poor results that they have been taken over—Paramount now being a part of Gulf & Western—that their lost opportunity has been made so obvious. If the logic of television as a means of distribution had been appreciated, the film companies might by now have had a large stake in television.

It remains to be seen whether films of traditional feature length and character can be made for television alone. The odd one has already appeared: Don Siegel's *The Killers* was shot originally for television. Many television series are produced like films and, in the case of *Uncle*, *Batman*, and *Thunderbirds*, transfer to the cinema. Ken Russell's work is midway between the Hollywood biopic and a *Monitor* documentary on an artist. Emil de Antonio's new film, *Rush to Judgement*, has been made principally for television and the B.B.C. has paid a record £14,000 for it. Remembering Antonio's previous *Point of Order*, it is hard to imagine that Hollywood will produce anything more exciting in 1967.

It has made nothing remarkable in 1966 except *The Chase*. Hitchcock's *Torn Curtain* epitomizes the general decline of talented directors; more minor, but still interesting directors have not even been able to work. The Samuel Fuller who appears in *Pierrot*, announcing his intention of filming *Les Fleurs du Mal*, went back to America empty-handed and has been idle ever since.

Two of the most interesting things about Arthur Penn's *Chase* are the way it denies so many Hollywood traditions, and the director's suppression of the personality of the producer,

31. Jeanne Moreau and Claude Mann in *Baie des Anges*. The Mediterranean sun sustains faith so that the fantastic excursions into luxury are experiences of paradise.

32. Françoise Prevost and Betty Schneider in *Paris Nous Appartient*. The spatial bond exists but is unreliable.

33. James Stewart's inspection schematizes Raymond Burr in *Rear Window* just as Hitchcock's image does Stewart's condition.

34. Edward G. Robinson and Joan Bennett in *The Woman in the Window*. The killing has been done but the scissors are clean, the bright apartment is unused and the duplication in the mirrors hints at dream.

35. Anna Karina in *Vivre Sa Vie*. The 'narrative' of her life is no more restricting than the prostitution is degrading.

36. Two of Rouch's interviewees in *Chronique d'un Été* are introduced and a friendship begins.

37. Who is offering Janet Leigh the money so tauntingly? A character in *Psycho*, or Hitchcock himself?

38. *Une Femme Mariée*.
Looking at Macha
Meril is like looking
at a camera.

39, 40. *Pierrot le Fou*.
Belmondo and Karina
are Crusoes. She plays
in the forest while he
writes his novel. They
drive into the ocean
and escape with their
belongings.

the conventionally liberal and socially conscious Sam Spiegel who made *On the Waterfront*, *Bridge on the River Kwai* and *Lawrence of Arabia*. The idea of social comment in a study of the lynch-mob mentality is not new; it is to be seen in *Fury*, *The Ox-Bow Incident* and *The Dividing Line*. But all these earlier films end with the actuality or the prospect of justice being done. The real gulf between law and society has never been faced as it is in *The Chase*. The ending has the beaten-up and defeated sheriff leaving town with his wife: in Hollywood terms this is Gary Cooper deserting the town in *High Noon*. The retreat amounts to a rejection of America—*The Chase* is the sort of film that the American expatriate in *Paris Nous Appartient* might have made. Significantly, even with all its stars, *The Chase* was a failure in America.

Yet it is not only the climactic re-enactment of Ruby's shooting of Oswald that makes *The Chase* seem so American and so untypical of Hollywood. It is as if the layer of allegory and convention that has separated American life from its cinematic expression had been abandoned. Penn has never been a restrained director and *The Chase* is not understated, but there remain disturbing and almost casual insights: the debauchery and malice bred by idleness; the acceptance of adultery; the conception of children as degenerates; the abounding treachery and self-interest. It is a film that might appeal to the Losey of *The Criminal*—another expatriate—for the escaped convict who provokes the action is plunged into the town like a victim. When he is trapped in the used-car lot he even seems the film's hero, and one can see how easily there might emerge from this view of America a new hero who lives in his own country as if it were occupied. This new Resistance demands existentialist energy and psychic participation that may only manifest themselves in behaviour the community considers criminal. Stephen Rojack in Mailer's *An American Dream* is such a figure and the passion with which he senses the interlocking conspiracy against man is expressed in Mailer's 'The shits are killing us'.

The unreasoned malevolence that shoots down the convict at the end of *The Chase* is a dramatic event imposed by fact, an excitement the audience had become accustomed to by television. America saw Ruby shoot Oswald live and, in the view of a man like Rojack perhaps, lived more intensely through witnessing that death. They may have noticed afterwards how like a fictional account it was and, indeed, in the ingenuity of paranoia may have wondered if the whole affair was not as contrived as Cary Grant's 'death' in *North by Northwest*. At any rate, as well as shocking, I think the spectacle entertained. Apart from Oswald's death I would cite as instances of this confused involvement, Kennedy's funeral, the riots in Watts, the exchanges between Fulbright and Dean Rusk at hearings of the Senate Committee for Foreign Relations and any of Cassius Clay's fights or impromptu dialogues with interviewers.

But the economics of television insist that the bulk of its time be devoted to deliberate, labelled 'entertainment'. A success like *Z Cars* is extended until its freshness becomes mannerism, and a programme that wins an audience slowly— interesting only four million at first, say—may be curtailed. There are people in television who regret this pressure. Thus David Susskind, a leading American producer: 'I'm an intellectual who cares about television. There are some good things in it, tiny atolls in the oceans of junk . . . I'm mad at TV because I really love it and it's lousy. It's a very beautiful woman who looks abominable. The only way to fix it is to clean out the pack who are running it.' But are Susskind's atolls any more than greater sophistication and better production values: *The Defenders*, say, instead of *Perry Mason*?

Perhaps we should examine the conception of entertainment more closely. With Susskind's paternal intellectualism, Schramm, Lyle and Parker, in *Television and the Lives of our Children*, concerned themselves with whether or not TV made children passive but seemed to disregard the passivity in the relationship that the idea of entertainment implied between public and authority. Just as a man expects the state to provide employment, housing and welfare, so the remaining hours of idleness have to be supplied with entertainment. The danger with this speculation is that it associates one with the generations that like to recall all the little ways they had of amusing themselves on long winter evenings. I believe earlier generations were just as confirmed in habit, but they were not so ideologically organized. They could contemplate without being accused of vacuity. For all the technical advances, and for all the increased prosperity, the range of human variety and potential does not seem to extend. There is an assurance for the individual that his day is taken up by work, relaxation and sleep. With that plan in mind he could live to the end of his life without worry or risk. He can turn the television on in the evening as he would his light, to show that the house is occupied.

I do not think television is a medium for indigenous entertainment; and yet every day it entertains more people than any other medium. If the entertainment on television continues within the current limits then I believe the public is depriving itself of the medium's and its own potential; and yet this is its right, and it is a taste that perpetuates the commercial infrastructure that relates viewing figures and the revenue from advertising. The information accruing from what is an information medium is no more than a side-effect.

Television remains a revolution—not in our nature but in our forms of organization. Its effectiveness is that of the cinema—television only increases it—in connecting people with events. When television is expressing opinions or forms of entertainment in which the quality of event is most spurious, then it is not harmful so much as wasteful. If the majority of our television consists of this, we have discovered our tragedy: that for most of the time our most vital medium is boring us.

The misuse gives television so bad a reputation that many mistrust it. This may have been why in November 1966 the House of Commons rejected even the private experiment for televising Parliament. Even if the experiment had been pursued and approved the system advocated in the *First Report of the Select Committee on Broadcasting of Proceedings* was only for an edited selection of the day's proceedings. This is the Englishness of revolution. In fact it is essential for the parliamentary sessions to be transmitted live in their entirety and for this coverage to apply to committees as well. Only thus will the institution of parliament be truly modernized. Some members object that the camera would intrude on and influence the nature of proceedings. Of course it would; that is the intention.

Parliament would be revealed as a focus for partisanship only by artifice and theatricality. It would have to conform to the administrative body that the camera revealed.

AMATEURISM

I should like to mention two Americans as examples of the potential that exists for the amateur film-maker: Andy Warhol and Abraham Zapruder.

Warhol may seem in many ways eminently professional; he is celebrated enough for expense to present him with little obstacle. At the same time he makes very long films absurdly cheaply and quickly. He is reported as having made 150 feature-length films in a year, at a cost of $500 each. His approach—as far as I can gather from reports and from a fraction of his output—is amateur and private. He asks the camera only to record: thus his films consist of rough and static images. He also complies with our experience of time, filming thirty consecutive minutes rather than a premeditated event. In a piece of Warhol film that I have seen a girl is asked to do no more than sit in front of the camera. In time she sheds inhibition, loses interest in the camera and becomes bored. She may even begin to behave like a girl alone with herself, and be forced to appreciate her own nature more imaginatively than ever before. The effect on the viewer is to juxtapose boredom and an almost hypnotized involvement. Without seeing more of his work I shall only say that I think Warhol may offer one of the most fruitful innovations in the use of film.

Abraham Zapruder is unarguably an amateur. He was out with his 8mm. camera on 22 November 1963 in Dallas, filming the president. His strip of film is the fullest of three amateur records of the moment of assassination and naturally it has been crucial to the debate that surrounds the Warren Report. The 28 November 1966 issue of *Life* magazine, which bought Zapruder's film, invited Governor Connally to examine the strip, frame by frame, under the microscope. As he did so, assessing his own movements and reactions, he concluded that he could not have been struck by the bullet that hit Kennedy.

As matters now stand on the case, if we believe Connally we can no longer say that there was only one assassin.

The Zapruder film is guileless but, possibly, no length of film may have a greater effect on the American people. The *Life* use of Connally shows the reflexivity of the medium: a man looking at himself as himself, and as an actor. As well as providing the best evidence of justice being seen to be done, it hints at a separation of mind and memory from physical presence that is the creative essence of film.

FUTURISM

It has been a theme of this book that our century is concerned to be modern. It senses the rate at which it is changing without necessarily being able to describe the various stages. Because the human being is already under such pressure it is inevitable that this sensibility begins to anticipate. At the beginning of *Alphaville*, Alpha 60 announces: 'There are times when reality becomes too complex for Oral Communication. But legend gives it a form by which it pervades the whole world.' For us, this is the legend of futurism.

Futurism is as dangerous as nostalgia; the enchantment with extrapolation may, as much as the illusory version of an imaginary past, detract from the observation of a dangerously practical present. I have already criticized this tendency in *Alphaville* and have now to do the same for Truffaut's *Fahrenheit 451*. Just as in *Alphaville* the proposals of the computer begin to penetrate the conventional humanist objections to a totalitarian society, so in *Fahrenheit* it is the sweet reason of Cyril Cusack— wildly miscast, but still the only credible human being in the film—which is of greatest interest when, simultaneously, he fondles the forbidden books and explains how they are the fruits of egotism and the cause of argument and unhappiness.

Cusack's portrayal makes one think of Marshall McLuhan if only because the condemnation of books is made within a society that has, as yet, been unable to replace them. It is rather that both Truffaut and McLuhan sense that books might become redundant. The world presented in *Fahrenheit*, and which Truffaut deplores, in which frustration may be alleviated by drugs, is a depressing prospect, but his alternative, of wholesome people living in the woods and memorizing good books—no bad books—is equally daunting.

But are books obsolete? Even the small eighteenth-century circle of *Emma* seems as brilliant and as present as it ever has. Is 'obsolete' then a proper word to apply to books—books of the quality, say, of Jane Austen's? Does it not imply a sense of function which the novelists may never have had of their books? Is the classical novel—and now the classical film—a work, which in economic terms, can only be seen realistically as a luxury? That neither the wit of Jane Austen nor the laconicism of Howard Hawks will be appreciated by even a reasonable proportion of our population cuts right through the imaginary traces that the protagonist for literature or cinema takes up and believes connect the author of genius with the world. This is particularly painful to acknowledge today because at no other time has this sort of connection seemed so necessary.

The idea in Bradbury's book, which Truffaut has faithfully adopted, is very much the frightened reaction of the alarmist liberal. Some time in the future the written word has been eliminated. The unimpeded bound forward science fiction begins with is necessary to support this suggestion; it does away with the description of how and by what the word has been replaced. The people are all able to read so that, by implication, they are unfulfilled by the withdrawal of words. There is no advancement of visual communication, simply a world very like our own, except that it has retrogressed. In fact it is another Resistance situation, as Truffaut was aware when making the film.

And here the legend of futurism relates to that of the past. The firemen in *Fahrenheit* are, like the authorities in *1984*, Gestapo figures. Renoir's admission of the Hitlerian alternative to the exercise of human appetites is reincarnated in the waiting evil genius of futurist extrapolations. But futurism is as intrigued by this prospect as it is frightened. There is an almost totalitarian pleasure in McLuhan's prognostications of an electronic society which encourages him to overstate his case. Thus he says the medium is the message—perhaps because, like Cusack, he has been sickened by all the conflicting messages—when he should only say the medium conditions the message. Above all, I think, the medium prescribes the way in which the message is understood.

In McLuhan's case it is a sign of his modernity perhaps that he describes complex hypotheses in vulgar and meretricious language. Let me liken his effect to that of a television commercial. I may say, as a commercial appears on television, that it is badly filmed or that past experience has taught me that the bread it proclaims tastes unpleasant. The fact remains that I cannot forget the name of the bread. McLuhan does not write sequentially, he does not choose or place words sensitively. But he is capable of producing single sentences which are very striking without, on examination, proving either accurate or true. Thus he says the world is a global village, as a commercial might say such a bread is the wheatiest. The nature of his own writing must have troubled McLuhan. His first books were printed and bound like ordinary books but they attempted to persuade their readers that, among other things, books were obsolete. The academic discipline of providing argued evidence for his claims was beyond McLuhan; consequently, his books consisted of as many of the single sentences as he could muster. These all repeated one fundamental wish: that the medium should be the message, in the way a commercial might say bread is life.

At last McLuhan has thrown off his unease with the conventional form and found one that fits the slogan. His latest book has great typographical variety and integrates text and illustrations like a comic. There is an order to the book which still shows the hopeful didact in McLuhan, but the book could as effectively be read backwards or forwards.

The book is called *The Medium is the Massage*, which is a good enough joke. That a printer's error can still make sense is not trivial but properly significant. That the medium can finally dominate any message as to massage or encapsulate the spectator against the content is a vivid thought, but it is a thought from science fiction. Julie Christie as the wife in *Fahrenheit* is massaged by her television as she is by her drugs.

On analysis, this striking title is as unsatisfactory as an advertising slogan. McLuhan has always been conscious of this *new* electronic age, and he has scorned fuddy-duddies who applied criteria from the age of print to current issues. But his adoption of 'massage' goes directly back to the prophecies of subservience that Orwell, Huxley and Bradbury have expressed. Just as he imagines circumstances are more advanced than in our experience they are, so the sense he has of a lost humanity is like a nuclear disarmer's unwillingness to face the tense realities of cold war.

For all the complexity of the society McLuhan describes, he suggests solutions that are simple if not ingenious, endorsing John Cage's adjuration 'to spread joy and revolution'—a policy advised by *I Ching*. Accepting another Cage precept—'One must be disinterested, accept that a sound is a sound and a man is a man, give up illusions about ideas of order, expressions of sentiment, and all the rest of our inherited aesthetic claptrap'—McLuhan seems to advocate the forms of Eastern mysticism which are now chiefly practised in the western states of the U.S.A.

Cage, McLuhan—and Godard—are on the borders of two possible conceptions of culture and civilization. Cage's 4 minutes, 33 seconds of silence has no intrinsic merit, but it is valuable for the contribution it makes towards the theory of music. *Pierrot le Fou*, on the other hand, is intrinsically valuable because it presents the disparities caused by our being on the borderland. Cage and McLuhan are iconoclasts who depend upon the stable body of convention. In Godard and Renoir there is a less startling but more plausible chance of revolution. It will not be a reversal in the structure of society or in the balance of human nature but an extension of our understanding. Belmondo in *Pierrot* and Renoir himself in *La Règle* are examples for us: men totally committed to the events that surround them but at the same time observing the spectacle thay make and looking to the future not with preconception but as Renoir sets out each day to film—as calm and as sensitive as his camera—'Je ne sais pas parce que, quand je tourne, j'ajoute beaucoup. J'ajoute, ou je retranche, de toute façon je change. Je crois absolument que le véritable sens d'un film ne se découvre qu'en le tournant, et quelquefois, après qu'on l'a tourné.'

FILMOGRAPHY

MICHELANGELO ANTONIONI b. 29 September 1912, Ferrara

1942–3—*Gente del Po* (S) (not released until 1947); 1948—*N.U.* (S); 1948–9—*L'Amorosa Menzogna* (S); 1949—*Superstizione* (S); *Sette Canne, Un Vestito* (S); 1950—*La Villa dei Mostri* (S); 1950–1951—*La Funiva del Faloria* (S); 1950—*Cronaca di un Amore*; 1953—*I Vinti*; *La Signora senza Camelie*; 'Tentato Suicidio' (an episode in the film *Amore in Citta*); 1955—*Uomini in Piu* (S); *Le Amiche*; 1957—*Il Grido*; 1960—*L'Avventura*; 1961—*La Notte*; 1962—*L'Eclisse*; 1964—*Il Deserto Rosso*; 1965—an episode in *I Tre Volti*; 1966—*Blow-Up*.

ALEXANDRE ASTRUC b. 13 July 1923, Paris

1948—*Aller-Retour* (S); 1949—*Ulysse ou les mauvaises rencontres* (S); 1952—*Le Rideau Cramoisi*; 1955—*Les Mauvaises Rencontres*; 1957—*Une Vie*; 1960—*La Proie pour l'Ombre*; 1961—*Éducation Sentimentale 61*; 1963—*Le Puits et le Pendule* (S); 1964—*Évariste Galois* (S); 1966—*La Longue Marche*.

JACQUES DEMY b. 5 June 1931, Pont-Château

1955—*Le Sabotier du Val de Loire* (S); 1957—*Le Bel Indifférent* (S); 1959—*Ars* (S); *Lola*; 1961—'Luxure' (S) (an episode from the film *Les Sept Péchés Capitaux*); 1962—*Baie des Anges*; 1964—*Les Parapluies de Cherbourg*; 1966—*Les Demoiselles de Rochefort*.

JEAN-LUC GODARD b. 3 December 1930, Paris

1954—*Opération Béton* (S); 1955—*Une Femme Coquette* (S); 1957—*Tous les Garçons s'appellent Patrick* (S); 1958—*Une Histoire d'Eau* (S);[1] 1959—*Charlotte et son Jules* (S); *A Bout de Souffle*; 1960—*Le Petit Soldat*; *Une Femme est une Femme*; 1961—'La Paresse' (S) (an episode from the film *Les Sept Péchés Capitaux*); 1962—*Vivre Sa Vie*; 'Le Nouveau Monde' (S) (an episode from the film *Rogopag*); 1963—'Le Grand Escroc' (an episode in the film *Les Plus Belles Escroqueries du Monde*[2]); *Les Carabiniers*; *Le Mépris*; 1964—*Bande à Part*; *Une Femme Mariée*; 'Montparnasse et Levallois' (an episode in the film *Paris Vu Par . . .*); 1965—*Alphaville*; *Pierrot le Fou*; 1966—*Masculin-Feminin*; *Made in U.S.A.*; *Deux ou trois choses que je sais d'elle.*

HOWARD HAWKS b. 30 May 1896, Goshen, Indiana
1926—*The Road to Glory*; *Fig Leaves*; 1927—*The Cradle Snatchers*; *Paid to Love*; 1928—*A Girl in Every Port*; *Fazil*; *The Air Circus*; 1929—*Trent's Last Case*; 1930—*The Dawn Patrol*; 1931—*The Criminal Code*; 1932—*The Crowd Roars*; *Scarface*; *Tiger Shark*; 1933—*Today We Live*; 1934—*Viva Villa!*;[3] *Twentieth Century*; 1935—*Barbary Coast*; *Ceiling Zero*; 1936—*The Road to Glory*;[4] *Come and Get It*;[5] 1938—*Bringing Up Baby*; 1939—*Only Angels Have Wings*; 1940—*His Girl Friday*; *The Outlaw*;[6] 1941—*Sergeant York*; *Ball of Fire*; 1943—*Air Force*; *Corvette K-255*;[7] 1944—*To Have and Have Not*; 1946—*The Big Sleep*; 1948—*Red River*; *A Song Is Born*; 1949—*I Was a Male War Bride*;[8] 1951—*The Thing*;[9] 1952—*The Big Sky*; 'The Ransom of Red Chief' (an episode in the film *O. Henry's Full House*); *Monkey Business*; 1953—*Gentlemen Prefer Blondes*; 1955—*Land of the Pharaohs*; 1959—*Rio Bravo*; 1962—*Hatari!*; 1964—*Man's Favourite Sport*; 1965—*Red Line 7000*; 1966—*El Dorado*.

[1] Co-directed with François Truffaut.
[2] Because of its length this film has not been released.
[3] After directing over half the film Hawks was replaced by Jack Conway, to whom it was credited.
[4] Not a remake of his own earlier film.
[5] Co-directed with William Wyler.
[6] Credited to Howard Hughes but the first half-hour is obviously Hawks and the whole conception is Hawksian.
[7] Directed by Richard Rosson after Hawks had advised.
[8] Also known as *You Can't Sleep Here*.
[9] Credited to Christian Nyby, Hawks's editor; again, the tone is unmistakable.

ALFRED HITCHCOCK   b. 13 August 1899, Leytonstone
1921—*Number Thirteen* (unfinished); 1922—*Always Tell Your Wife*;[1] 1925—*The Pleasure Garden*; 1926—*The Mountain Eagle*; 1927—*Downhill*; *Easy Virtue*; *The Ring*; 1928—*The Farmer's Wife*; *Champagne*; 1929—*The Manxman*; *Blackmail*; 1930—*Juno and the Paycock*; *Murder*; 1931—*The Skin Game*; 1932—*Rich and Strange*; 1933—*Waltzes from Vienna*; 1934—*The Man Who Knew Too Much*; 1935—*The Thirty-nine Steps*; 1936—*The Secret Agent*; *Sabotage*; 1937—*Young and Innocent*; 1938—*The Lady Vanishes*; 1939—*Jamaica Inn*; 1940—*Rebecca*; *Foreign Correspondent*; 1941— *Mr and Mrs Smith*; 1942—*Suspicion*; *Saboteur*; 1943—*Shadow of a Doubt*; *Lifeboat*; 1944—*Aventure Malgache* (S); *Bon Voyage* (S);[2] 1945—*Concentration*[3] (abandoned); *Spellbound*; 1946—*Notorious*; 1947—*The Paradine Case*; 1948—*Rope*; 1949—*Under Capricorn*; 1950—*Stage Fright*; 1951—*Strangers on a Train*; 1952—*I Confess*; 1953—*Dial M for Murder*; 1954—*Rear Window*; 1955—*To Catch a Thief*; *The Trouble with Harry*; 1956—*The Man Who Knew Too Much*;[4] 1957—*The Wrong Man*; 1958—*Vertigo*; 1959—*North by Northwest*; 1960—*Psycho*; 1963—*The Birds*; 1964—*Marnie*; 1966—*Torn Curtain*.

FRITZ LANG   b. 5 December 1890, Vienna
1919—*Halb-Blut*; *Der Herr der Liebe*; *Der Goldene See* (Part One of the film *Die Spinnen*); *Hara Kiri*; *Das brillanten Schiff* (Part Two of *Die Spinnen*[5]); 1920—*Das wandernde Bild*; 1921—*Vier um die Frau*; *Der müde Tod*; 1922—*Dr Mabuse, der Spieler* (Part One of the film *Dr Mabuse, der Spieler*); *Inferno* (Part Two of *Dr Mabuse, der Spieler*); 1924—*Siegfrieds Tod* (Part One of the film *Die Niebelungen*); *Kriemhilds Rache* (Part Two of *Die Niebelungen*); 1926—*Metropolis*; 1928—*Spione*; *Frau im Mond*; 1932—*M*; *Das Testament von Dr Mabuse*; 1933—*Liliom*; 1936— *Fury*; *You Only Live Once*; 1938—*You and Me*; 1940—*The Return*

---

[1] Co-directed with Seymour Hicks.
[2] Both shorts directed in 1944 were in French for the Ministry of Information.
[3] The concentration camps were the intended subject of this film.
[4] A re-make of Hitchcock's own film.
[5] Two further parts were planned for *Die Spinnen* without coming to fruition.

of Frank James; *Western Union*; 1941—*Man Hunt*; *Confirm or Deny*;[1] 1942—*Moontide*;[2] *Hangmen Also Die*; 1943—*The Ministry of Fear*; 1944—*The Woman in the Window*; 1945—*Scarlet Street*; 1946—*Cloak and Dagger*; *Secret Beyond the Door*; 1949—*House by the River*; 1950—*Winchester 73*;[3] *American Guerrilla in the Philippines*; 1951—*Rancho Notorious*; *Clash by Night*; 1952—*The Blue Gardenia*; 1953—*The Big Heat*; 1954—*Human Desire*; *Moonfleet*; 1955—*While the City Sleeps*; 1956—*Beyond a Reasonable Doubt*; 1958—*Der Tiger von Eschnapur*; *Das indische Grabmal*;[4] 1960— *Die 1000 Augen des Dr Mabuse*.

JOSEPH LOSEY b. 14 January 1909, La Crosse, Wisconsin
1939—*Petroleum and his Cousins* (S); 1941—*A Child Went Forth* (S); *Youth Gets a Break* (S); 1945—*A Gun in His Hand* (S); 1948—*The Boy with Green Hair*; 1949—*The Dividing Line*;[5] 1950—*The Prowler*; *M*; 1951—*The Big Night*; *Stranger on the Prowl*;[6] 1954—*The Sleeping Tiger*;[7] 1955—*The Man on the Beach*;[8] *The Intimate Stranger*;[9] 1956—*Time Without Pity*; 1957— *The Gypsy and the Gentleman*; 1959—*Blind Date*; 1960—*The Criminal*; 1961—*The Damned*; 1962—*Eve*; 1963—*The Servant*; 1964—*King and Country*; 1965—*Modesty Blaise*; 1966—*Accident*.

ANTHONY MANN b. 30 June 1906, San Diego, California
1942—*Dr Broadway*; *Moonlight in Havana*; 1943—*Nobody's Darling*; 1944—*My Best Gal*; *Strangers in the Night*; 1945—*The Great Flamarion*; *Two O'clock Courage*; *Sing Your Way Home*; 1946—*Strange Impersonation*; *The Bamboo Blonde*; 1947—*Desperate*; *Railroaded*; *T-Men*; 1948—*Raw Deal*; 1949—*Reign of*

---

[1] Taken over from Lang by Archie Mayo, to whom it was credited.

[2] Taken over from Lang by Archie Mayo, to whom it was credited.

[3] Substantially an Anthony Mann film.

[4] These two films running, respectively, 1 hour 37 minutes and 1 hour 40 minutes, were cut down and dubbed and released in this country as *Tigress of Bengal* at 1 hour 38 minutes.

[5] Also known as *The Lawless*.

[6] Filmed in Italy after Losey had left America, this film was taken from Losey and cut and released with Andrea Forzano credited as director.

[7] Directed under the pseudonym 'Victor Hanbury'.

[8] A 30-minute film in colour and CinemaScope.

[9] Directed under the pseudonym 'Victor Canning'.

Terror; *Border Incident*; *Side Street*; 1950—*Devil's Doorway*; *Winchester 73*;[1] *The Furies*; 1951—*Quo Vadis*;[2] *The Tall Target*; 1952—*Where the River Bends*; 1953—*The Naked Spur*; *Thunder Bay*; 1954—*The Glenn Miller Story*; *The Far Country*; 1955— *Strategic Air Command*; *The Man from Laramie*; 1956—*The Last Frontier*; *Serenade*; *Men in War*; 1957—*The Tin Star*; *God's Little Acre*; 1958—*Man of the West*; 1959—*Spartacus*;[3] 1960—*Cimar-ron*; 1961—*El Cid*; 1963—*The Fall of the Roman Empire*; 1965— *The Heroes of Telemark*.

MAX OPHULS   b. 6 May 1902, Sarrebruck; d. 26 March 1957, Hamburg

1930—*Dann Schon Lieber Lebertran*; 1931—*Die Verliebte Firma*; 1932—*Die Verkaufte Braut*; *Die Lachenden Erben*;[4] *Liebelei*; 1933— *Une Histoire d'Amour*;[5] 1934—*On a Volé un Homme*; *La Signora di Tutti*; 1935—*Divine*; 1936—*Valse Brillante de Chopin* (S); *Ave Maria de Schubert* (S); *Komedie um Geld*; *La Tendre Ennemie*; 1937—*Yoshiwara*; 1938—*Werther*; *Sans Lendemain*; 1940—*De Mayerling à Sarajevo*; *L'École des Femmes* (uncompleted); 1941— *Vendetta*;[6] 1947—*The Exile*; 1948—*Letter from an Unknown Woman*; 1949—*Caught*; *The Reckless Moment*; 1950—*La Ronde*; 1952—*Le Plaisir*; 1953—*Madame de . . .*; 1955—*Lola Montes*.

OTTO PREMINGER   b. 5 December 1906, Vienna

1936[7]—*Under Your Spell*; 1937—*Danger, Love at Work*; 1943— *Margin for Error*; 1944—*In the Meantime Darling*; *Laura*; 1945— *Czarina*;[8] *Fallen Angel*; 1946—*Centennial Summer*; 1947—*Forever*

---

[1] This film was begun by Fritz Lang.

[2] Mann shot the scenes of Rome's burning.

[3] Mann shot some of the early part of the film and was then replaced by Stanley Kubrick.

[4] Some sources give 1951 as date, see *L'Avant-Scène*, No. 25.

[5] French version of *Liebelei*.

[6] Ophuls began this film but was replaced in turn by Preston Sturges, Stuart Heisler, Howard Hughes (the producer) and Mel Ferrer, to whom the film was credited.

[7] Preminger had already made some films in Vienna, including *Die Grosse Liebe*.

[8] Also known as *A Royal Scandal*, produced by Ernst Lubitsch.

Amber; *Daisy Kenyon*; 1948—*That Lady in Ermine*;[1] 1949—
Lady Windermere's Fan; *Whirlpool*; 1950—*Where the Sidewalk
Ends*; *The Thirteenth Letter*; 1952—*Angel Face*; 1953—*The Moon
Is Blue*;[2] 1954—*River of No Return*; *Carmen Jones*; 1955—*One
Man Mutiny*;[3] 1956—*The Man with the Golden Arm*; 1957—*St
Joan*; *Bonjour Tristesse*; 1958—*Porgy and Bess*; 1959—*Anatomy
of a Murder*; 1960—*Exodus*; 1961—*Advise and Consent*; 1962—
The Cardinal; 1964—*In Harm's Way*; 1965—*Bunny Lake Is
Missing*; 1966—*Hurry Sundown*.

JEAN RENOIR   b. 15 September 1894, Paris
1924—*La Fille de l'Eau*; 1926—*Nana*; 1927—*Marquitta*; *Charles-
ton*; 1928—*La Petite Marchande d'Allumettes*;[4] *Tire au flanc*;
1929—*Le Tournoi*; *Le Bled*; 1931—*On Purge Bébé*; *La Chienne*;
1932—*La Nuit de Carrefour*; *Boudu Sauvé Des Eaux*; 1933—
Chotard et Cie; 1934—*Madame Bovary*; *Toni*; 1935—*Le Crime de
M. Lange*; 1936—*La Vie Est à Nous*;[5] *Une Partie de Campagne*;[6]
Les Bas-Fonds; 1937—*La Grande Illusion*; *La Marseillaise*; 1938—
La Bête Humaine; 1939—*La Règle du Jeu*; 1940—*La Tosca*;[7]
1941—*Swamp Water*; 1943—*This Land Is Mine*; 1944—*Salute
to France* (S); 1945—*The Southerner*; 1946—*The Diary of a
Chambermaid*; *The Woman on the Beach*; 1950—*The River*; 1952—
Le Carrosse d'Or; 1954—*French Can-Can*; 1956—*Elena et les
Hommes*; 1959—*Le Testament du Docteur Cordelier*; *Le Déjeuner
sur l'Herbe*; 1961—*Le Caporal Épinglé*.

JACQUES RIVETTE   b. 1 March 1928, Rouen
1956—*Le Coup de Berger* (S); 1958-60—*Paris Nous Appartient*;
1965—*Suzanne Simonin, La Religieuse de Diderot*.

---

[1] Credited to Lubitsch but partly directed by Preminger after Lubitsch's death.

[2] A German version was shot simultaneously, *Die Jungfrau auf dem Dach*.

[3] Also known as *The Court-Martial of Billy Mitchell*.

[4] Co-directed with Jean Tedesco.

[5] Banned by the censor.

[6] Originally uncompleted, completed in 1940 by Jacques Becker and Marguerite Renoir.

[7] Renoir shot the opening five set-ups; completed by and credited to Carl Koch.

JOSEF VON STERNBERG b. 29 May 1894, Vienna
1925—*The Salvation Hunters*; *The Exquisite Sinner*; *The Masked Bride*;[1] 1926—*A Woman of the Sea*;[2] 1927—*Children of Divorce*;[3] *Underworld*; 1928—*The Last Command*; *The Drag Net*; *The Docks of New York*; 1929—*The Case of Lena Smith*; *Thunderbolt*; 1930—*The Blue Angel*; *Morocco*; 1931—*Dishonoured*; *An American Tragedy*; 1932—*Shanghai Express*; *Blonde Venus*; 1934—*The Scarlet Empress*; 1935—*The Devil Is a Woman*; *Crime and Punishment*; 1936—*The King Steps Out*; 1937—*I, Claudius*;[4] 1938—*The Great Waltz*;[5] *I Take This Woman*;[6] 1939—*Sergeant Madden*; 1941—*The Shanghai Gesture*; 1943—*The Town* (S); 1946—*Duel in the Sun*;[7] 1951—*Jet Pilot*;[8] 1952—*Macao*;[9] 1953—*The Saga of Anatahan*.

ORSON WELLES b. 6 May 1915, Kenosha, Wisconsin
1941—*Citizen Kane*; 1942—*The Magnificent Ambersons*; *It's All True*;[10] *Journey Into Fear*;[11] 1946—*The Stranger*; 1947—*The Lady from Shanghai*; 1948—*Macbeth*; 1952—*Othello*; 1955—*Confidential Report*; 1958—*Touch of Evil*; *Don Quixote*;[12] 1962—*The Trial*; 1965—*Chimes at Midnight*.

[1] Completed by and credited to W. Christy Cabanne.
[2] The producer, Charlie Chaplin, never released the film.
[3] Credited to Frank Lloyd but partly reshot by von Sternberg.
[4] Abandoned when Merle Oberon had a car crash.
[5] Von Sternberg made some additions to Julien Duvivier's film.
[6] Von Sternberg began the film, was replaced in turn by Frank Borzage and W. S. Van Dyke II, to whom the film was credited.
[7] Von Sternberg directed one week while King Vidor was ill.
[8] Reshot and re-edited by Jules Furthman and released in 1957.
[9] Rumoured to have been reshot in part by Nicholas Ray.
[10] A project on Argentine, Brazil and Mexico, Welles shot about 100,000 feet of film before being recalled.
[11] Partly directed by Welles but credited to Norman Foster.
[12] Made for American television, but not yet completed.

INDEX

Numerals in italic refer to the plates

225